T0339842

MINIMUM WAGE POLICY IN GREAT BRITAIN AND THE UNITED STATES

Minimum Wage Policy in Great Britain and the United States

Jerold Waltman

Algora Publishing
New York

Library of Congress Cataloging-in-Publication Data —

Waltman, Jerold L., 1945-
  Minimum wage policy in Great Britain and the United States / Jerold L. Waltman.
    p. cm.
  Includes bibliographical references and index.
  ISBN 978-0-87586-600-0 (trade paper: alk. paper) — ISBN 978-0-87586-601-7 (hard:
alk. paper) — ISBN 978-0-87586-602-4 (ebook) 1. Minimum wage—United States. 2.
Minimum wage—Law and legislation—United States. 3. Minimum wage—Government
policy—United States. 4. Minimum wage—Great Britain. 5. Minimum wage—Law
and legislation—Great Britian. 6. Minimum wage—Government policy—Great Britian.
I.Title.

  HD4918.W2647 2008
  331.2'30941vdc22
                            2007048167

Front Cover: Minimum wage protesters demonstrate outside the Labour Party
conference in Brighton. England, 1995.
  Image: © Sean Aidan; Eye Ubiquitous/CORBIS
  Photographer: Sean Aidan

Printed in the United States

To

Abraham Attrep, who first stimulated my interest in British politics

and

Deborah Littman and Neil Jameson, for their tireless efforts to bring dignity to all those who work

[T]he function of the State is to secure conditions upon which its citizens are able to win by their own efforts all that is necessary to a full civic efficiency. . . . The "right to work" and the right to a "living wage" are just as valid as the rights of person or property.
— Leonard Hobhouse, 1911

Our Nation so richly endowed with natural resources and with a capable and industrious population should be able to devise ways and means of insuring to all our able-bodied working men and women a fair day's pay for a fair day's work.
—Franklin D. Roosevelt, 1937

ACKNOWLEDGEMENTS

This book began one afternoon over ten years ago while I was barbecuing in my backyard. A visiting friend from Britain, a police officer, and I were discussing the relationship between poverty and crime. I had just begun working on the politics of the minimum wage in the United States and casually asked what the minimum wage was in Britain. He answered that the U.K. had no minimum wage; I silently thought that he must be mistaken, as surely no advanced industrial country did not have a minimum wage. I discovered, of course, though, that he was indeed right.

Soon after that, Labor coasted to its 1997 electoral victory, bringing with it the promise of Britain's first national minimum wage. When I completed my American work, I began looking into the background and details of the policy. From the beginning, I was struck by both the parallels and the differences between the British experience and our own. Yet the most striking aspect of minimum wage policies in both countries, I came to believe, was how they had evolved from a central component of social policy to an all but free-standing issue. Although I provide an abundance of policy details and historical background in what follows, that theme forms the bedrock of the book.

I have had an enormous amount of help along the way in the research for and the writing of this book. On my first research trip to Britain, I had the good fortune to meet Bharti Patel, of the now defunct Low Pay Unit, and Victor Patterson, then an official at the Department of Trade and Industry. Both of them are extremely knowledgeable and gracious people who gave me a more than generous portion of their time. On my next trip, I met two of the people to whom the book is dedicated, Deborah Littman of UNISON and Neil Jameson of TELCO. Through Deborah, I made arrangements to interview Rodney Bickerstaffe, the father, it is fair to say, of the British minimum wage. To all these British friends, I owe a hearty thanks.

My friend Michael Hayes of Colgate University has been a continual source of inspiration as well as a sounding board for many of the ideas contained in the following pages. I also have three friends I have never met face-to-face, but who have been lively and enlightening email correspondents regarding the minimum wage. They are Tim Babbidge, Luke Shaefer, and Brock Haussamen, all of whom have had a hand in keeping my enthusiasm up and shaping my ideas.

Baylor University provides its faculty with the best of environments and resources for the conduct of research. The University Research Council provided the funds to travel to London. The library staff, especially the people of the Interlibrary Loan Department, has gone far beyond the call of duty in tracing down obscure materials and delivering them to me efficiently. My department chair, Mary Nichols, was encouraging throughout the project. My graduate research assistants, Tuoya Wulan, Stephen Block, and Jerome Foss, were all superb, especially in guiding me in the use of data bases. Sara Savill and Leah Gatlin proved to be remarkable when it came to taking my scratchings and converting them into readable tables and figures. But my greatest debt at Baylor is due Jenice Langston and Cynara Butler, the department's administrative personnel. They spent many hours helping me with various aspects of the manuscript preparation and did it all with unmatchable good humor.

Thanks is also due the editorial staff at Algora Publishing. Martin DeMers and Andrea Secara have had confidence in the project since its inception and have done their usual more than praiseworthy job in moving the manuscript through production. Every author should be so fortunate.

Of course, it is time to insert the usual caveat, and I follow the tradition: None of these people bears any responsibility for errors of fact or for faulty interpretations; those are my responsibilities alone.

Finally, I must express my gratitude to my wife Diane. Although she shares my enthusiasm for a high minimum wage as a way to give people both income and dignity, she has had to endure many dinner-time conversations about all manner of technical issues, put up with my perpetual distractedness, and be patient when I was glued to the word processor. To her, then, is owed the greatest thanks of all.

TABLE OF CONTENTS

INTRODUCTION

At their inception, minimum wage policies in both Great Britain and the United States were intimately tied to other aspects of social welfare: pensions, housing, health care, and public assistance. In the United Kingdom, the same pre-World War I Liberal government that produced the Trade Boards Act 1909, Britain's first minimum wage statute,[1] also passed the Old Age Pensions Act 1908, the Labor Exchanges Act 1909, the Housing and Town Planning Act 1909, and the National Insurance Act 1911, which set up systems of unemployment and health insurance. In the United States, the Progressive movement of the early twentieth century sought to attack social ills on a variety of fronts, and it was this movement which produced the first state minimum wage statute, in Massachusetts in 1912. At the federal level, it was the New Deal coalition that finally managed to secure passage of the Fair Labor Standards Act of 1938, the national minimum wage law, after an initial experiment with minimum wage demands in 1933 as part of the National Industrial Recovery Act. Sandwiched between these efforts, it obtained congressional approval for the Social Security Act of 1935, which not only created systems of old age pensions and unemployment insurance but also contained what became the nation's chief public assistance program, Aid to Families with Dependent Children. In both countries, policy planners envisaged a close connection among all these pieces of legislation, the com-

---

[1] This act created minimum wages for only four industries. The level of the wage was to be set by a separate board for each, the details of which are discussed more fully in chapter 2.

bined effects of which it was hoped would go some distance in alleviating poverty and reducing inequality.

This seamless policy web continued for a while, but in time the minimum wage got severed from its welfare state parentage. In the United Kingdom, after a rapid expansion of the trade board system during the First World War and an unsuccessful effort to establish a uniform national minimum wage in 1921, the minimum wage retreated to the margins of the state. Serious discussion of the matter largely disappeared, and by the late 1920s even the Labor Party had stopped mentioning it. The trade boards receded to the shadows. Then, when Ernest Bevin became Minister of Labor in the wartime cabinet he set about transforming the entire trade board apparatus from one designed to secure a minimum income for low-wage workers into a system for encouraging collective bargaining, something he accomplished with the Wages Councils Act of 1945. Meanwhile, William Beveridge was drawing up his famous blueprint for postwar social policy. His widely hailed 1943 plan focused solely on social insurance and public assistance as ways to relieve destitution, failing to even mention the minimum wage. The Labor Government of 1945-1951 subsequently married his proposals to long-advocated measures for health care and housing as it set about erecting the postwar welfare state. At no time during these years of reform were any serious discussions held regarding a national minimum wage. In the postwar years, as the recession Bevin feared did not materialize, the trade boards limped along; for all intents and purposes, they remained largely invisible to most of the public. When Mrs. Thatcher entered office, though, her implacable animosity to economic regulation of any kind led to their being first emasculated then completely abolished.

The minimum wage's place in the national policy matrix lasted a while longer in the United States. President Truman viewed it as a cornerstone of his Fair Deal program, and even as late as 1961 the Kennedy administration was devoting more effort to broadening and raising the minimum wage than it was to improving public assistance. In fact, in the early days of the New Frontier, the minimum wage was taken up before any other anti-poverty proposals. It was only with the Johnson administration's War on Poverty that the minimum wage was decidedly eclipsed by public programs. Although not hostile to the minimum wage, the Johnson administration's policy planners did not see it as a major approach to fighting poverty. Pushed from the center ring, it has since remained consigned mostly to the periphery of welfare state debates. A fierce but brief controversy flares when proposals to raise it move onto the floor of Congress, but little serious thought has been given to its place in the overall system of social welfare.

Several explanations come to mind for the difficulties that plague the minimum wage. For one, public expenditure programs are undeniably more efficient poverty-fighting instruments in one sense: they channel money to people more directly. Whether set up as social insurance or as public assistance, transfer programs can put cash straight into the hands of all qualified recipients. In principle, a rational system can be set up to establish whether a person qualifies, either by having made contributions to a social insurance fund or by demonstrating a lack of resources. A formula can then be applied to determine how much he or she should receive, and the funds can be automatically dispersed. The designated beneficiary now has the monies available to move himself or herself out of poverty. The minimum wage, on the other hand, is a bit more cumbersome. It cannot, for instance, help the unemployed. Further, a certain number of minimum wage workers — spouses in casual employment or young people earning pocket money (historically more common in the United States than Britain) — are not necessarily from families that are in poverty.

The long postwar boom was also partly responsible. Once cash transfer programs were created, they could grow almost effortlessly as public budgets of the period grew. Economic growth generated ample revenues for government, and allocating a certain percentage of this bounty to social welfare programs seemed a humane thing to do. The public, political elites, and policy makers could all feel good about society's efforts to make life decent for all, and it cost almost nothing to do so.

Minimum wage politics were decidedly different. Business interests remained and remain adamantly and resolutely opposed to the whole idea of a minimum wage. The legislation is ideological anathema to much of the business community, mainly it seems because it interferes with what in their view is a basic business decision. It legitimates, that is, governmental regulation in general. Moreover, on the practical side, there is indeed a certain burden involved in having to maintain the required records and then being subjected to the annoying demands of inspectors. Overcoming this opposition demanded that those favoring broader and/or higher minimum wages win bruising political battles at each turn. These were political struggles that progressive forces could and sometimes did win, of course, but there was a natural reticence to stoke these fires, especially when increasing the social welfare budget produced so much less controversy.

Additionally, the nature of policy making provided another advantage for social welfare expenditure programs over the minimum wage. Each expenditure program gave birth to a governmental agency charged with the tasks of determining eligibility and dispersing the funds. As usual, such bureaucracies became embedded in the policy making process, as they continually put forth policy proposals to "improve" their field of responsibility. Furthermore, they developed a "turf" that had to be defended, in part to protect the recipients but also in part to protect jobs and promotions. These bureaucratic institutions were highly visible parts of the state, and both political appointees in the executive branch and important legislators became accustomed to working with them. Aside from a handful of inspectors, however, minimum wage laws have no bureaucracy with a vested interest in the policy's continuation or expansion.

Nevertheless, by far the most important reason for the marginalization of the minimum wage was intellectual. The British sociologist T.H. Marshall laid out one of the earliest and clearest statements of this position, and his position became the bedrock of welfare state theory.[2] Marshall argued that rights had gone through a three-stage process. First, basic civil liberties had been secured in the eighteenth century, followed by the acquisition of participation rights in the nineteenth. The third set of rights, developed and codified in the twentieth century, was the right to share in the largesse of the society. Marshall and his followers came to argue that the right to receive benefits from the state, therefore, was as fundamental an aspect of citizenship as freedom of speech and the right to vote.

This position was neither economically, politically, nor morally sustainable. It was not economically sustainable because the postwar boom could not last forever. It was not politically sustainable because it drew no distinction between contributory social insurance programs, which maintained their popularity because of their universality, and public assistance programs which divided the public, in people's perception in any event, into givers and takers. Finally, it was not morally sustainable because it neglected any obligation to contribute to society.[3]

---

2 T.H. Marshall, *Citizenship and Social Class* (Cambridge: Cambridge University Press, 1950).

3 There is some doubt whether Marshall himself believed that social rights came without responsibilities, including the obligation to work. See Stuart White, *The Civic Minimum* (Oxford: Oxford University Press, 2002), 139-140 and Martin Powell, "The Hidden History of Social Citizenship," *Citizenship Studies* 6(2002), 229-244. However, whatever Marshall's true feelings, his modern day disciples do not believe benefits should be tied to work. See Desmond King, *In the Name of Liberalism: Illiberal Social Policy in Britain and the United States* (Oxford: Oxford University Press, 1999) and Nancy Fraser and Linda Gordon, "Civil

It is perhaps impossible to know whether an attack on the welfare state would have occurred in any event. In fact, though, it coincided with the economic constrictions that began in the mid-1970s. Personified by the administrations of Ronald Reagan and Margaret Thatcher, but backed by an intellectual vanguard schooled in neoliberal economics, the assault on the welfare state has been unrelenting since those years. Faced with this onslaught, supporters of the welfare state in both Britain and the United States opted to vigorously defend public expenditure programs. It was a battle, however, that they were destined to lose, though some continue a guerilla campaign even yet.

Their failure was rooted in a confusion of ends and means. The goals of a viable welfare state are twofold: to do everything humanly possible to eliminate poverty and to provide a corrective to the economic inequality produced by the operation of the market. The means selected to accomplish these ends need to be honestly evaluated in terms of their economic and social consequences, their administrative practicality, and their long-run political viability. Cash transfer programs indeed have a role to play; however, they are not the essence of the welfare state, but only one aspect of it. The direct provision of services and a minimum wage are equally important strategies. No effective defense of the welfare state can rest solely or even primarily on policies engendering cash payments to individuals.

Minimum wage policies and their surrounding politics are, consequently, at an important crossroads in the United States and Britain. In the United States, there is a new vitality to minimum wage policies at the state level, but even more importantly a vibrant living wage movement has sprung up at the local level. As with the original minimum wage movement, the current effort is following a hallowed American tradition of securing new policies first at the state and local level. In Britain, the Blair Government adopted and steadfastly defended a National Minimum Wage. In fact, as Blair prepared to leave office, the British public overwhelmingly accorded it the honor of being his greatest legacy.[4] It outdistanced the other top two items — finding a peace settlement in Northern Ireland and securing steady economic growth with nearly full employment and low inflation — considerably, 54% to 42% and 36% respectively.[5] At the same time, a small but dedicated group of citizens based largely in East London has been working for a living wage.

Citizenship against Social Citizenship: On the Ideology of Contract-Versus-Charity," in Bart van Steenbergen, ed., *The Condition of Citizenship* (London: Sage, 1994), chap. 8.

4 YouGov/*Daily Telegraph* Poll, May 2, 2007.

5 Nothing else rose above 13%.

Their efforts there have borne some fruit in both the private and public sec-tors, resulting in improved wages at several banks, for instance, the recent establishment of a living wage unit within London's city government, and the securing of a living wage agreement to accompany London's successful Olympic bid.

In what follows, I have sought to accomplish two objectives. First, I want to describe and analyze the current operation of minimum wage policies and politics in both countries. Where are we and how did we get here? For Britain, I chronicle the events leading up to the enactment of the National Minimum Wage, and then discuss its subsequent evolution. Turning to the United States, I cover the almost moribund but still important federal mini-mum wage, and then trace developments on the state and local front. After that, I take up the accomplishments of the living wage movement in each nation. Second, I want to assess whether or not contemporary advocates for heightened minimum wages are laying the groundwork for a rejuvenated welfare state. Are they fashioning a public philosophy that will make the minimum wage once again a central feature of the welfare state, or are they heading down other paths?

Before we embark on these two tasks, though, we need to lay some foun-dation stones by surveying the general aspects of minimum wage policy and examining the history of minimum wages in the two countries.

Chapter 1. The Political Economy of the Minimum Wage

The starting point for understanding the minimum wage is the fact that it lies in two policy domains. In *purpose* it is a social welfare policy, in that its primary goal is to attack poverty. In *design* and *operation*, however, it is a labor market regulation. This fundamental fact is hugely important in the administration of the policy, of course, but it is of even more importance in its politics.

At the broadest level, those favoring minimum wage policies are the same individuals and groups who favor other measures to alleviate poverty. Opponents, again very generally, are a combination of free market ideologues and business interests. The answers to two questions will therefore determine a country's minimum wage policy: 1) How important is the minimum wage to social welfare reformers? There are a number of available policy options for overcoming poverty, such as public services, social insurance, and public assistance, and social reformers have to decide which one or ones to emphasize. Furthermore, there are other ways to raise wages, collective bargaining, for instance, or a tax rebate for earned income. Thus, the initial questions to be asked are Where does the minimum wage rank in the minds of social welfare advocates and How much political effort are they willing to expend on its behalf? 2) How successful will the opponents be? What political resources will they bring to bear, and with what intensity will they marshal them? Will the minimum wage become a major battle ground, or will only token opposition be offered?

Both steps are vital in determining a country's minimum wage, but the first question is perhaps the most crucial. The central theme of this book is that in the early twentieth century, when minimum wage policies were first being promulgated in the United Kingdom and the United States, their backers viewed them as a critical component of the nascent welfare state. They held a central place in what might be called the preferred policy matrix, alongside public services such as education and health care and social insurance policies covering unemployment and old age. Public assistance — cash payments on a need basis — would be the most marginal welfare state policy. Low wages, unemployment, sickness, and old age were seen as the chief culprits in causing poverty. Therefore, setting a minimum wage that allowed working people to enjoy a decent life was an essential part of any genuine system of social welfare. However, in time, the minimum wage moved to the margins of social welfare thinking, and hence to the margins of politics.

How and when this happened is a tale to be told in later chapters. What is important to note here is that the consequences have been little short of calamitous for those who struggle to live on low wages. Yet, in recent years, there has been a renewed focus on the minimum wage, and it has taken on a new vitality. This, too, is part of our story, in fact a major part of the pages that follow. How far will the minimum wage rise, though, in the policy hierarchy? How far will social welfare advocates will go in reestablishing it as a cornerstone of social policy? This, in turn, is directly connected to theoretical thinking about the welfare state. For, ultimately, while political energy comes from activists and organizations, it is ideas that drive politics. In the concluding chapter, we will survey current thinking on the welfare state and try to predict how these developments might influence the future of the minimum wage.

The Goals of Minimum Wage Policy

The primary goal of any minimum wage policy is to increase the incomes of those at the very bottom of the wage scale. Low wages are a prime contributor to poverty and misery, and they therefore provide fodder for other social pathologies. Using legal means to attack the problem of low pay at its source will therefore alleviate at least some of this misery.

Minimum wage policy can take one of three forms, however. It might be, first, strictly an antidote to the most base kind of poverty, forcing employers to pay wages that are at least slightly above the bare subsistence level. Or, second, it might be designed to provide something approaching a "living wage," that is an income that would furnish the decencies of life as defined by the society at large. Or, third, it might be hoped that the minimum wage would lift all wage earners into at least the rungs of the lower middle class. In whatever guise, though, it is a policy whose chief goal is to make work more rewarding for the lowest paid people in the work force.

There are two secondary goals of minimum wage policy as well. The first of these is to reduce economic inequality. Since wages and salaries are the major components of income, wage compression will reduce the gap between the top and bottom. A minimum wage will lift the income of those at the very bottom, and it will also have a spillover effect up the wage scale, as those earning above the lowest wages being paid will insist on retaining a differential. However, this differential will dissipate as one moves up the wage scale. Therefore, setting a minimum wage will have a compressing effect on wages. Of course, how much of a compressing effect occurs will depend on how high the minimum wage is. In general, the higher the minimum wage, the greater the compression.

The other secondary goal is to reduce industrial unrest.[1] Disputes over wages have always been the main cause of strikes and work stoppages. If the setting of wages is transferred to a public body, then, the need for such actions will diminish, with salutary effects for the economy as a whole.

ARGUMENTS FOR AND AGAINST A MINIMUM WAGE

Arguments for and against the minimum wage can usefully be divided into those based in morality and those based in economics. However, they tend to overlap and bleed into one another, defying efforts to put them into neat categories.

Moral Arguments For a Minimum Wage

The oldest moral argument for a minimum wage is the "just wage" tradition, a tradition which traces its lineage to St. Thomas Aquinas and the medieval Scholastics.[2] Prices of products and services are generally just if they are set in open, competitive markets, they thought. However, that does not mean that any specific transaction is just. For that to be the case, the Scholastics held that, first, there must be no hint of violence, coercion, or fraud. But in addition there is the problem of unequal bargaining power. Both par-

---

1 Actually, this was a primary goal of the early minimum wage laws in Australia. See H.B. Higgins, *A New Province for Law and Order* (London: Constable and Co., 1922).

2 A discussion of the just wage can be found in Steven Epstein, "The Theory and Practice of the Just Wage," *Journal of Medieval History* 17 (1991), 53-69.

ties must be equally able to say no to the transaction. This is the core of the problem in wage bargaining, especially concerning people who work at low wages, for seldom are the bargaining positions equal.

Employers therefore have a duty "to give every worker what is justly due him."[3] What the Scholastics ignored and what can lead from just wage theory to a legally mandated minimum wage is the problem of enforcement. Having established the principle, Catholic theologians have often been content to rely solely on moral exhortation. The problem then is that the business person who is persuaded to pay the just wage may well be put at a competitive disadvantage. Therefore, to secure a just wage to all employees and to be fair to the ethical business person, the coercive apparatus of the state must be called forth.

A second moral strand concerns poverty, and here we find a tangle of both religious and secular threads.[4] Judaism, Catholicism, mainline Protestantism, and evangelical Protestantism all agree that care for the poor is a religious duty. Where they diverge is whether the obligation falls exclusively on individuals and religious organizations or whether the state should take up a role also. Several strands of Judaism and most of evangelical Protestantism emphasize the responsibility of individuals and religious organizations, and are skeptical of the state. Other strands of Judaism, most of mainline Protestantism, and virtually all of Catholic thought, on the other hand, while not denigrating the efforts of individuals and organizations, believe that public authorities also have a responsibility to care for the "least of these."

From this starting point, the question is then a tactical one. Which public policies are most effective in fighting poverty? Which ones have the fewest negative side effects? Which ones build or reinforce virtue? On all these fronts, the minimum wage usually more than holds its own. It measurably increases the incomes of the poor. (In candor, there is a debate about this, an issue that will be taken up momentarily.) It has few negative side effects for the poor themselves. There is disagreement, of course, over other side effects, such as whether heightened unemployment results, but that is in principle an empirical question. Further, it places a premium on work, which in itself is a moral good. In short, the path from a public responsibility for attacking poverty to the minimum wage is one that can be walked quickly and briskly.

---

3 This quote is from the Papal encyclical *Rerum Novarum* (1891).
4 I have discussed these foundations more fully elsewhere, Jerold Waltman, *The Case for the Living Wage* (New York: Algora, 2004), chaps. 2 and 3.

Religious people and secularists come together when the fair remuneration for work done is at issue. The religiously inclined will say that no child of God who labors should be denied a fair wage. Matthew 10:10 ("the worker is worth his keep") and Luke 10:7 ("the laborer is worthy of his hire") put this rather clearly. For those who have more secular leanings, a simple notion of fundamental fairness seems to demand a "fair day's pay for a fair day's work." Once again, if you accept this position for either reason, and if you believe that some employers will deny the worker a fair wage, then you almost have to endorse a legal minimum wage.

Then, there is a more general secular vein regarding poverty as well. At times, it flows from simple moral outrage that people could be allowed to live in the conditions found in slums. At other times, it is connected to a position that can be stated as "In a country as rich as ours surely we can bring everyone up to some decent level." Or, in a related variant, "Inasmuch as everyone contributes to the economic well being of society, everyone has a claim on a reasonable slice of the pie." There is also a more "hard left" version that sees the poor as hapless victims of a capitalist order. The first three groups see the minimum wage as one way to help lift people out of poverty, and therefore as a highly desirable policy. The last group prefers more radical surgery on the economy and polity, but will ordinarily support the minimum wage as a stopgap ameliorative measure in the meantime.

Among both the religious and the secularists, there is sometimes a whiff of the old Victorian distinction between the deserving and the undeserving poor, or perhaps as they would more likely put it, the deserving poor and the really deserving poor. Who could be more deserving than someone who is working full time, year round in a perfectly legal occupation? If anyone deserves the solicitude of public policy makers, then it is surely he or she. And what could be more helpful than increasing the return to that person's work?

A final moral position takes it cue from the demands of democratic citizenship. One version of this is an updated Jeffersonianism. People need economic independence in order to exercise their political rights and obligations responsibly. Beholden to no one for their daily bread, they can weigh the merits of candidates for office or proposals for new public policies without any outside influence. If so, again, it is a tactical question: Which public policies will produce such independent citizens with the least cost? Another version holds that poverty stunts the capacity for democratic citizenship. Especially in an affluent society, it produces a sense of exclusion, which brings in its train a number of unhealthy consequences. Public institutions — schools, parks, the military, for instance — lose support. Public order becomes harder to maintain. Psychological disorders grow, particularly when they are linked to addiction. A healthy democratic society requires active, informed citizens, not those beset with heavy doses of alienation. Here, too, while few would believe that modern alienation is solely the product of low incomes, low incomes and the lack of dignity they sow have certainly played a part.

Another group concerned with democratic citizenship worries about the growth of inequality. Too much disparity between those at the bottom and those at the top erodes the sense of common purpose that all societies need, especially democratic ones. To the extent that a minimum wage can help close this gap, it can contribute to making people feel that their fates are linked together.

Economic Arguments For a Minimum Wage

Although it is not heard as much today as formerly, one economic argument for a minimum wage is that it increases purchasing power. There is first a more or less standard version of this argument. Edward Filene, an early twentieth century American businessman, used to try to convince his fellow entrepreneurs that higher wages were better for everybody.[5] With higher wages, workers could buy more products. But Filene was realistic enough to know that it would have to be mandatory. Otherwise, the temptation to let others pay the high wages and enjoy the benefit of increased revenue while keeping one's own cost low by paying low wages (to be a "free rider" in modern parlance) would be too much for many business owners. Then, there was the Keynesian inspired variant. The key to restoring or maintaining prosperity, according to Keynes, was to keep aggregate demand high.[6] While this could be done by several different techniques, putting money in wage earners' pockets via a minimum wage was (and is) definitely one possibility. In both cases, it is good for business generally and good for the economy as a whole.

A second economic argument is that it increases productivity. Higher productivity — more output per person hour worked — is a goal everyone agrees is worth pursuing. Sidney and Beatrice Webb were the first, in the late nineteenth century, to emphasize that a minimum wage can enhance

---

5 See the compilation of his speeches in Edward Filene, *Speaking of Change* (New York: Privately published, 1939).
6 Although it is somewhat dated, an excellent summary of Keynes' ideas is Robert Lekachman, *The Age of Keynes* (New York: Random House, 1966).

productivity.[7] When labor costs go up, firms seek more efficient ways of doing things: they give workers more training, they provide better supervision, and they investigate new techniques for producing goods and services. These efficiencies, the very essence of higher productivity, aid economic growth, and make the supply of goods and services more plentiful for everyone. In the long run, too, they create more jobs at higher wages.

Another economic reason for imposing a minimum wage is that it removes public subsidies from certain types of businesses. Suppose a business is paying wages that do not even provide for subsistence. Unless a society is prepared to literally let people starve (and then there would be fewer workers anyway), then some way must be found to bring those people up to subsistence level. In the late nineteenth and early twentieth centuries, the shortfall was usually made up by charities. Thus, those who provided the charities' wherewithal were subsiding low wage industries. These firms, in short, were not bearing the full cost of manufacturing their products, which they should if a market is to work properly. Today, the subsidy is more likely to come from a combination of public assistance and charities. Either way, the low wage firm is a parasite. Neither those people who donate to charities nor the taxpayers should be asked to defray the cost of manufacturing certain products. If a company cannot successfully bring a good to market when bearing the full cost of making it, then obviously buyers do not want it badly enough. In a market economy, put simply, that firm should go out of business.[8]

A final argument is more political than economic, but it turns on financial considerations. It is that the minimum wage is one of the few poverty fighting strategies that requires no commitment from taxpayers. Aside from the miniscule costs of enforcement, the public treasury does not have to make any expenditure whatsoever in order to increase the incomes of the poor. Now, to be sure, any economist will reply that while there may be no direct costs to the taxpayers there may still be costs. Suppose, for instance, that unemployment were to go up as a result of a minimum wage hike and more people applied for unemployment benefits. Or, suppose that prices went up and consumers had to pay more for a variety of goods and services. In short, the minimum wage could be seen as a tax on the business firms which have to pay the increased wages, and, as in all tax policy, there is shifting and incidence. However, as will be detailed below, we still don't know exactly how

---

7 Sidney and Beatrice Webb, *Industrial Democracy* (London: Longmans, 1897).
8 Business activity as a whole will not shrink, though, as whatever consumers spent on the old product will be spent elsewhere.

the minimum wage affects business firms. Thus, the costs to the public are unknown, while the lack of direct public expenditures is definite.

Moral Arguments Against a Minimum Wage

A moral position against a minimum wage is harbored by those who believe the market has a theological status. Individual economic choice, the foundation of market economics, is a sanctified right. The outcomes produced by markets are therefore in themselves "moral."

Any interference in market prices is consequently not only wrong headed but sinful. The minimum wage, as such an interference, is therefore close to an abomination. In fact, the most prominent modern spokesman for market theology, Milton Friedman, listed it as one of the policies he would instantly repeal. He even advocated adding an amendment to the US Constitution reading "Congress shall make no laws abridging the freedom of sellers of goods or labor to price their products or services."[9] As constitutional protections for the free exercise of religion and freedom of speech grew out of natural rights theory, so too this "right" to sell one's labor at any price is part of an "economic bill of rights" based on unalterable principles of justice.

Economic Arguments Against a Minimum Wage

By far, the most commonly voiced economic argument against a minimum wage is that it leads to unemployment, and, further, that the job layoffs will be concentrated among the most vulnerable workers, those new to the labor market and those with the fewest skills. In the United States especially, these people will often be minority youth, it is said.

The logic is straightforward, "Economics 101," as its proponents like to say. The prices of goods and services are determined by the forces of supply and demand. If government sets an artificially high price for any product or service, it will dampen the demand for it since less will be bought at a higher price than a lower price. When the cost of labor goes up, therefore, employers will be forced to lay off workers (or at the least reduce hours and benefits).

True, gains are had by those fortunate enough to keep their jobs, but they come at the cost of unemployment to others. Furthermore, fewer jobs are offered, as the required price exceeds the return a business can expect from adding additional workers. Both the layoffs and the reduced job opportunities adversely affect especially those most in need of entry level jobs. Thus,

---

9 Milton and Rose Friedman, *Free to Choose: A Personal Statement* (New York: Harcourt Brace Jovanovich, 1980), 305.

for both business and for those gaining a first toehold in the labor market, the consequences are adverse. And, of course, the higher the wage, the more adverse the consequences.

A second economic argument is that the minimum wage leads to inflation. The most common assertion here comes from the truism that businesses naturally seek to pass on to consumers cost increases of any kind. When labor costs go up therefore thanks to a minimum wage, firms will raise prices. As a matter of course, consumers will end up footing the bill, then, for the increase in wages. And, of course, to a degree even those who gain via the higher wage will be faced with higher prices. Another way that a minimum wage can lead to inflation begins by noting that the policy is redistributive.[10] It takes money from some — businesses and consumers — and transfers it to low wage workers. Since the recipients are as a whole less well off than the people who lose, a higher percentage of the amount transferred will be spent than would have been the case had it remained in its original hands. The increased spending will add to aggregate demand without any concomitant increase in production, a formula for inflation.

Along with unemployment and inflation will also come business failures. A minimum wage places a business in a difficult position. It has three choices: it can reduce the higher labor costs by pruning workers or hours; it can raise prices; or it can absorb the increased costs by accepting lower profits. If it opts for layoffs or giving workers fewer hours, it may find that it cannot meet the demands of its customers, and they will go elsewhere. If it raises prices, it will lose some customers' dollars or pounds as buyers now want less of the product or service at the higher price. And, finally, some firms do not have a sufficient enough profit margin to absorb the costs. As a result of any or all of these three factors, some businesses will be forced to fold. Again, the most vulnerable are smaller and newer businesses, the very ones often credited with being the most innovative, as well as the most important furnishers of new jobs.

A final economic critique of the minimum wage is that as an antipoverty measure it is poorly targeted. Many if not most minimum wage workers are young people living with their parents, so this argument goes. They do not come from poor households and are not really supporting a family. Thus, the bulk of the benefits will go not to the poor but to relatively affluent teens. There are far better ways to target help to the poor, it is said, the most popu-

---

10 Of course, it is redistributive *only* if efficiency gains do not outpace the increase.

lar of which is some form of tax credit for earnings that slowly phases out as income rises.

Opponents of the minimum wage often contend that the real way to lift people out of poverty is through economic growth and increased productivity. These will create more jobs and higher wages, and those at the bottom of the economic ladder will then benefit along with everyone else. Public policies, therefore, should be designed to encourage business expansion and the creation of a more highly trained work force.

THE ECONOMICS OF THE MINIMUM WAGE

There are two ways to perform economic analysis. One is to erect a model of how individuals, firms, or the macro-economy behave. Then, one reasons from the model to solve particular problems. This approach need not neglect data. However, the data are often collected and analyzed through the lens of the model. The problem is that the more comprehensive the model and/or the greater attachment to it one has, the harder it will be to accept that the data do not conform to the model. The other is to begin with no *a priori* model and simply gather data from the real world and analyze it. Generalizations are formulated based on the data, and then tested against other data. Theory emerges from cautiously connecting the generalizations developed in several studies. The danger here is the opposite faced by the model builders, that the generalizations will be too guarded and important theoretical insights missed. The ideal, of course, is a combination of the two, but that is always difficult to attain.

Wide swaths of contemporary economics are decidedly more influenced by the former way of thinking than the latter.[11] In particular, they work from a rather rigid neoclassical model, and this seems especially true of many who study labor markets.[12] This framework, it must be pointed out, also reinforces a neoliberal, anti-statist political platform. For some, that is, it is a science, for others a religion, and for still others some of both. The "institutionalists," as the inductive camp is known, have been in the minority for some time. However, their approach seems to be making some headway, and that may be at least partly attributable to research on the impact of the minimum

---

11 For an overview of economic thought see Michael Bernstein, *A Perilous Progress: Economists and Public Purpose in Twentieth Century America* (Princeton, NJ: Princeton University Press, 2001). For how economic thinking has influenced contemporary political discourse, see Kenneth Hoover, *Economics as Ideology: Keynes, Laski, Hayek and the Creation of Contemporary Politics* (Lanham, MD: Rowan and Littlefield, 2003).

12 The highly regarded *Journal of Labor Research* is indicative of this trend.

wage. In the chapters that follow, we will have several occasions to examine this research, but some introductory notes are appropriate here.

Take first the matter of rising unemployment accompanying the introduction or the raising of the minimum wage, a hypothesis deduced solely from the model of price theory. The long and short of it is that there is simply no evidence that this is true. After Britain adopted the Trade Boards Act 1909, which established trade boards to set minimum wages in four industries, one of the twentieth century's most noted economists, R. H. Tawney, was commissioned to find out if unemployment had resulted. He and his associates found none.[13] In the 1940s, Richard Lester studied cotton mills in the United States, and failed to uncover any significant correlation between minimum wage increases and decreases in employment.[14]

In our day, the most thorough, and most controversial, work on minimum wages and employment was David Card and Alan Krueger's 1995 book, *Myth and Measurement: The New Economics of the Minimum Wage.*[15] They examined fast food restaurants lying near the New Jersey-Pennsylvania border after New Jersey raised its state minimum wage. Using a telephone survey to gather information, they found that rather than falling, employment increased faster in the higher minimum wage state. The book was subjected to withering criticism, but Card and Krueger's conclusions more than held up when they utilized aggregate data for a follow-up study.[16] We will have an opportunity to look in detail at the studies of the employment effects at the British National Minimum Wage, the US federal minimum wage, and state and local minimum wages in the following chapters. In none of these cases is there any evidence that minimum wages, at least to the level they have been raised so far, have any measurable negative employment effects. It is also worth mentioning here a recent New Zealand study.[17] New Zealand long had a tiered minimum wage, with a youth subminimum. In 2001, they abol-

---

13 R.H. Tawney, *The Establishment of Minimum Rates in the Chain Making Industry under the Trade Boards Act of 1909* (London: Bell, 1914); R.H. Tawney, *The Establishment of Minimum Rates in the Tailoring Industry under the Trade Boards Act of 1909* (London: Bell, 1915); Mildred Emily Bulkley, *The Establishment of Minimum Rates in the Boxmaking Industry under the Trade Boards Act of 1909* (London: Bell, 1915).

14 Richard Lester, "Shortcomings of Marginal Analysis for Wage-Employment Problems," *American Economic Review* 36 (1946), 63-82.

15 David Card and Alan Krueger, *Myth and Measurement: The New Economics of the Minimum Wage* (Princeton, NJ: Princeton University Press, 1995).

16 David Card and Alan Krueger, "Minimum Wages and Employment: A Case Study of the Fast-Food Industry in New Jersey and Pennsylvania: Reply," *American Economic Review* 90 (2000), 1397-1420.

17 Dean Hyslop and Steven Stillman, *Youth Minimum Wage Reform and the Labour Market*, New Zealand Treasury Department, February 2004.

ished the difference, which meant the youth minimum wage went up 41%. Surely, if there was going to be an employment effect, it would occur under these circumstances. Dean Hyslop and Steven Stillman, however, found no unemployment effects whatever in the months following the increase. We might hasten to add, though, that this was not an unmitigated good for New Zealand. The increased minimum wage did tend to pull some teenagers out of school, something that will harm their long-term earning power, to say nothing of how it will limit their lives in other ways. But this is a different matter entirely from unemployment effects.

Representative James Saxton of New Jersey blustered in 1995 that if it were true that minimum wage increases had no employment effects "Why then don't we just raise the minimum wage to $300 or $400 an hour and pay everyone lawyers' wages?"[18] The absurdity of this position ought to be painfully self-evident. No one believes that at some point a minimum wage would not have adverse employment effects (but we don't even know that for sure). Saxon's view is akin to saying that if the doctor tells you one dose of a medicine will do you good, you should drink the whole bottle at once.

When Tawney reflected on why his findings ran counter to standard economic theory, he penned a thought that is as pertinent today as then. "The ingenuity of employers and workpeople so greatly exceeds that of economists that discussions of what 'must' happen, unsupported by evidence of what happened or is happening, are usually quite worthless."[19] Today, the wonder is that so many economists continue to have faith in the model over the accumulated evidence.

Several explanations can be offered as to why unemployment does not seem to follow in the wake of minimum wage increases. Among them three seem to stand out, although they are not the only possible ones. One is that the new purchasing power available to low-wage workers offsets the costs to businesses. That is, low-wage workers often patronize the very types of firms that are most sensitive to minimum wage increases. Thus, increased revenues more than pay for the wage hikes. Another is that low-wage labor "markets" simply do not conform to textbook models. In reality, the facts on the ground regarding low wage workers and how they go about searching for a job are so at variance with the assumptions of a market that perhaps the word "market" should not even be used here. Polly Toynbee, who spent time working at several minimum wage jobs in London and environs, made

---

18 US Congress, Joint Economic Committee, *Evidence against a Higher Minimum Wage*, February 22, 1995, 86.
19 Tawney, *Minimum Rates in the Chain Making Industry*, 105.

this point over and over.[20] Third, it is back to the Webbs. If minimum wage increases lead to increased productivity, then there would be no need for layoffs at all. In fact, hiring would likely increase, something we will actually find in the chapters below. There is much more research to be done here, though, before it will be clear what is going on. For the moment, however, what is important is that we need to search for an explanation for what is actually happening, usually no or even positive employment effects accompanying minimum wage increases.

What about the evidence for inflation? There do seem to have been some price hikes associated with various minimum wage increases, but they have been meager.[21] The reason is that labor costs are only a small fraction of total costs, and vary a lot by type of business. Food service establishments, the industry most sensitive to minimum wage increases, is the most prone to raise prices, but not by much. We will look closely at some of these studies, especially in the chapter on state and local minimum wage laws.

There is no evidence whatever to support the idea that minimum wage increases lead to decreased profits or to business failures. The return to capital seems to stay steady when minimum wages are increased, as we will see from the most thorough data on the matter, collected in Britain. As for the number of businesses in existence, both generally, and in the low-wage sectors, there is actually an increase. This holds true in both the UK and the US. Thus, it is hard to see how a minimum wage increase harms business.

Turning to poverty, the evidence is mixed. It is simply not true that the majority of minimum wage workers are young people earning a little extra spending money. A majority are adults and a surprising number work full time. Furthermore, more of the increase goes to people in the lower income brackets than to those more fortunately situated. The households containing minimum wage workers are not spread evenly throughout the population; they are heavily skewed toward the lower end. Thus, it is reasonably well targeted, but certainly not perfectly so.

In sum, the minimum wage does contribute to lowering poverty, and it does so without any noticeable effects on employment levels or business profits. While there are some inflationary effects, granted, they are not very significant. Tawney said something else nearly a hundred years ago that is also worth quoting. "[O]wing to recent departures in legislation evidence is now coming to light which can be used as a partial criterion of the social

---

20 Polly Toynbee, *Hard Work: Life in Low Pay Britain* (London: Bloomsbury, 2003).
21 See Daniel Aaronson, "Price Pass-Through and the Minimum Wage," *Review of Economics and Statistics*, 83 (2001), 158-169.

and economic effects produced by the intervention of a public body to fix minimum rates, and it is therefore possible to appeal, for a solution of certain primary problems, to the light of experience."[22]

But the appeal to such evidence only bears fruit when two conditions are met: a willingness by academics and analysts to abandon models that do not accord with the evidence and a willingness of political partisans to set aside political prejudices. Neither of these conditions holds in either the United Kingdom or the United States, and we are therefore led directly into the domain of politics. It is here, and not in a seminar room guided by Tawney's appeal to careful inquiry, that minimum wage policy is forged.

THE POLITICS OF THE MINIMUM WAGE

Many models of democratic politics are based on the notion that individual citizens all pursue their own self interest. If the institutions of the polity are properly constructed, the ensuing outcomes will be both acceptable and morally justifiable. As in a smoothly functioning market, the "goods," in this case public policies, will maximize satisfaction for the people at large.

Middle Class Leadership

Whatever validity this model may have in some policy areas, it is a far cry from what goes on in minimum wage politics. The prime beneficiaries, the young and the poor, are among the least powerful segments of society, and have great difficulty making their voices heard. This is because the major sources of political power in a democracy are voting and interest group lobbying, and in neither of these are the young and the poor to be found.

Begin with voting. In the first place, those under 18 are legally barred from voting. In addition, every voting study has shown that the young and the poor turnout in much lower numbers than other sectors of the electorate.[23] Thus, their interests do not get as much attention from politicians as their sheer numbers would warrant. As for interest groups, one of the consistent findings is that the higher one goes up the income and educational ladder, the more likely are people to join groups of any kind, politically oriented groups included.[24] The reasons for this are not hard to see. For one thing, the poor spend most of their time finding ways to stretch their meager incomes

---

22 Tawney, *Minimum Wages in the Chain Making Industry*, xi.

23 For the US, see the report by the Pew Research Center *Who Votes, Who Doesn't, and Why*, October 18, 2006. For Britain, see John Curtice, "Turnout: Electors Stay Home — Again," in Pippa Norris and Chris Wlezien, *Britain Votes 2005* (Oxford: Oxford University Press, 2005), 120-129.

24 See Jeffrey Berry and Clyde Wilcox, *The Interest Group Society* (New York: Longmans, 2007).

and have little time to attend meetings. Moreover, the collective action problem makes it hard for them to mentally link their needs to the long-run advantages of getting organized. Thus, organizations formed by the poor are quite rare, and even when they are planted they obviously lack the financial clout and political savvy of groups representing, say, doctors. In short, if the success of the minimum wage relied only on the efforts of the poor, it is unlikely any country would have ever had one.

In minimum wage policy, therefore, others must take the lead. In most cases, it has been and is middle class reformers who push for minimum wage legislation, who provide the political energy to generate petitions, who write position papers and editorials, and who contact members of the legislature and other public figures.[25] To be sure, they often form organizations and invite the poor to join, and have some success at doing this; however, the leadership role of dedicated middle class elites is absolutely critical.

Public Opinion

Three facets of public opinion regarding the minimum wage are noteworthy.[26] First, the public overwhelmingly supports the minimum wage. Second, while support for the policy is lower among wealthier and more ideologically conservative segments of the population, it is still high in absolute terms. Third, the support is shallow rather than intense.

As for absolute levels of support, the minimum wage very rarely gets less that 80% approval. For example, 88% of the British public endorsed the minimum wage in 1999.[27] Similarly, in the most recent American poll, 83% favored increasing the minimum wage.[28]

Table 1-1 shows how support breaks down across income and ideological lines in the United States. There is a clear difference between Democrats, Independents, and Republicans, but it is significant how strong the support — nearly three out of four — is among Republicans. It is also clear that support for the minimum wage decreases as income rises; again, however, an equally pertinent fact is that there is overwhelming support even among the well off.

---

25 Although he pays inordinate attention to the possible economic motivations of activists to the exclusion of their moral concerns, an interesting review of the matter is Richard Freeman, "Fighting for Other Folks' Wages: The Logic and Illogic of Living Wage Campaigns," *Industrial Relations* 44 (2005), 14-31.

26 I have analyzed public opinion on the minimum wage more thoroughly in *The Politics of the Minimum Wage* (Urbana: University of Illinois Press, 2000), chap. 3 (US only) and *The Case for the Living Wage*, chap. 8 (US and UK).

27 Roger Jowell, *et al..*, eds., *British Social Attitudes, the 17ᵗʰ Report* (London: Sage, 2000), 329.

28 Pew Research Center, *Maximum Support for Raising the Minimum*, April 19, 2006.

	Favor	Oppose	Don't Know
	TABLE 1-1. SUPPORT FOR RAISING U.S. MINIMUM WAGE FROM $5.15 TO $7.25, IN 2006		
	%	%	%
All adults	83	14	3
Income Levels (household)			
Below $20,000	91	7	1
$20–$50,000	85	13	2
$50–$75,000	86	11	3
Above $75,000	76	22	2
Party identification			
Democrats	91	8	1
Independents	87	11	2
Republicans	72	24	4

Source: Pew Research Center.

At the same time, when people are asked to list the most important problems they want government to address, the minimum wage is seldom mentioned. For example, in a 2000 MORI poll, only 2% of the British public mentioned the minimum wage as an important issue. Similarly, in Gallup's monthly polls asking the American public to name the most important public problems, the minimum wage is usually off the radar screen.

The picture changes somewhat, though, when people are handed a list of items and asked which ones an incoming Congress should address. The numbers were arguably inflated in 2006, because Democrats had put so much emphasis on the minimum wage during the campaign, but that only presents us with a stronger version of the general point. For instance, in a *Newsweek* poll taken immediately after the election, 68% said raising the minimum wage should be a top domestic priority, second only to providing for ways Americans could get lower prices on drugs (75%). In short, the minimum wage always scores well when it is mentioned by pollsters in this context.

What all this means is that politicians can always win points with the public by standing in favor of a minimum wage hike. However, the relatively low intensity of the issue allows opponents to stall for time, and, crucially, means that those in favor of it have a hard time keeping momentum going. There will always be many who sympathize but who have no sense of urgency. This explains why, despite enormous public backing, unless there is some regular mechanism to put them before the legislative body, minimum wage increases will often fail to pass.

Interest Groups

A goodly number of interest groups are active in minimum wage politics, on both sides of the issue. It is here more than anywhere else that we glimpse the importance of the *pro* side being grounded in social welfare advocacy and the *anti* side coming at the issue from the perspective of labor market policy. The minimum wage is the only arena in which these two sides confront each other directly.

In the United States especially, but also in Britain to a degree, one of the most important players in minimum wage politics is self-styled "community organizations." These entities are founded and run mostly by a dedicated group of reformers, most of whom come from middle-class backgrounds. Sometimes they have risen from the ranks of minimum wage workers, but more often they are imbued with an admirable idealism. In advocating increased minimum wages, they usually have nothing to gain personally. The organizations customarily make Herculean efforts to recruit the poor and involve them in all facets of the organization, including decision making. In truth, though, the poor are very difficult to organize, and while these organizations have indeed had some successes, the challenges are overwhelming.

The prime example of this type of entity in the United States is the Association of Community Organizations for Reform Now (ACORN). Begun in the 1970s in Little Rock, Arkansas, its main focus until the mid-1990s was housing reform and increasing the opportunities for the dispossessed to participate in politics.[29] In the mid-1990s it took up the living wage issue at the local level, and was the prime mover in spreading this idea throughout the United States. Then, too, it has made state and federal minimum wage policies a central concern. Its organizers were the principal force behind the successful Florida minimum wage effort in 2004, for example, and the group has mounted major letter writing and lobbying campaigns regarding the federal minimum wage.

In Britain, The East London Citizens Organisation (TELCO) and the closely linked Citizens Organizing Foundation (COF) make up the closest parallel group. Begun about ten years ago, it too has worked on several fronts. Nonetheless, one of its central planks has long been advocacy of a living wage.

---

29 A history of the organization is offered at its website, www.acorn.org.

Many religious groups are closely allied and even organizationally linked to ACORN and COF. For example, COF counts among its constituent members a large number of Catholic parishes in London, along with a multiplicity of Protestant churches and mosques. ACORN too has a variety of congregations allied to it. However, many other religious groups work independently on behalf of the minimum wage. For example, in January 2007, American Catholic Bishops sent a letter to Congress renewing their "support for an increase in the minimum wage. For us it is a matter of simple justice for a decent society."[30] Protestant churches have been equally emphatic. At its 2005 General Assembly, the Christian Church (Disciples of Christ) passed a resolution asserting that the denomination "supports national movements toward the passage of legislation that guarantees workers sufficient wages to supply adequate food, clothing, shelter, and health care for themselves and their families."[31] In 2006, a wide array of American religious leaders banded together to form the "Let Justice Roll" network, whose central purpose was supporting the minimum wage increase then pending in Congress.[32] In the United Kingdom, the Church Action on Poverty group has an active living wage campaign as part of its efforts; Caritas, the Catholic Church's social action agency, has called for making the minimum wage a living wage; and the Church of England's May 2006 report *Faithful Cities* called for a living wage.[33]

Of vital importance to minimum wage politics is the role of unions, but it is a role that has historically been ambivalent. At the outset, in both the UK and the US many of the largest and most powerful unions were actually opposed, even adamantly opposed, to the introduction of minimum wage laws. To some degree, this reflected unabashed gender discrimination. Many of the workers who would be covered by minimum wages, in fact in Britain and in law in the United States, were women. Skilled workers were often of the opinion that women should not really be in the labor market at all, in part because men felt they should be the family breadwinner and also in part because it was felt women workers drove down wages. Another dimension, though, was that many union leaders felt that setting a minimum wage would undermine collective bargaining. In their view, a minimum wage, which would invariably be low, might become some kind of benchmark. In the United States, Samuel Gompers, the American Federation of Labor (AFL)

---

30 Office of Media Relations, United States Conference of Catholic Bishops, January 8, 2007.
31 Complete text available at the denomination's website, www.disciples.org/
32 Its letter to Congress and associated materials can be found at www.letjusticeroll.org/
33 Information on all these is available at the respective websites.

leader, remained strongly opposed to minimum wage laws until the end.[34] In Britain, the major unions continually used their position in the Labor party to block the party's endorsement of a minimum wage; in fact, it was not until the 1980s that many British unions would drop their opposition.

However, there were always exceptions. Unions organized for women, naturally, were quite hospitable to the minimum wage. Then, too, some other union leaders were at least sympathetic, such as John L. Lewis of the United Mineworkers in the United States and regional union leaders in Boston.

Today, unions representing many low-paid workers, chiefly UNISON in Britain and the Service Employees International Union (SEIU) in the United States, are among the most reliable and steady backers of minimum wage policies at every level of government. They have full time employees dedicated to working for minimum and living wages, and they eagerly seek out alliances with other groups interested in promoting minimum wage policy. The unions' peak organizations, the TUC in Britain and the AFL–CIO in the United States, have also come around, and are now enthusiastic backers of the minimum wage. Both maintain an active interest in raising the minimum wage, and can be counted on to put their financial and political muscle into the fight.

Two other sets of groups will also attempt to make their voices heard regarding the minimum wage. The first is most women's groups. As we will see, in both countries the minimum wage work force contains a significantly disproportionate number of women. Thus, minimum wage politics cannot be divorced from gender politics. The other is groups representing minorities. It has long been more evident in the United States than in Britain that minorities stand to benefit more than the general population from minimum wage increases. Thus, American civil rights groups regularly weigh in and enter the fray. In Britain too, now, as cleaners especially have come to have a more heavily immigrant profile, something similar is beginning to occur there as well.

In the United States particularly, and also in Britain but to a lesser degree, the pattern is for these groups — community organizations, religious bodies, unions, and often women's and civil rights groups — to form a loose umbrella organization to push for minimum wage increases. This allows them to co-ordinate their lobbying and public awareness efforts. However, between minimum wage battles, these umbrella organizations tend to fade away. The reason that this pattern is less prevalent in Britain is structural. In

---

34 Gompers' opposition to minimum wage laws is discussed in Bernard Mandel, *Samuel Gompers: A Biography* (Yellow Springs, OH: Antioch Press, 1963), 174-180.

the United States, each minimum wage hike at the federal level has to be obtained through regular legislation, securing the assent of both houses of Congress and the president. (Until recently, when indexing provisions have been added, state minimum wage increases could only be passed by a similar process.) In Britain, Parliament has established the Low Pay Commission (LPC) to recommend periodic adjustments to the minimum wage. Thus, much of the lobbying effort goes into preparing submissions to this body, and there is less need for building a broad-based coalition. There is intense lobbying as the proposal moves from the LPC to the cabinet, but again the time frame is relatively short, and each group can work with friendly forces within the parliamentary party. Thus, there is certainly some co-ordination of efforts, but it is less formally organized. Interestingly, when the initial British minimum wage was under consideration immediately prior to the First World War, though, the modern American pattern was replicated almost exactly, a story that will be told in some detail in chapter 2.

One factor that deserves mention is the role of philanthropists. Many of the community organizations have only the thinnest of financial bases, and into this breach often steps a wealthy underwriter. For example, George Cadbury, the chocolate magnate, was instrumental in helping the British minimum wage movement establish and maintain its momentum. In like manner, Rob McKay, heir to the Taco Bell fortune, gave generously to the San Francisco living wage campaign. Similarly, during the 2006 campaign in Arizona to initiate a state minimum wage, the Tides Foundation of San Francisco made important monetary contributions. Without these people, minimum wage advocates would be hard pressed to keep their campaigns going.

Opposition to the minimum wage flies in from several fronts. There is first a reliable cadre of editorial writers, commentators, and economists who can be counted on to fervently denounce the minimum wage as a violation of market principles and a barrier to job creation. Their shrillness sometimes takes on a quasi-religious quality, as the minimum wage is pronounced an abomination that must be strenuously resisted. In other cases, the stress is merely on the deleterious effect raising the minimum wage will have on the poor. In these diatribes, minimum wage advocates are depicted as naïve idealists, at best.[35]

---

35 Examples are legion. A mild version of the position can be witnessed in George Will's column in the *Washington Post*, January 4, 2007, while more strident articles can be found in *Reason* magazine.

Business interests are also usually to be found among the ranks of the opposition.[36] First in line are the peak business organizations, such as the Confederation of British Industry and the Institute of Directors (UK) and the United States Chamber of Commerce. These organizations are general business groups, though, and many of their members will be only marginally affected if at all by a minimum wage increase. Their opposition often appears to be therefore almost reflexive, a ritualistic protest against the symbolic role of the minimum wage in legitimating government regulation of the economy in general. They add their names to the opposition, but do not draw lines in the sand.

Small business associations, on the other hand, will often mount an all-out effort to kill, or alternatively to minimize, any type of minimum wage increase. Statements from these organizations echo the free market editorial writers, and often sound dire notes. For example, the American National Federation of Independent Businesses issued the following statement as the most recent minimum wage increase was under consideration:

> NFIB opposes any increase in the minimum wage. Mandatory wage increases hurt not only small businesses, but their employees as well. Big corporations do not have to absorb the cost because most minimum-wage jobs are offered by small businesses. Government manipulation of the starting wage has failed as [a] tool of social and/or economic justice. It has not been proven to reduce poverty or narrow the income gap and puts a stranglehold on America's top job creators: small businesses.[37]

In a similar vein, although dramatically less apocalyptic, Britain's Federation of Small Business said in a January 2007 press release: "Inflation-busting increases in the NMW [National Minimum Wage] are beginning to hit some small businesses hard. The situation may become critical if the NMW is geared towards average earnings instead of inflation."[38]

The strongest opponents are naturally the businesses most affected by minimum wage policies, chiefly restaurants and retailers. In the United Kingdom, the British Hospitality Association and others expressed serious doubts when the National Minimum Wage was being introduced in 1998-1999. However, they now more or less live with the policy, and devote their efforts merely to keeping the increases modest. In the United States, on the other hand, the National Restaurant Association keeps up a drumbeat of opposition to the minimum wage, and has even established its own research organization (the Employment Policies Institute) to churn out studies sup-

---

36 But, of course, there are always exceptions.
37 www.nfib.com/page/minimumwage
38 www.fsb.org.uk/news.asp

portive of their position. A letter sent to Senators during June of 2006 captures the tone of the Association's position:

> On behalf of the National Restaurant Association . . . we want to make you aware of our strong opposition [to a minimum wage increase].
>
> The [proposed] starting wage . . . is the largest increase in the entry-level wage ever proposed, and would result in a *41 Percent Hike In Labor Costs!* Small employers and labor-intensive businesses such as restaurants are most impacted by entry-level wage increases. . . The restaurant industry . . . believes the market should determine entry level compensation around the country, rather than force businesses to cope with a one-size-fits-all federal requirement.
>
> The National Restaurant Association encourages your opposition to [this increase]. **This amendment will be a key vote for the restaurant industry.** (Emphasis in original.)[39]

Political Parties

It goes without saying that the parties on the left are in favor of the minimum wage and those on the right opposed. Thus, it is no surprise whatever that the Democratic Party in the United States and the Labor party in Britain have been the ones who inaugurated minimum wage policies and remain the ones more hospitable to expanding the coverage and increasing the level of the minimum wage. However, it is not a simple for and against dichotomy.

There is first the matter that support for the minimum wage varies inside the parties of the left. Within the Democratic Party almost every prominent politician now supports minimum wage increases; however, when the party harbored a strong Southern wing in Congress there were often opponents among its ranks. In addition, the ardor with which the contemporary party elites support the minimum wage is not uniform. Some, especially Senator Edward Kennedy of Massachusetts, lose no opportunity to push the minimum wage, and those most closely allied to unions tend to put on their battle armor whenever the measure is mentioned. Other Democrats fall into two camps. On the one hand, there are those whose policy commitments are rooted elsewhere, in environmental issues or education, for example. On the other, many Democrats are still wedded to social welfare expenditure policies and the Earned Income Tax Credit. People in both camps can certainly be counted on to support minimum wage increases, but they are followers not leaders, falling in line but cheering with only muted enthusiasm.

---

39 The restaurant industry has long called minimum wage jobs "entry level jobs." The 41% increase figure is also disingenuous. It was slated to occur in steps. Besides, it was only because the minimum wage had been stuck at $5.15 for a decade that a sharp increase was needed.

Then, there is the fact that Republicans are not monolithic either. To be sure, the more liberal generally Northeastern wing of the party is only a shadow of its former self. And it is certainly the case that many Republican members of Congress are market fundamentalists when it comes to the minimum wage. In 1996, for instance, when the Republican leadership had agreed to pass a minimum wage increase coupled to tax cuts, several House members insisted that the measures be brought to the floor in two separate bills so that they would not have to cast a vote for a minimum wage increase. However, there are Republicans who are more moderate on the issue. For most, it seems that it is practical politics. Given the popularity of the minimum wage, there is a political cost to be paid in being too adamantly opposed; and given the negligible impact minimum wage increases seem to have, unbridled opposition is not worth the political costs. Moreover, some Republicans have union members in their constituencies and believe that the success of the party depends on winning them over. Standing in the way of minimum wage increases makes this pitch harder. For a small contingent, the minimum wage is an acceptable policy to fight poverty, as long as it is not too high. Consequently, when minimum wage increases are debated in Congress, it is possible to win over a few Republicans in the critical votes. In fact, after the necessary compromises are struck, most Republicans can even be persuaded to vote for final passage.

The Labor party's approach to minimum wage policy has been determined by the stance of the unions. So long as the major unions were opposed to a universal minimum wage, the party avoided the issue. Then, when union opposition dissolved, the party moved quickly to include calls for a minimum wage in its manifestos, beginning in 1987. The current division in the party is between those who are strongly committed to the minimum wage as a way to ensure a decent life for those at the bottom and those who are especially keen to be seen as sensitive to the needs of business. New Labor's success, in this latter view, has been based on courting the approval of the business community, and one way to keep that boat sailing is to be sure that Labor party officials themselves include the needs of business when making decisions. Being hesitant on the minimum wage is a perfect way to do this. Thus, while virtually all Labor party elites endorse the minimum wage in principle, there is substantial disagreement about how far it should reach into the labor force and how high it should go.

The Conservative party has moderated its views on the minimum wage. During the Thatcher and Major years, they demolished the old Wages Councils (tri-partite bodies which had set minimum wages in selected industries) as a blemish on free market principles. When, later, Labor proposed adopting a universal minimum wage, Conservatives denounced it in the strongest possible terms. After its adoption, though, the party gave way. Whether because of practical politics (fearing public wrath, given the immense popularity of the minimum wage) or a sincere change of heart, the party has officially said that it will not repeal the measure, and has even given it a grudging endorsement. However, there is still no real enthusiasm in the party for the idea. Hence, it seems likely that when given the opportunity to govern they will avoid any direct attacks on the measure, but allow it to atrophy through neglect instead.

Intraparty politics is more critical in Britain than in the United States since power is more concentrated, and there is no need for interparty politics. Given the realities of the parliamentary system as it currently operates, decisions are made within the governing party. Labor does not need to win over a handful of Conservatives in order to approve minimum wage increases in the way that Democrats must rope in a few Republicans, especially to reach the 60 votes needed in the Senate to break a filibuster. Within a British governing party, the decisions taken by the leadership will become policy, but backbench rebellions are not without impact, as we will see when we discuss how increases to the National Minimum Wage have developed.

POLICY MAKING ARENAS

Once a minimum wage law is enacted, subsequent policy development can take one of three forms.[40] The first option is to establish a public body outside the legislature and endow it with the power to make changes in the law, especially the setting of the level of the wage. A second approach is to create an outside body, but only give it the power to make recommendations, recommendations that then come to the legislature. The final way of doing business is to keep all aspects of minimum wage policy in the hands of the legislature.

The first approach has been the one utilized in Australia. The composition of and the statutory guidelines under which the public body operates have changed from time to time, as has its name. Today, minimum wages are set by the Fair Pay Commission, and the Howard government has introduced more business friendly strictures into the statutory regime that con-

---

40 A complete discussion of this matter, although they use rather different categories, can be found in Francois Eyraud and Catherine Saget, *The Fundamentals of Minimum Wage Fixing* (Geneva: International Labour Office, 2005).

trols its deliberations.[41] However, the principle of setting minimum wages by an extra-legislative entity remains.

Britain has looked to the second option. Parliament created the Low Pay Commission to make initial recommendations regarding the minimum wage, and later made it a statutory body. Each year it is given a charge by the government about what it should consider. It then accepts submissions from interested parties, conducts hearings, and holds deliberations. Its recommendations are then taken under advisement by the government, but do not become policy until approved by it.

The United States, in contrast, uses the third model, as Congress has repeatedly resisted creating even a recommendatory body. Thus, each alteration in the minimum wage must run the entire legislative gamut, as any other statute.

Although the British system is still in its infancy, and has not been thoroughly tested by an alteration of party control of government, two generalizations can be drawn. First, the very existence of the Low Pay Commission keeps the minimum wage on the agenda. The government must provide a charge each cycle and it must at least make a public response to the recommendations. In contrast, one of the major hurdles minimum wage advocates face in the United States is just getting the issue on the political front burner. Congressional time is always limited, and Democratic leaders (the only ones to ever try to bring minimum wage increases out of the political firmament), whether presidents or congressional leaders, always have a long list of other matters competing for attention. Second, the need to secure passage in both houses of Congress, especially to garner the 60 votes necessary to cut off debate in the Senate, and then get presidential approval puts all the trump cards in the hands of the opponents. As with any legislation in the United States, the opponents need win only once, while the proponents must come out on top each time, all the while fending off debilitating amendments.

There is also the matter of campaign finance. American politicians are always in need of funds, and business interests furnish most of these. Minimum wage advocacy organizations are not without power in campaigns, as they have prestige in certain quarters and sometimes a small staff of campaign workers; however, they are no match for business lobbyists. Hence, every member of Congress cannot help but be influenced by the needs of business. The situation is Britain is rather different, especially as regards the Labor party. While the need for campaign contributions has grown, many

---

41 See Mark Wooden, "Minimum Wage Setting and the Australian Fair Pay Commission," *Journal of Australian Political Economy* 56 (2005), 81-91.

MPs are still more beholden to unions. Thus, as a whole, the political dynamics are more open and more interests are brought to bear in minimum wage politics in Britain than in the United States.

THE STRUCTURE OF A MINIMUM WAGE

A number of important structural issues are inherent in minimum wage legislation. For starters, both the level of the wage and to whom it should apply must be addressed. In addition, there is the matter of whether the wage should be identical for everyone covered, or whether certain people should be subject only to some type of subminimum wage. On another front, there are various peculiarities relating to certain occupations or to certain economic sectors. Finally, enforcement mechanisms must be established.

Universal versus Sector Specific Minimum Wages

The first decision to be taken when setting up a minimum wage law is whether there shall be one wage applicable to all who are covered by the law or whether different wage mandates shall prevail in different industrial sectors. All the early laws in Britain and the United States (and in Australia and New Zealand as well) were cast in the latter mold, usually referred to as "trade board" type statutes. A law would establish a trade board, customarily a tripartite affair with representative from business firms, workers, and "the public," with authority to establish minimum wages throughout a certain industry. Typically, a list of factors the board had to bear in mind when setting the wage was included in the statute. The board was ordinarily further empowered to update the wage periodically, as economic conditions changed in the country as a whole and in the given industry.

These early laws were restricted to those sectors where wages were the lowest, but where they were retained the number of boards expanded steadily. In practice, though, they proved cumbersome. Classifying individual firms as falling into this industry or that was never easy. Plus, the dynamic nature of the economy meant that new industries were always rising and old ones fading away. In addition, these laws bore an inherent contradiction. If the purpose of a minimum wage policy is to provide a certain minimum income to workers, then why should where the work is done be germane at all?

The theoretical and practical difficulties involved in the operation of trade boards led in time to calls for a nationally uniform minimum wage, a call that was heeded almost everywhere except in Britain. However administratively simple and politically expedient a universal minimum wage is, though, it has inherent difficulties of its own. The chief one is geographical, as living costs always vary enormously from one locale to another. Then, there is always the fact that some industries could pay well above the minimum but will perhaps not do so unless compelled.

When the Roosevelt administration initially proposed what was to become the Fair Labor Standards Act of 1938, they tried to combine the two types. Their proposal set a universal minimum wage, but at the same time gave the Secretary of Labor the authority to establish industry committees that could set enforceable minimum wages for their industry that were above the statutory level. This part of the bill survived the legislative struggle, and the Secretary did set up a few such committees. They did not work well, however, and their use was soon abandoned.[42]

In Britain, the Trade Boards (rechristened Wages Councils in 1945) continued to operate until wound up in 1993. When the Labor government brought forward its minimum wage proposal in 1998, there was no talk of having it be anything but uniform. (See chapter 3.)

The Level of the Wage

Whether it is done by industrial sector or generally, the most common referent for setting the level of the wage is the needs of the worker. But there is no agreement on how this standard ought to be calculated. Should it be the bare subsistence of one person? The amount it takes one frugal person to live very modestly, say, above the society's poverty line? For one person to live reasonably comfortably, at a "decent" level? If so, how are we to measure "decently"?[43] What about the worker's family? Should he/she be able to support a family of two? Three? How many people in a family should be expected to work?

Another alternative is to set some type of benchmark. For example, British unions have set a goal of one-half median male earnings. President Jimmy Carter once proposed tying the American minimum wage to half the average hourly manufacturing wage. Any number of other benchmarks could also be developed and defended.[44]

Then, there is the question of whether or not some assessment ought to be made regarding what business can afford. If separate minimum wages are to be maintained for various industrial sectors, then conditions in the

---

42 These boards and their problems are discussed in Willis Nordlund, *The Quest for a Living Wage: A History of the Federal Minimum Wage Program* (Westport, CT: Greenwood, 1997).

43 The usual way of doing this is to compile some type of family budget, and then compute a per hour rate that would allow monthly earnings to reach this level.

44 I discuss my own preferences in *The Case for the Living Wage*, 117-125.

industry may well warrant consideration. If a uniform minimum wage is established, then the argument is that macroeconomic conditions should be brought to bear on the matter of the wage level. Or, in a related vein, should other economic factors be considered, such as the economic cycle, the current unemployment rate, the competitiveness of the country's firms in international markets, and so forth?

Coverage

Coverage, at its simplest, would be universal. However, there are sometimes economic arguments for certain exceptions, and there is *always* political pressure to grant exceptions. The most commonly raised ones involve sectors, occupations, or small firms.

Political pressure to exempt is usually strongest where the minimum wage is needed the most, in fields such as agriculture, hospitality and food service, and retail. If the goal is to help the low paid, then none of these exceptions makes any sense. However, minimum wage proponents have sometimes had to grant such exclusions in order to get a law on the books, hoping to win the fight another day.

The occupations that most often present the hardest cases are either those involving legitimate training (such as apprentices) or those in which the hours worked are difficult to compute (domestic service or home health care, for example). Most of the time, though, these exceptions are negligible.[45]

A more pervasive dispute involves whether or not the smallest of firms should be exempt or not. The argument is often made that these "mom and pop" businesses cannot really afford the increased wages coverage would entail, and that the paperwork requirements are unduly burdensome. Two major problems come to the fore immediately, though, even if the argument is granted. First, by what criteria do you distinguish "small," and where do you draw the line? The United States has used a gross sales test, which is probably the easiest metric; but the question of where to establish the cutoff point is a morass. Second, as noted above regarding sectors, if the needs of the worker are the rationale for a minimum wage law, why should the size of the firm for which the work is done matter?

---

45 In the United States all workers subject to the minimum wage are also subject to the maximum hours provision of the FLSA (requiring time and a half pay for all hours over 40 per week). Several occupations have remained exempt from FLSA coverage, but the real reason the exemption is sought is the hours requirements, not the minimum wage rates.

Subminimums or a Tiered System

Two arguments are advanced to justify paying some workers below the minimum wage. One is that some workers are not productive enough to justify the minimum wage. The other is that certain groups of workers are especially vulnerable to the unemployment effects of a minimum wage (assuming there are any) and that allowing employers to hire them at a subminimum wage will mitigate this effect.

One group in the first category that is seldom controversial is the physically or mentally disabled. Almost everyone agrees that if these citizens can find satisfying and productive work, they should be allowed to pursue it and, if it is true that their output falls short of the minimum wage, their compensation can be adjusted. The balance can then be made up from public funds.

The real controversy swirls around new workers and young people. Some analysts have argued that new workers need training to become valuable to their employers, and that therefore a reduced wage is justified for some initial period, such as 90 or 180 days. Unions always oppose this proposal, taking the position that if it is adopted employers will constantly churn their work force in order to keep paying the lower wage. Neither one of these arguments seems to hold much validity. The training required for most low skill jobs takes less than a day. On the other side, what rational business will dismiss workers at the end of 90 days to take on a fresh crop of novices (who will surely know what their fate is likely to be in 90 days and work accordingly)? For the most part, it is symbolism at work here, not economic reality.

Concerning young people, though, the arguments are more serious. *If* you want to push the adult minimum wage up to a reasonably high level, and *if* you want to encourage as many young people to take jobs as possible, and *if* you believe a high minimum wage has unemployment effects, then some kind of case can be made for creating a youth differential. This is precisely the argument Gordon Brown, British Chancellor of the Exchequer from 1997 to 2007, and his allies made, and cited as justification the fact that the youth unemployment rate was consistently higher than the adult rate. Combine the rates, they said, and the picture will be even worse. Of course, it cannot be proven that youth unemployment would have been any different with a uniform rate. In the United States, there is a seldom used youth and student differential, in part because the administrative requirements are relatively stringent but in part also because the minimum wage has been so low anyway.

Two Complexities

One complexity involves people who earn tips. Should an employer be exempt from paying the minimum wage if the workers' tips exceed the required wage? This problem is known as the "tip credit" controversy, and we will examine how it has played out below.

The other involves payments in kind. The most common one is housing, often offered for the employer's convenience to agricultural workers and seasonal workers at holiday resorts and the like. However, all kinds of other candidates present themselves, an issue that has flared in Britain in particular.

In both these cases, there is a plausible argument on the employers' side. However, there is a wide open door to abuse here as well. Who will verify the tips? Who will decide how much the payment in kind is worth?

Enforcement

Although it is not a subject we will be discussing in this book, adequate enforcement is critical, as anemic enforcement is an invitation to avoidance.[46] All entities subject to the act must be required to maintain and produce accurate payroll records. The agency charged with enforcement must have an adequate corps of inspectors, and these people must not only be suitably qualified but must also have ample powers. A useful supplement to agency enforcement powers is granting individual workers and anyone speaking on their behalf (usually unions) the right to bring a suit for back wages. Too, the penalties for evasion must be sufficiently severe to act as a deterrent. Those designing enforcement powers must always remember that the beneficiaries of a minimum wage law are the least likely people to know their rights and the most likely ones to be intimidated by an overbearing employer.

Conclusion

As a policy to ameliorate poverty, the minimum wage is dependent, in the first instance, on whether or not social reformers deem it important. If it is thought to be worthwhile, then where it lies among the various conceivable strategies to address poverty becomes critical. But even when it is put high on the social welfare agenda, the minimum wage's status as a labor market policy will shape the political struggle, as unions and employers accompanied by free market ideologues enter the scene. The support, or at a minimum

---

46 On enforcement of minimum wage policy, see Richard Croucher and Geoff White, "Enforcing a National Minimum Wage: The British Case," *Policy Studies* 28 (2007), 145-162.

the acquiescence, of the former will make or break a minimum wage, while the entrenched opposition of the latter must be overcome.

We turn now to a discussion of how these elements have played out in Britain and the United States.

Chapter 2. Origins

Public policies, or at least domestic public policies at any rate, result from the interaction of social conditions, ideas, and the dictates of practical politics. This was certainly true in the long road to the adoption of a minimum wage in the United Kingdom and the United States. The continuing presence of poverty into the late nineteenth and early twentieth century, when the optimistic predictions of the founders of political economy concerning the benefits that would automatically flow from sustained growth turned out to be false, prompted a search for new ways to analyze the world. New models of thought produced, in turn, a sheaf of innovative proposals for increasing the role of the state in the society and the economy. After a period of gestation, these proposals moved from the pages of journals and books into the minds of those actively involved in politics. When political conditions were apt, in 1909 in Britain, in 1912 in Massachusetts, and in 1938 at the US federal level, minimum wage policies emerged.

It is imperative to understand, though, that the minimum wage was not a policy developed in isolation. It was, from inception to adoption, part of a broader program of social reform. Once on the books, it slowly became detached from this social welfare base, with significant consequences for both the minimum wage and social welfare policy generally. What Adrian Vinson said of Britain was equally true of the United States: "If the essentially Edwardian combination of the minimum wage with family endowment offered the model for *a* welfare state, it was not to become the model for *the* welfare

---

state after 1945."[1] Social welfare advocates were to turn to social insurance and public assistance, and in so doing pushed the minimum wage to the sidelines. However, that was not where it began, either in the realm of ideas or the realm of politics.

THE ROAD TO THE TRADE BOARDS ACT 1909

The Trade Boards Act 1909 was enacted after the Liberal party's election victory of 1906, in which they were victorious in 400 constituencies compared to the Conservatives' 157. (There were also 30 Labor M.P.s) Dominated now by the New Liberals, the party stood prepared to adopt a comprehensive program of reform. In addition to the Trade Boards Act 1909, they secured the Old Age Pensions Act 1908, the Workmen's Compensation Act 1906, the Housing and Town Planning Act 1909, the Labour Exchanges Act 1909, the National Insurance Act 1911 (which laid the foundations of health and unemployment insurance policies), and of course the redistributive taxation contained in the 1909 Budget.[2]

New Liberalism

At the broadest level, the story of the minimum wage begins in the intellectual shift away from the liberalism epitomized by John Stuart Mill to what is called the New Liberalism. The older version of liberalism had glorified and sanctified the individual as the building block of society. Maximizing the scope of individual liberty while simultaneously limiting the reach of the state was not only morally correct; it would produce the greatest amount of good for all concerned.

The shift to a revised version of liberalism derived, in the first instance, from the absorption of newer intellectual currents. Many analysts of the period point to the pivotal role of the Idealists, in particular T.H. Green. Green insisted on the existence of a concept of the common good that was not merely the summation of individual desires. Moreover, a central role of the state, in his view, was to remove the barriers that kept people from contributing to the common good.[3] Others have argued that biological and evolutionary ideas were more important in the transformation.[4] That is, society

---

1 Adrian Vinson, "The Edwardians and Poverty: Towards a Minimum Wage?" in Donald Read, ed., *Edwardian England* (New Brunswick, NJ: Rutgers University Press, 1982), 90.

2 For an overview of the Liberal government's work, see Peter Rowland, *The Last Liberal Government*, Vol. I: *The Promised Land, 1905-1910* (New York: Macmillan, 1969).

3 Kenneth Hoover, "Liberalism and the Idealist Philosophy of Thomas Hill Green," *Western Political Quarterly* 26 (1973), 550-565.

4 Michael Freeden, *The New Liberalism* (Oxford: Oxford University Press, 1978).

is able to evolve into a better form, and that, consequently, what is today is not determinative of what will be tomorrow. British intellectuals of the late nineteenth century, then, did not discard liberalism; instead they modified and extended it.

At the same time, liberalism could not escape the growing influence of empirical social science. Repeated investigations, some of which are detailed below, produced undeniable evidence that despite huge leaps in average income and the large-scale charitable efforts of the Victorians, poverty and misery were still prevalent and deep-seated. "The idea of a free, self-regulating market, reflecting natural law and epitomizing social justice," Michael Freeden has said, "collapsed in the face of the facts uncovered by the increased awareness of socio-economic ills."[5]

Advocates of New Liberalism came to embrace two propositions. On the one hand, they did not abandon the pursuit of individual liberty as a social good. However, they believed that the state could be used to enhance rather than threaten individual liberty. This led them straight to the idea of a "national minimum" to be provided through enlightened public policies. On the other, they removed individual liberty, especially in its economic guise, from its pedestal as the only social good to be sought. It was important, they emphasized, but not the only goal worthy of pursuit. There were higher ends towards which both individuals and society should march. Alan Sykes put it as follows:

> Much of the New Liberalism of the late nineteenth and early twentieth centuries was a conscious reaction against mid-Victorian libertarianism. Its ideas were conditioned by the increasingly influential biological interpretation of man and his world; by the advancing secularization that was eroding the cohesive morality which bound Liberalism together despite its intellectual contradictions, and by an awareness of the poverty and social injustice to which traditional Liberalism had no answer. . . Individual liberty was no longer an end in itself, nor its preservation the purpose of government. It was merely one condition amongst others for the achievement by society and its constituent individuals, under the direction of the state, of the higher end for which it was established, the "good human life."[6]

There were any number of ways public policy could be used to help bring about the good life. State-provided education and public health measures were important components, for example. In keeping with their view that policies to aid the lower rungs of society would benefit everyone, they were

---

5 Freeden, *New Liberalism*, 19.
6 Alan Sykes, *The Rise and Fall of British Liberalism* (New York: Longman, 1997), 17. However, Jose Harris has cautioned against drawing too distinct a line between the Old and the New Liberalism. Jose Harris, "Political Thought and the Welfare State 1870-1940: An Intellectual Framework for British Social Policy," *Past and Present* 135 (1992), 116-141.

also led to sweeping notions of extensive work place regulation and provisions for maximum hours and minimum wages. Sidney and Beatrice Webb, for example, wrote that:

> When any European statesman makes up his mind to grapple seriously with the problem of the "sweated trades" he will have to expand the Factory Acts of his country into a systematic and comprehensive Labour Code, prescribing the minimum conditions under which the community can afford to allow industry to be carried on, and including not merely definite precautions of sanitation and safety, and maximum hours of toil, but also a minimum of weekly earnings.[7]

The Campaign against Sweating

"The fundamental intention of the 1909 Trade Boards Act," Sheila Blackburn notes, "was to eradicate sweating."[8] The term "sweating" was used most often to refer to the system of outwork or homework, whereby manufacturers supplied materials and sometimes tools to individuals or small workshops and then collected the finished goods, for which the worker was paid by the piece. Frequently, especially as the nineteenth century wore on, the term was given a more inclusive meaning, covering those who worked in factories as well. The report of the House of Lords Select Committee on Sweating (1890) defined it as those trades characterized by: "A rate of wages inadequate to the necessities of the workers or disproportionate to the work done; excessive hours of labour; [and] the insanitary state of the houses in which the work is carried out." By these definitions, the Committee, which heard from nearly 300 witnesses, found that 1,086,439 men and 647,930 women in 27 trades fell into this category. This was fully 24% of the industrial workforce. The report amplified further:

> [T]hese evils can hardly be exaggerated. The earnings of the lowest classes of workers are barely sufficient to sustain existence. The hours of labour are such as to make the lives of the workers periods of almost ceaseless toil, hard and often unhealthy. The sanitary conditions under which the work is conducted are not only injurious to the health of the persons employed, but are dangerous to the public.[9]

At the time, though, the Committee only made suggestions regarding the safety and health aspects of sweating, recommending additional factory inspectors and a modest tightening of the factory acts. When it came to wages, the Committee had only the vaguest suggestions.

---

7 Sidney and Beatrice Webb, *Industrial Democracy* (London: Longmans, 1897), 767.
8 Sheila Blackburn, ""Ideology and Social Policy: The Origins of the Trade Boards Act," *The Historical Journal* 34 (1991), 46.
9 House of Lords Select Committee on Sweating, *Fifth Report*, PP 1890, pp. 42-43.

When legislation has reached the limit up to which it is effective, the real amelioration of conditions must be due to increased sense of responsibility in the employer and improved habits in the employed. We have reason to think that the present inquiry itself has not been without moral effect. And we believe that public attention and public judgment can effectively check operations in which little regard is shown to the welfare of workpeople and to the quality of production, and can also strongly second the zealous and judicious efforts now being made to encourage thrift, promote temperance, improve dwellings, and raise the tone of living.[10]

While these are the same bromides heard often, even today, as remedies for low pay, it is easy to sympathize with the Committee. The intellectual search for policies to fight poverty had not yet come up with the idea of a general minimum wage, it not being floated at all until 1896.[11] Nevertheless, in response to the Committee's findings, Parliament did pass a Fair Wages Resolution in 1891, which required government contractors (such as those manufacturing army and navy uniforms and boots) to pay "fair wages." Local governments were likewise urged to do the same, and many of them did so. However, the chief contribution of the report was that it generated a significant amount of public discussion.

At the same time, both the attention and the conscience of the public were prodded by a number of empirical investigations into poverty and working conditions. The most systematic of these were Charles Booth's investigations of London and Seebohm Rowntree's studies of York.[12] Rowntree, for example, found that 15% of the working class population lived in dire poverty. In over half these cases, this was directly attributable to low wages. Another 22% of the working class, he demonstrated, earned wages totally inadequate for a larger family.[13]

Another critical fact is that among the lowest paid workers there was a preponderance of women. Here is where the Victorian political economy came into conflict with its social ideals. The political economists taught that any regulation of the labor market was inherently wrong and bound to fail; the social norms of the day cherished the wife and mother who stayed home. Yet, the realities of working class life were such that families depended, often heavily depended, on women engaging in paid work. Not only was this detrimental to the prevailing ideal of the family, the conditions under which many of these women worked were threatening to their well being. Any campaign

---

10 Select Committee on Sweating, *Fifth Report*, 301.

11 J.A. Hobson, "The Living Wage," 1 *Commonwealth* (1896), 128-129; 165-167.

12 Charles Booth, *Life and Labour of the People in London* (London: Macmillan, 1902); Seebohm Rowntree, *Poverty: A Study of Town Life* (London: Macmillan, 1901).

13 These figures are discussed in Vinson, "Edwardians and Poverty," 75.

to eradicate low wages was by definition, therefore, an issue deeply affecting women.

Many reformers believed that the path to better wages for the low paid lay in organizing trade unions. Clara Collet, for example, an associate of Charles Booth who later took a post at the Board of Trade, took this position.[14] However, there were almost insurmountable obstacles to this approach working. First, women workers were often in and out of the labor market; second, they often worked in small dispersed settings, and often in fact at home. Furthermore, the male dominated unions were seldom hospitable to women members (sometimes in fact banning them altogether), and at times even hostile to the idea of women working at all.[15] The Secretary of the Amalgamated Society of Tailors told the Royal Commission on Labour in 1891, for example, that women and foreigners were responsible for driving down wages and should be banned from the labor market. Other trade unionists argued that it was much better for everyone if women would stay at home, with a man earning a "family wage."

Slowly, the idea of a minimum wage took hold. As noted above, the first person to propose it was J. A. Hobson in 1896, the same year that the Australian state of Victoria adopted the world's first minimum wage. Six years later, Sidney and Beatrice Webb endorsed the idea in their book *Industrial Democracy*. To them, it would be part of a "national minimum," which included an array of factory legislation in addition to a minimum income. Hobson, too, thought in terms of a general minimum standard; but for him the standard was composed of far more than basic individual physiological needs. It included "good air, large sanitary houses, plenty of wholesome, well-cooked food, adequate changes of clothing for our climate, ample opportunities of recreation," and even "art, music, travel, education, social intercourse."[16]

We might note here that there were three different concepts on the table. A "minimum wage" would be one that would put the worker at least somewhat above the subsistence level. Here are the Webbs:

> [T]he minimum wage for a man or woman respectively would be determined by practical inquiry as to the cost of the food, clothing, and shelter physiologically necessary, according to national habit and custom, to prevent bodily deterioration. Such a minimum would be low [and] . . . would not at all correspond with the conception of a "Living Wage."[17]

14 The role of women in the sweated industries is covered in John Sheldrake, "The Sweated Industries Campaign," *Socialist History* 3 (1993), 43-45.

15 The role of the trade unions is discussed in Jenny Morris, *Women Workers and the Sweated Trades: The Origins of Minimum Wage Legislation* (Aldershot: Gower, 1986), 112-123.

16 J.A. Hobson, *The Social Problem* (London: Nisbet and Co., 1902), 79.

17 Webbs, *Industrial Democracy*, 774-775.

But what should be the unit? The individual or the family? Since many low-wage workers were young single women, should the wage be calculated by reference to their needs? Or, should there be different levels of the minimum wage? Alternatively, if one talked of a "living wage," this often implied enough for one person, usually the male breadwinner, to earn to support the average family.[18] This is what the miners union had in mind when it broached the idea. Finally, a "national minimum" implied a certain standard of living that was not necessarily tied to paid employment. Accepting the national minimum entailed first erecting a variety of public policies, covering unemployment, health, education, disability, old age, and so forth, to accompany a minimum, or even a living, wage. But it also meant embracing the notion of the "endowment of motherhood." The idea was that if a mother did not have a male breadwinner, she should be given an income from public funds sufficient to allow her to stay home and raise her children. In the words of the Minority Report of the Royal Commission on the Poor Laws of 1909, "When the breadwinner is withdrawn by death or desertion . . . [or] unable to earn the family maintenance, . . . [i]t seems to us clear that, if only for the sake of the interest which the community has in the children, there should be adequate provision made from public funds for the maintenance of the home."[19] This position clearly points the way to family allowances.

Parenthetically, we should add that the proponents of a minimum wage sought even at this early date to answer some oft-leveled objections. The most common then as now was that a minimum wage would lead to unemployment, especially among the most vulnerable workers. The Webbs answered this by arguing that a minimum wage would lead to greater efficiency.[20] As the cost of labor increased, employers would search for more efficient means to produce goods, which would be beneficial to everyone in the long run. Too, they and others took the "parasitic" approach. Industries that pay less than a living wage actually live on the community, for charities and the state must somehow take up the slack. Thus, even if whole industries disappeared after the introduction of a minimum wage, the community would actually benefit. As for the workers, they would be absorbed in whatever industries consumers now patronized with the money they did not spend on goods produced by the parasites.

---

18 See Wally Sercombe, "Patriarchy Stabilized: The Construction of the Male Breadwinner Norm in Nineteenth Century Britain," *Social History* 2 (1986), 53-76.

19 Minority Report, *Royal Commission on the Poor Laws and Relief of Distress*, PP (1909), 1160.

20 In fact, they later were enthusiastic supporters of the national efficiency movement. See Geoffrey Searle, *The Quest for National Efficiency: A Study in British Politics and Political Thought, 1899-1914* (Berkeley: University of California Press, 1971).

Political Factors

"Late Victorians continued to be reminded that many who were 'morally' worthy did not secure a fair day's pay for a hard day's work, and they were driven to conclude that some general failure in social and economic organization must be at least partly to blame."[21] Such sentiments undoubtedly penetrated much of late Victorian society. Nonetheless, public policies are not produced by general sentiments; it takes organizations to push for reform and it takes those near or in the seats of power to push for specific statutes. One common pattern, of course, is for public policies to be advocated and then secured by pressure brought to bear by those who stand to benefit. However, the minimum wage is never like that, and was not here.

For starters, those who would benefit most, women workers, were legally politically powerless, not even possessing the right to vote. Moreover, even if they could have voted, they would have faced huge obstacles in getting organized, having little income, little education, and little time. Thus, it fell to middle class reformers, both women and men, to push their case. A scattering of women tried to pursue the trade union route, both to secure collective bargaining and to mobilize political power. However, far more influential were organizations such as the Women's Industrial Council, a grouped linked to the Liberal party. They thought legislative action the more likely route to reform. Of course, though, they had to seek their goals by going through men.

Another political fact of life in this period was the apathy or at times hostility of some of the trade unions to the idea of a minimum wage. Pinpointing the reasons for this position is a little difficult. Part of the apathy was simply the fact that most trade unions were composed of skilled workers; thus, it did not concern their members. Part of it was just pure discrimination against women; even the small unions of the unskilled contained few women, and often then there were separate divisions for women. Part of it was the pride union members took in being independent, "holding one's own corner," as the Secretary of the London Trades Council explained to the Select Committee on Sweating.[22] A major part, though, was the fear that a minimum wage would undermine collective bargaining. This was the position Ramsay McDonald took, for instance.[23] However, the union movement

---

21 Duncan Bythell, *The Sweated Trades: Outwork in Nineteenth Century Britain* (London: Batsford Academic, 1978), 11.

22 Quoted in Helen Hohman, *The Development of Social Insurance and Minimum Wage Legislation in Great Britain* (Boston: Houghton Mifflin, 1933), 365.

23 Valerie Hart, *Bound by Our Constitution: Women, Workers, and the Minimum Wage* (Princeton, NJ: Princeton University Press, 1994), chap. 3, *passim.*

was not monolithic, and there were scattered supporters of the minimum wage, although it was not a major part of any union platform.

Yet another aspect of early twentieth century politics was the rise of the Labor party. Despite union apathy, there was a vibrant minimum wage coterie within the party, especially among those affiliated with the Fabian Society. Furthermore, the party intelligentsia, including almost every M.P. (30 of whom, recall, took seats in 1906), was in favor of the idea. However, the most important political effect of the growth of the Labor party was how it affected the internal dynamics of the Liberal party, in that it strengthened the hand of the New Liberals.[24] Although their attempt to fend off the Labor party by moving to the left ultimately failed, in 1906 that position was a strong argument for a period of Liberal sponsored reform. When the Liberals entered office in 1906 and Lloyd George was appointed Chancellor of the Exchequer and Winston Churchill soon went to preside over the Board of Trade, it was clear that the pair "would use the opportunities of . . . office to promote the sort of comprehensive reform of which New Liberals had been dreaming."[25]

Adoption of the Trade Boards Act

In the same year as the election, a loose coalition favoring the minimum wage persuaded George Cadbury, the wealthy chocolate merchant and owner of the *Daily News*, to sponsor an Exhibition of Sweated Industries. Forty-five workers sat in stalls at Queen's Hall, London, and plied their trade while visitors strolled through the building. Printed tables were provided showing how much the products cost and how much the workers earned, along with information on how much it cost workers to live. These live displays were supplemented by a variety of lectures presented during the evenings. The Exhibition was a sensational success. Over 30,000 people visited, as it became an event in the London social season. At its close, it moved to regional cities, with equal success. According to contemporaries, it fastened the attention of the nation on the issue of sweating and led many to believe that something must be done.[26]

Not wishing to lose the momentum created by the Exhibition, minimum wage advocates created the National Anti-Sweating League. Its public announcement laid out the rationale and the goal:

24 See David Powell, "The New Liberals and the Rise of Labour, 1886-1906," *The Historical Journal* 29 (1986), 369-393.

25 John Grigg, *Lloyd George: The Peoples' Champion, 1902-1911* (Berkeley: University of California Press, 1978), 160-161.

26 See the quotations from G.P. Gooch reported in Blackburn, "Ideology and Social Policy," 55.

> It was the common feeling of those who visited the Exhibition that the interest and indignation that it excited ought not to be allowed to pass away, but ought to be used as motive power for a constructive attack on Sweating. Consequently, it was resolved to form the Anti-Sweating League, and, taking inspiration from Australia and New Zealand, to work towards the setting up of machinery to deal with Sweating on lines of a compulsory Minimum Wage in specified industries.[27]

The League immediately organized a conference to be held at the Guildhall, London in October of 1906. The Lord Mayor opened the proceedings, and a list of prominent public figures spoke in favor of a minimum wage. Delegates came from all segments of the reform coalition: women's' groups, unions, churches, "enlightened" employers, economists, politicians. In order to keep the coalition as broad as possible, the League kept the conference resolutions and its subsequent goals modest. It agreed that the minimum wage should only apply to selected industries, not across the board, and, clearly playing on social sympathies, the industries most often mentioned consisted primarily of women workers. It also acknowledged that what the particular industry could pay should enter into the calculation of the wage.

Feeling the pressure, in January 1907 the government dispatched a civil servant, Ernest Aves of the Home Office, to Australia to report on the operation of the minimum wage there. Some historians believe this was a delaying tactic, as the details of the Australian system and its impacts were already well known.[28] Later that year, the House of Commons created a Select Committee on Homework. After taking extensive evidence, its conclusion was that legislation was the only way to cure the problem of low pay, but opted for wage boards over a universal minimum wage. In early 1908 a delegation from the Anti-Sweating League, led by the Archbishop of Canterbury, paid a call on the Prime Minister to urge his support for a minimum wage bill.

Charles Dilke, a Liberal M.P., had been introducing minimum wage bills into the House of Commons since 1900. Churchill now took the cause under his wing, over the objections it might be noted of senior civil servants at the Board of Trade. Dilke and Churchill both thought a universal minimum wage the proper route, Churchill even proposing to cover one-third of the work force. The Anti-Sweating League, though, afraid of losing some of its support and therefore the entire program, urged a more cautious approach. In the end, a bill covering only four trades — tailoring, paper box making, lace making, and chain making — was passed. In fact, it encountered little opposition, given how restricted it was.

---

27 National Anti-Sweating League, *Report of a Conference on a Minimum Wage held at the Guildhall, London, October 24, 25, and 26, 1906*, 3.

28 Aves' report was, in fact, somewhat ambiguous. See Hart, *Bound by Our Constitution*, 46.

In the end, then, Britain got a minimum wage, even though it was to apply to a very limited number of cases. Why, several historians have asked, was the legislation so watered down? Some have laid the blame on or given credit to high officials at the Board of Trade, officials who were known to be hostile to the idea of a minimum wage and worked on Churchill until he relented. Others, more convincingly, have taken the position that the Anti-Sweating League, with its desire to keep its coalition intact and its fear of losing any bill at all, was able to move Churchill in a more modest direction. For example, when the League's deputation met with the Prime Minister in 1908, they reportedly found him "sympathetic" to their position, but unwilling to give any "trace of any pledge of immediate, or indeed of any, action."[29] One needed little political education to get the message and start worrying about the project's fate.

Even if unduly modest in scope and stingy in how the minimum wages were to be calculated (by a tripartite board in each industry considering not only the needs of the worker but the economic conditions in the industry), Britain had now endorsed the principle of state regulation of wages. Many in the pro-minimum wage camp hoped that this was but a first step, that either a universal minimum wage would soon replace the trade boards, or, at the least, that the trade board system could be expanded into most of the economy. Constance Smith wrote soon afterward, "The minimum rate is not the living wage; but it has made the attainment of the living wage even for the poorest and least skilled among those who work with their hands a question of practical politics."[30] Expansion of the system did indeed occur through the workings of practical politics, but very shortly the trade board regime, owing again to practical politics, was to begin to decay, and become before long but a marginal aspect of British social welfare policy.

American State Legislation

The origins of American minimum wage legislation divide into two distinct periods. Prior to and immediately after the First World War, a number of states, beginning with Massachusetts in 1912, adopted minimum wage laws. Federal legislation, though, did not come until 1938, with the passage of the Fair Labor Standards Act (FLSA). The first of these stages was a product of the Progressive movement, while the second was the last major reform

---

29 Quoted in Hart, *Bound by Our Constitution*, p. 54.
30 Constance Smith, "The Working of the Trade Boards Act in Great Britain and Ireland," *Journal of Political Economy* 22 (1914), 629.

of the New Deal. In both cases, as in Britain, it is important to keep in mind that the minimum wage was part of a broader, general program of reform.

Progressivism

Progressivism was the American variant of the movement for social reform that touched most Western countries in the late nineteenth and early twentieth centuries.[31] In many ways, it was similar to the New Liberalism then taking hold in Britain. It shared, particularly, in the notions that a common good existed and that reaching for this required state action. They "denied the liberal contention," James Kloppenberg has written, "that the pursuit of personal interest insures optimal social benefits. The public interest, like the ethical ideal, emerges from the concrete struggle among competing conceptions of the good."[32] Ethical ideals were therefore paramount, and if achieving them meant public action, they were not inhibited by the limited role assigned the state by liberals of an earlier era. Robert Prasch has stressed that "A unifying feature of Progressive era political economy was the belief that direct government action could serve the economic and moral needs of the American people."[33] At the same time, they were hardly radicals, as they never challenged the idea of private property or the general beneficence of the market.

Furthermore, they did not view policies to aid the poor as helpful to them alone. Poverty, and the deplorable working conditions in which the poor labored, damaged the entire society. Sometimes this damage was direct, as in the diseases that might spread to the broader public from unsanitary conditions. At other times the damage was indirect, as when stunted lives led to stunted democratic citizens. Richard T. Ely, a prominent Progressive economist, asserted that "Whenever we truly advance the interests of wage-earners we necessarily advance the interests of all society."[34] Or, as Shelton Stromquist has put it more recently, "The idea of the people resonated powerfully with reformers. They focused on inclusion not exclusion, social amelioration not division, harmony not conflict."[35]

---

31 For a discussion of the international character of progressivism, see Daniel Rodgers, *Atlantic Crossings: Social Politics in a Progressive Age* (Cambridge, MA: Harvard University Press, 1998).

32 James Kloppenberg, *Uncertain Victory: Social Democracy and Progressivism in European and American Thought, 1870-1920* (New York: Oxford University Press, 1986), 173. Kloppenberg was referring specifically to William James in this sentence, but the sentiment is more generally applicable.

33 Robert Prasch, "American Economists in the Progressive Era on the Minimum Wage," *Journal of Economic Perspectives* 13 (1999), 221-230.

34 Richard T. Ely, "A Programme for Labor Reform," *Century* 39 (1890), 939.

35 Shelton Stromquist, *Reinventing "The People": The Progressive Movement, the Class Problem, and the Origins of Modern Liberalism* (Urbana: University of Illinois Press, 2006), 34.

There were some uniquely American aspects to Progressivism, however. For one, it was more religiously based than that in Britain. While religious ideals and religious figures were not absent in Britain, both were more pronounced in the United States. The Social Gospel, preaching salvation through making conditions better in this world, became dominant in many branches of Protestantism. Moreover, one student has pointed out that almost all the major Progressive economists were active members of mainline Protestant churches, and that their writings had a strong religious flavor.[36]

For another, the character of citizenship was more central to American Progressive thought. In part, this was because creating democratic citizens was a continuing concern in the United States. But another dimension was that the late nineteenth century witnessed an influx of immigrants from Eastern Europe, who mostly crowded into the industrial cities of the North and Northeast (and became ripe candidates for machine driven politics). Since they often took low-paid industrial jobs, the problem of integrating them into American society was economic as well as social and political. Thus, issues of wages, public health, education, and political participation merged together more strongly than in Britain.

For yet another, Progressivism was broader and more amorphous than New Liberalism. People identified as Progressives advocated a breathtaking array of reforms, touching almost every aspect of life. Thus, there was no parallel to the "national minimum" that was discussed in Britain. Instead, reform proposals developed in an uncoordinated and often piecemeal fashion. Nevertheless, no Progressive believed any single reform stood alone. They always pointed out how given policies were connected to others. Therefore, the minimum wage never stood alone.

We might use Henry Seager as an example. His chief interest was social insurance, and he explained in some detail how his plan for covering health, unemployment, and so forth would work.[37] Yet, he also saw the minimum wage as an important component of an overall program.

> Any program of social reform for wage earners may be analyzed into two parts. One part aims to protect them in the continued enjoyment of their present standards of living. The other endeavors to assist them to advance these standards to even higher levels. The proposal to establish minimum, or living, rates of wages by law for individuals and classes that

---

36 Eldon Eisenach, *The Lost Promise of Progressivism* (Lawrence: University Press of Kansas, 1994), 31-36.

37 Henry Seager, *Social Insurance: A Program of Social Reform* (New York: Macmillan, 1910).

are now so unfortunate as to fail to secure them is the link which connects these two parts into a consistent and comprehensive program.[38]

When it came to justifying the minimum wage, Progressives turned to the same arguments as their British counterparts: ending extreme poverty, driving out parasitic industries, efficiency, and the like.[39]

From Idea to Concrete Proposal

While Progressivism was the impetus for and the backdrop to the development of minimum wage measures, as in Britain, ideas only moved onto the statute books through the conduit of political organizations. In line with what happened in Britain, the initiative in the United States came largely from middle class women. Also paralleling what occurred in Britain, the unions were often either apathetic or hostile. However, there were some exceptions; in the end, though, even these unions were often only lukewarm to the idea. One critical difference between the two countries, though, was that in the United States there was no analogue to the Liberal party. American parties were more fragmented and more amorphous. Progressives had, consequently, to pursue a broader political strategy, seeking allies where they could. This, of course, could be either an asset or a liability.

One of the most important groups involved with early agitation for a minimum wage was the National Consumers League (NCL). Founded in New York City in 1890, the League was not entirely opposed to efforts then underway by some to organize women workers. However, its favored approach was the development of "Fair House Standards." This meant developing a list of conditions under which products should be manufactured. Companies that agreed to abide by these conditions could attach the League's label to their wares. Women would then be encouraged to buy only those goods bearing the label, with the hope that the ensuing economic pressure would make the standards universal. Echoes of this approach still sound today and are about as effective as they were then. The administrative and practical difficulties were (and are) simply overwhelming. There was also an organization known as the Women's Educational and Industrial Union (WEIU), which focused on research into the conditions under which women worked. The fledgling Women's Trade Union League (WTUL), which also had heavy representation from middle class reformers, began advocating a minimum

---

38 Henry Seager, "The Minimum Wage as Part of a Program for Social Reform," *Annals of the American Academy of Political and Social Science* 38 (1913), 3.

39 See, for example, the exposition of Arthur Holcombe, "The Legal Minimum Wage in the United States," *American Economic Review* 2 (1912), 21-37.

wage in 1909, and soon several state branches of the NCL swung behind the idea, often, it must be said, reluctantly, though.

Union organization in the United States was more diffuse than in Britain. The major craft unions had formed the American Federation of Labor, and its president Samuel Gompers, was a lifelong opponent of minimum wage laws, fearing they would undermine collective bargaining. However, he could not control state branches, and sometimes they were somewhat more sympathetic to the cause. As for unions of unskilled workers, while seldom enthusiastic, few were overtly hostile. Moreover, unions had some political experience, having been active in securing both state and federal legislation mandating maximum hours and minimum wages for government workers and for those working on government contracts.[40] Thus, in some of the states labor proved a useful ally.

There was one unique American matter, though, that threatened to render any generally applicable minimum wage proposal stillborn. In the late nineteenth and early twentieth centuries, the Supreme Court had interpreted the due process clause of the constitution's Fourteenth Amendment to create a "liberty of contract." The justices had construed "No State . . . shall deprive any person of . . . liberty . . . without due process of law" to mean that each individual had a constitutional liberty to enter into any economic arrangement he or she (perhaps) should choose. The high point of this view was the case of *Lochner v. New York*, decided in 1905.[41] The case involved a New York maximum hours law for bakers. While the Court acknowledged that the state may interfere with contracts in certain instances, it held that this regulation was beyond the scope of state powers. As for the general principle,

> In every case that comes before this court . . . where legislation of this character is concerned, and where the protection of the Federal Constitution is sought, the question necessarily arises: Is this a fair, reasonable, and appropriate exercise of the police power of the state, or is it an unreasonable, unnecessary, and arbitrary interference with the right of the individual to his personal liberty, or to enter into those contracts in relation to labor which may seem to him appropriate or necessary for the support of himself and his family.

However, the court seemed to leave a door open when it applied this principle to the case at hand, even though it voided the law. It argued that "There is no contention that bakers as a class are not equal in intelligence

---

40 These laws are covered in Conrad Fritsch and Steven Connell, "Evolution of Wage and Hour Laws in the United States," *Report of the Minimum Wage Study Commission*, 1981, Vol. 2, 3-4. Many of these laws, though, were hobbled by narrow judicial interpretations and haphazard enforcement.

41 198 US 45.

and capacity to men in other trades or manual occupations, or that they are not able to assert their rights and care for themselves, without the protecting arm of the state." Furthermore, they noted that their hours of work did not affect "any other portion of the public than those engaged in that occupation." Under these guidelines, a minimum wage law covering men was clearly doomed. However, since women, for any number of reasons, were not able to assert their rights in the workplace, and because their health affected children yet to be born, a case might could be made that legislation applying to women could survive judicial scrutiny. Oregon tested this approach with a maximum hours law which applied to women only. The Supreme Court held the door ajar in *Muller v. Oregon* (1908).[42] After asserting the general right of contract, the justices observed that for most women "in the struggle for subsistence she is not an equal competitor with her brother," and further that the health of present and potential mothers is a legitimate object of community concern. A law regulating hours for women was therefore valid. Thus, while today the justices' attitudes seem patronizing and limiting, at the time, they gave minimum wage advocates a ray of hope. For this reason, they carefully crafted early minimum wage legislation to apply only to women.[43]

State Action

The campaign against sweating aroused as much public concern as in Britain. Several inquiries, both private and governmental, documented the low wages and harsh working conditions prevalent in many industries. The federal government's Bureau of Labor Statistics conducted, for example, a wide ranging study in 1907-09, and similar reports were also undertaken in several states.[44]

In time, between 1912 and 1923, 15 states enacted minimum wage laws covering women, and Congress adopted a similar law for the District of Columbia in 1918.

Massachusetts was the first to act, and the pattern that was followed there was fairly typical.[45] Minimum wage advocates, driven by the three organizations mentioned above, first proposed a conference in 1910 "to consider bringing in a minimum wage board bill."[46] It was not until 1911, though,

---

42 208 US 412.

43 A contemporary discussion of this issue can be found in Thomas Reed Powell, "The Constitutional Issues in Minimum Wage Legislation," *Minnesota Law Review* 2 (1917), 1-21. A shorter review is in Oren Levin-Waldman, *The Case of the Minimum Wage: Competing Policy Models* (Albany: State University of New York Press, 2001), 61-70.

44 These reports are discussed in Hart, *Bound by Our Constitution*, 63-66.

45 The Massachusetts campaign is covered in Hart, *Bound by Our Constitution*, chap. 4.

46 Quoted in Hart, *Bound by Our Constitution*, 68.

that a committee, modeled on the Anti-Sweating League, but including, importantly, the Boston Central Labor Union, had been set up to lobby the legislature for a wage board measure. In the spring of 1911, the legislature established a commission to "study the matter of wages of women and minors." The commission reported in 1912, and recommended a series of wage boards. Employer opposition in the legislature turned out to be minimal, most of them apparently assuming that the boards would have little effect. In fact, they turned out to be correct. The only penalty for employers found in violation was having their name publicized. However, the Massachusetts law had an important effect: it emboldened minimum wage advocates in other states.

Indeed, in the following year, eight states — California, Colorado, Minnesota, Nebraska, Oregon, Utah, Washington, and Wisconsin — passed laws.[47] Within a few more years, similar statutes were on the books in Arizona, Arkansas, Kansas, North Dakota, South Dakota, and Texas. Most of these actually carried some type of penalty for employers who violated the measure, but it was usually minimal. In any event, all the effort and work was to soon come to nil, when the Supreme Court took up the case of *Adkins v. Children's Hospital* in 1923.[48]

The case involved a challenge to the congressional statute mandating minimum wages in the District of Columbia; however, since the wording of the Fifth Amendment's due process clause, applicable to the federal government only, was identical to that in the Fourteenth Amendment, the court's decision would affect state statutes as well. In short, the court held that regulation of wages was fundamentally different from limitations placed on hours worked, and that therefore the law could not be sustained under the *Muller* precedent. Within a short period, employers mounted legal attacks on most of the state minimum wage laws, and both state and federal courts generally struck them down, citing *Adkins*. The others were repealed outright, or enforcement simply waned.

The Fair Labor Standards Act of 1938

While it was five years into the New Deal before President Roosevelt was able to push through a minimum wage law, interest in using the minimum wage as a policy tool was present from the beginning. As was true for the Progressives, it was an outgrowth of a set of ideas about political economy,

---

47 A table detailing the laws can be found in Clifford Thies, "The First Minimum Wage Laws," *Cato Journal* 10 (1991), 718-719.
48 261 US 525.

and as with the Progressives too, it was part of a much broader strategy, not something to be considered alone.

New Deal Philosophy

While New Deal theorists shared many connections to the Progressive movement, they were not merely its latter day incarnation. Political economy had moved away from its moral base, making New Dealers decidedly less religious. Moreover, they had absorbed the ideas of people such as John Maynard Keynes, and believed in the possibilities of macroeconomic management. William E. Leuchtenberg has contended that "Unlike the earlier Progressives, the New Dealers shied away from being thought of as sentimental. Instead of justifying relief as a humanitarian measure, the New Dealers often insisted it was necessary to stimulate purchasing power or to stabilize the economy or to 'conserve manpower.'"[49]

Nevertheless, the New Dealers shared with the Progressives a faith that government could make people's lives better, and they remained decidedly sympathetic to those on the bottom of the economic ladder. Pragmatists imbued with technical economic analysis they may have been, but policy was to be purposely bent to help those with little. In so doing, of course, they believed, also in tune with the Progressives, that they would be helping the society as a whole. The minimum wage, many of them thought, would be the ideal way to combine the raising of incomes for the poor with the stimulation of purchasing power. In calling for Congress to enact a minimum wage in 1937, Roosevelt said:

> Today, you and I are pledged to take further steps to reduce the lag in the purchasing power of industrial workers and to strengthen and stabilize the markets for the farmers' products. The two go hand in hand. Each depends for its effectiveness on the other.[50]

Early Initiatives

As the Depression deepened, even before Roosevelt took office in 1933, activists were succeeding in spurring the states to try again to legislate minimum wages. Legal advisers to the National Consumers League had argued that the defect with the District of Columbia law, in the Supreme Court's view at least, was that the wage was based on the needs of the worker. If a state were to require a "fair wage," as a legitimate payment for services

---

49 William E. Leuchtenberg, *Franklin D. Roosevelt and the New Deal, 1932-1940* (New York: Harper and Row, 1963), 338.
50 Message to Congress, May 24, 1937. *The Public Papers and Addresses of Franklin D. Roosevelt* (New York: Macmillan, 1941), Vol. 5, 210.

rendered, this difficulty might be surmounted. The NCL drafted a model bill (still applying only to women, though) along these lines, and it was soon taken up in several states.[51]

In filling out his administration, Roosevelt turned to Frances Perkins, a long time activist for labor rights, to become Secretary of Labor. Before taking the post, Perkins forced the new president to pledge himself to a large-scale program of social insurance and minimum wage and maximum hour legislation.[52] Perkins drew up a minimum wage bill soon after taking office, but it was pushed to one side by the president's legislative planners. They were instead drafting what was to become the National Industrial Recovery Act.

It is often forgotten that this act contained an important minimum wage component. In fact, Paul Douglas and Joseph Hackman have said that Roosevelt favored the NIRA primarily because of its wage provisions.[53] The act required each business grouping to adopt a code of fair competition, which would be submitted to the president for approval. If approved, it would then have the force of law. At the outset, before business groups even began work on their codes, the administration drafted a "blanket code," called the President's Re-employment Agreement, which went into effect immediately. The central part of this code set minimum rates of pay and maximum hours of work. The plan was that as codes were developed and promulgated, they would replace the blanket code; and the administration clearly hoped most would include rates of pay above their already declared minimum. Meanwhile, the president continued to urge states to follow the NCL's suggestions and pass minimum wage laws for women.

Unfortunately for the administration, the Supreme Court struck down the NIRA system in 1935, both on the grounds that it exceeded congressional authority under the commerce clause and that it delegated too much discretion to the executive branch.[54] Perkins then tried to persuade Roosevelt to throw his backing behind a general federal minimum wage law, but the administration's legal advisers feared that even if a new bill could be passed, it would simply run aground on judicial shoals.[55] Nevertheless, the 1936 Demo-

---

51 On the NCL, see Landon Storrs, *Civilizing Capitalism: The National Consumers' League, Women's Activism, and Labor Standards in the New Deal Era* (Chapel Hill: University of North Carolina Press, 2000).

52 George Paulsen, *A Living Wage for the Forgotten Man* (Selinsgrove, PA: Susquehanna University Press, 1996), 37-44.

53 Paul Douglas and Joseph Hackman, "The Fair Labor Standards Act of 1938, I" *Political Science Quarterly* 53 (1938), 492.

54 *Schechter Poultry Corporation v. United States* 295 US 495 (1935).

55 Much of this sparring is discussed in Paulsen, *Living Wage*, chap. 3

cratic platform contained an unambiguous plank favoring a national minimum wage, and even proposing a constitutional amendment if the Supreme Court failed to approve it.

In 1935 and 1936, along with the NIRA, the Supreme Court had also struck down a number of other New Deal initiatives, often with 5-4 votes. An exasperated president was seeking any way possible to circumvent the hard liners among the justices. Pending before the court were still other important new statutes, the National Labor Relations Act, the Social Security Act, and the Public Utilities Holding Company Act. In 1936 the court signaled its entrenched position when it struck down (again by a 5-4 vote) New York's new minimum wage law, which had tried to use the NCL recommended "fair wage" as the ruling standard. This led the president to set in motion his ill-fated court-packing scheme.[56] Even though his proposal won little support in Congress, the court changed course in 1937 and 1938. It first upheld the National Labor Relations Act (expanding the possible scope of federal power under the commerce clause), and then a Washington state minimum wage law.[57]

Passage of the Fair Labor Standards Act

Almost immediately after the upholding of the National Labor Relations Act, the administration drafted a minimum wage bill (onto which were tacked maximum hour provisions and a ban on the use of child labor). The president's address accompanying the bill contained the famous phrase "one-third of our population . . . is ill-nourished, ill-clad, and ill housed."[58] According to Roosevelt, the proposed bill had three objectives: 1) protecting workers from ruinous competition; 2)halting the downward spiral of wages; and 3)increasing purchasing power.

Unlike the British and Massachusetts laws, this proposal encountered shrill opposition. Business interests denounced it across the board. The National Association of Manufacturers saw it as constituting "a step in the direction of communism, bolshevism, and Nazism." A congressional opponent said it was a "tyrannical industrial dictatorship." Another held forth sarcasti-

---

56 See Marian McKenna, *Franklin Roosevelt and the Great Constitutional War: The Court-Packing Crisis of 1937* (New York: Fordham University Press, 2002).

57 *National Labor Relations Board v. Jones and Laughlin Steel Corporation* 301 US 1 (1937); *West Coast Hotel v. Parrish* 300 US 379 (1938).

58 Quoted in Douglas and Hackman, "Fair Labor Standards Act," 493.

cally that "we ought to add the millennium to the program. Otherwise, it will not be complete."[59]

Despite these cries, the administration's bill was actually rather modest. Most importantly, though, it jettisoned the trade boards approach and opted instead for a flat minimum wage. It would apply to all workers engaged in manufacturing, mining, transportation, and public utilities, if the products or services they produced moved in interstate commerce. Wide swaths of workers were either exempt entirely or explicitly excluded if covered: professionals, executives, supervisors, agricultural workers, and retail workers. Moreover, a Labor Standards Board could grant further exemptions to small firms generally or to people employing apprentices.

However, a remnant of the trade boards system was retained. The Labor Standards Board could set wages above the statutory minimum in specific industries. It could only do this, though, after conducting investigations and hearing from affected parties.

Even though Democrats controlled both houses of Congress by lopsided margins, the fractious nature of the party, especially the disaffection of southerners, made securing the bill a difficult task for the administration. Probably to blunt some southern criticism, Roosevelt convinced Senator Hugo Black of Alabama to be the floor leader for the bill, even though he had little background in labor matters. Black managed to get Senate approval for the bill, but had to accept a slew of amendments substantially watering down its provisions. For example, the agricultural exemption was broadened. Then, the powers of the Labor Standard Board were reversed; it was now given power to set minimum wages below the statutory minimum. Furthermore, it was given authority to introduce regional differentials, something desired by many southern manufacturers who believed it would allow them to keep one of their few competitive advantages.[60] In addition, the board now had to consult industry committees when setting wages. In the end, this watered-down measure, even though a disappointment to most minimum wage advocates, passed by a two-to-one margin.

The House of Representatives presented a different picture. The floor of the House was more hospitable to the New Deal, and therefore to the bill,

---

59 A number of quotations are contained in Willis Nordlund's discussion of the FLSA's passage, *The Quest for a Living Wage: A History of the Federal Minimum Wage Program* (Westport, CT: Greenwood, 1997), chap. 3. Also see Jonathan Grossman, "Fair Labor Standards Act of 1938: Maximum Struggle for a Minimum Wage," *Monthly Labor Review* 101 (1978), 22-30.

60 A good analysis of the position of an important southern industry is James Hodges, *New Deal Labor Policy and the Southern Cotton Textile Industry, 1933-41* (Knoxville: University of Tennessee Press, 1986).

than the Senate. During these years, though, much of the power of the body was dispersed to its committees, and within these committees the chairs wielded extraordinary power. A rather anomalous practice, selecting as chair the longest-serving member of the majority party, was a major defect to normal democratic politics. This had a two-edged effect. In the south of that day, the Democratic Party was unchallenged, and voters there tended to return the same member election after election. At the same time, urban machines in northern cities also tended to be mostly Democratic, and this often ensured long-serving members from these districts as well. As a result, the House Labor Committee was in hands friendly to the New Deal, and actually strengthened the bill slightly. It outlawed gender discrimination, required regional representation on the Labor Standards Board (to prevent southern dominance), and mandated that the board could only act if collective bargaining was ineffective. However, bills could not move to the floor of the House without approval of the Rules Committee, which was chaired by an unreconstructed southern opponent of the bill. He simply refused to let the bill come to a vote, and, according to House procedures, the only way the bill's backers could override this stranglehold was by a discharge petition, a document that had to be signed by 218 members (a majority). The session ended with the bill still in the Rules Committee.

Roosevelt responded by calling a special session of Congress, and made the Fair Labor Standards Act a top priority. The Senate quickly repassed its bill from the regular session, but the House Rules Committee again bottled up the measure. Fate seemed to intervene, though. A Democratic primary in Florida was to be held to fill an empty Senate seat, and in those days winning the Democratic primary in a southern state guaranteed election. A candidate who made the minimum wage almost his sole campaign issue scored a huge victory. In less than three hours, the discharge petition had secured the number of needed signatures, and the Labor Committee's bill moved to the House floor. With the House now in favor of a stronger bill, the conference committee removed some of the Senate's amendments. The wage was set low, but was to rise in a series of steps through 1945. No regional differentials were to be allowed, and a division of the Department of Labor, a newly created Wage and Hour Division, was to be charged with enforcing the act. The Division was also empowered, after due consultation, to set higher wages in certain industries. By and large, it seems, the administration was pleased. Roosevelt told a fireside chat audience that:

> Except perhaps for the Social Security Act, it is the most far-reaching,
> far-sighted program for the benefit of workers ever adopted here or in any
> other country. Without question it starts us toward a better standard of
> living and increases purchasing power to buy the products of farm and
> factory.[61]

The act was of course immediately challenged in the courts as exceeding Congress' authority under the commerce clause. However, the Supreme Court followed its National Labor Relations Board precedent, and upheld the act.[62] The United States now had a fixed minimum wage applicable to all who were covered. According to the best estimate, approximately 300,000 workers received a raise, and minimum wage advocates hoped that number could be made to grow with subsequent expansion of the act.[63] Federal action, it was felt at the time, had eclipsed state minimum wage laws.

CONCLUSION

Enacting a minimum wage had proved a daunting task in both countries. Those who stood to benefit the most were some of the politically weakest people in society. Thus, others, with more education and more resources, both economic and political, had to take the lead. Then, delicate coalitions had to be built to secure passage, and they were often fleeting and fragile. Moreover, the opposition could only be silenced, and not always even then, by emasculating and defanging the statute. In the end, statutes with limited scope, low wages, and cumbersome administrative machinery emerged in all three cases.

However similar though the political events leading to passage were in both countries, the laws' subsequent paths were strikingly different. After an initial push to strengthen minimum wage policy, British politicians laid the idea to one side. It took ninety years for the idea to regain a footing. In the United States, on the other hand, for nearly three decades the minimum wage was a central feature of federal policy, and it was steadily broadened in coverage and regularly raised. However, it too lost out in time to social insurance and public assistance as major poverty fighting tools. After that, within 15 years, it fell victim to a combination of conservative dominance of national politics and weakened unions. In time, once again the states became the major arena for minimum wage laws. The British story is told in the following chapter, while the American experience is taken up in chapter five.

---

61 *The Public Papers and Addresses of Franklin D. Roosevelt* (New York: Macmillan, 1941), Vol. 7, 392.
62 *United States v. Darby Lumber Company* 312 US 100 (1941).
63 Paulsen, *Living Wage*, 137.

Finally, even at the risk of repetition, it cannot be stressed too strongly that in all these cases — New Liberalism, Progressivism, and the New Deal — the minimum wage was part of a whole fabric of legislation. It stood alongside factory regulation, social insurance, public health measures, housing and urban renewal policies, and public assistance programs. Its specific goals were primarily to mitigate poverty and lessen economic inequality, but it looked beyond that to larger purposes. Coupled with other reform measures, it was to give people dignity and ensure that they were fitted for democratic citizenship. Its tragedy was that it was to become severed from that base. In the final chapter I will examine how it is being reconnected to the ideas that gave it birth.

Chapter 3. Decay, Death, and Rebirth

Launching the Trade Boards, 1909-1921[1]

The Trade Boards Act created boards to set minimum wages in four industries: ready-made and bespoke tailoring, paper and cardboard box making, chain making, and the finishing of machine-made lace. Altogether, about 400,000 people worked in these industries, the vast bulk of whom were women.[2]

Administratively, the boards were placed under the Board of Trade, which Winston Churchill headed at the time. According to the act, each board was to be composed of representatives of both employers and employees in the industry, some "independent members," and two officials from the Board of Trade, one of whom would be the chair and one the secretary. The size of the Boards ranged between 17 and 41, and a system of tripartite District Committees was also authorized.[3] In the chain-making industry (largely because of its small geographical spread), employee members of the board were elected directly; in all the others, the Board of Trade solicited names and chose the members from those lists. Employer organizations selected their members. Initially, the same government official was appointed to chair all four boards.

---

1 I am omitting consideration of the Agricultural Wages Boards.

2 Fred Bayliss, *British Wages Councils* (Oxford: Basil Blackwell, 1962), 10.

3 Detailed information on the administrative operations of the boards is given in Constance Smith, 'The Working of the Trade Boards Act in Great Britain and Ireland," *Journal of Political Economy* 22 (1914), 605-629.

The operational procedures were somewhat cumbersome, and seemingly designed to impede quick action. Fred Bayliss explains:

> The Act laid down a procedure which meant that in practice it took at least a year from the Board's first meeting to bring legal minimum wages into force. Each Board had to determine, by a majority vote if necessary, minimum time rates of wages and, if it wished, general minimum piece-work rates. These were the only minimum rates of wages it had the power to determine. All employers and workers had to be notified of its proposals, and during a period of three months objections could be lodged against them. Having considered the objections, the Board had then to ask the President of the Board of Trade to ratify its recommendations. If he did so, the rates become obligatory at the end of six months. . . The legal time limits alone, which the Board could do nothing to shorten, meant that nine months had to elapse between the Board's decision to propose certain wage rates and their legal enforcement throughout the trade.

It is small wonder that the implementation of the minimum wages went slowly. The tailoring board did not secure legally binding rates until over two years after the act had gone into effect. Still, though, according the Jenny Morris, wages rose for most workers in the covered industries.[4]

The act contained a procedure by which new trade boards could be created, although it limited them to industries in which "the rate of wages prevailing in any branch of the trade is exceptionally low, as compared with that in other employments, and that the other circumstances of the trade are such as to render the application of this Act to the trade expedient." The President of the Board of Trade could propose the new boards, but it took a vote in the House of Commons to actually establish them. In 1913, the Anti-Sweating League pushed for several more boards, and five were eventually set up. These covered the sugar confectionary, shirt making, hollow-ware making, and linen and cotton embroidery trades, along with a portion of the laundry industry, all industries with an almost exclusively female work force. About 140,000 additional workers were now covered.[5]

The outbreak of war in August of 1914 affected every aspect of the British economy. As the war dragged on, the need for economic coordination and planning grew, meaning an expansion of the state into labor-management relations. Government-sponsored tribunals were set up for a number of industries, given the remit to set conditions of work, including wages in many cases, and prevent strikes. The trade boards soon more or less fell into line with these designs.

---

4 Jenny Morris, *Women Workers and the Sweated Trades: The Origins of Minimum Wage Legislation* (Aldershot: Gower, 1986), 231-232.
5 Morris, *Women Workers*, 232.

Thus, the early experience with the trade boards was rocky. The original four had barely had time to begin operating before they were eclipsed by the war. As for the second batch of five, none of them had even issued a wage order when war came.

The end of the war brought serious economic dislocations and a concomitant wave of strikes, resulting in a great wave of policy ferment. The Ministry of Reconstruction chartered a committee (labeled the Whitley Committee after its chairman) to examine the postwar relationship between employers and employees and make recommendations. The majority on this body favored a universal system of Joint Industrial Councils through which the government would compel collective bargaining. In their view, the trade boards could be utilized as a stepping stone to this end. Therefore, they recommended that the criteria for establishing new boards be changed so that it would be easier to erect them. Their proposals greatly influenced the drafting of the Trade Boards Act 1918, which empowered the Minister of Labor to constitute a board in any case for which "no adequate machinery exists for the effective regulation of wages throughout the trade, and that accordingly, having regard to the rate of wages prevailing in the trade, or any part of the trade, it is expedient that the Act should apply."

Meanwhile, Lloyd George, now prime minister, convened a National Industrial Conference (NIC) composed of representatives of both employers and unions. It issued a report in 1919 calling for "the establishment by legal enactment of minimum time rates of wages, such rates to be universally applicable."[6] Cabinet members and senior civil servants were badly split on the subject. The Minister of Labor was especially concerned about how the purported wage would be calculated. Should the needs of the worker be the central criteria, he feared, it would have serious negative economic consequences.

> The fundamental difficulty is that such a wage is likely to be either too low to give any satisfaction or too high for certain trades to bear. If it was based on generally accepted ideas of a reasonable living wage, it would certainly stamp out some industries. If on the other hand, it were so low as not to injure the least profitable in the country, the number of workers affected would be negligible.[7]

As always, political considerations played a major role in the various maneuverings. Liberal party leaders of the day were keenly mindful of the rise of the Labor Party. In the election of 1918, it had flexed a good deal of muscle,

---

6 Cited in Rodney Lowe, "The Erosion of State Intervention in Britain, 1917-24," *Economic History Review* 31 (1978), 273.

7 Quoted in Lowe, "Erosion of State Intervention," 274.

a signal that it was a serious contender to replace the Liberals as the party of the left. A 1918 Labor party policy document called *Labour and the New Social Order* had set out four central objectives, including the creation of a univer-sally enforced "national minimum."[8] This objective was to be met by a living wage and a full employment policy. At its 1918 conference, Labor delegates had approved a resolution saying that a minimum wage should be "extended and developed so as to ensure to every adult worker of either sex a statu-tory base line of wages (to be reviewed with every substantial rise in prices) not less than enough to provide all the requirements of a full development of body, mind, and character."[9] For the 1918 election campaign, the party's manifesto called for "an altogether new status for labour," for which "[t]he national minimum is the first step." The hand of the Webbs is evident in all these pronouncements, as the "national minimum" and a "minimum" or "liv-ing" wage are used more or less interchangeably. Importantly, however, in time the party would come to believe that the national minimum could be achieved without a minimum wage.

For the moment, though, the central political fact was that the Liberals were cross-pressured. Intense debate ensued within the Government, with Lloyd George at one point drafting a letter to the Provisional Joint Council of the NIC (its executive committee) declaring that:

> Every worker should be ensured a minimum wage which will enable him or her to maintain a becoming standard of life for himself and his fam-ily. Apart altogether from considerations of humanity it is of the highest interest to the State that children should be brought up under conditions that will make them fit and efficient citizens.[10]

In the end, however, the opponents of the minimum wage carried the day in cabinet, and Lloyd George had to back off. To smooth things over, two compromises were cobbled together. First, a bill was presented to Par-liament authorizing the appointment of a Minimum Wage Commission to inquire into the issue. Before the bill was voted on, though, a constitution-al controversy led the entire Provisional Joint Council to resign in a huff.[11] With its supporters disbanded, the bill languished and soon died. Second,

---

8 G.D.H. Cole, *A History of the Labour Party from 1914* (London: Routledge and Kegan Paul, 1948), 56. The other goals were democratic control of industry, a revolution in national finance, and the use of the nation's surplus wealth for the common good.

9 Quoted in Cole, *History of the Labour Party*, 66.

10 Quoted in Lowe, "The Erosion of State Intervention," 274.

11 The NIC had called for the creation of a permanent National Industrial Council to make and enforce industrial policy. (Actually, this was in line with what the government had said when it called for "home rule for industry.") Under British constitutional practice, be-cause of parliamentary sovereignty the government may not delegate any official power to an outside body.

the Minister of Labor utilized his power under the Trade Boards Act 1918 to expand the number of boards, bringing the total to 63 by the end of 1920. An obvious ploy to undermine the case for a national minimum wage, his action nevertheless brought the number of workers covered to about three million. Around 70% of these people were women.[12]

THE DIMINISHING ROLE OF THE TRADE BOARDS, 1922-1939

Three factors shaped trade board policy in 1921. First, a number of employers were never reconciled to the introduction of minimum wages of any kind, and the expansions undertaken after 1918 increased their numbers. Second, the rapid increase in the number of trade boards had led to severe administrative difficulties.[13] Third, unemployment had begun to increase.

Consequently, the government appointed yet another committee, this one called the Caves Committee, to examine the work of the trade boards and make recommendations. Its 1922 report suggested, first, that the trade boards' work be restricted to ameliorating sweating, not encouraging collective bargaining. Second, they urged that the procedures for creating additional boards be altered to make it more difficult to christen new ones. Part of the proposed administrative procedures, the requirement for a public inquiry to be held before the establishment of a new board, did not require legislation, and was put into effect immediately. A bill was introduced to implement the other recommendations, but it was still on the legislative docket when an election was called in late 1923. Even though a minority Labor Government was returned at this election, the Caves Committee's report "determined the place of the Trade Boards in wage settlement for the next ten years."[14]

During its brief tenure in office (January-October 1924), the first Labor Government did act in the minimum wage area. The Minister of Labor started some inquires with a view toward establishing new boards, and a bill was introduced to resurrect the discarded Minimum Wage Commission. Neither bore fruit, however, when the Government was removed from office by the 1924 election. The new Conservative ministry promptly scuttled both of these initiatives.

Thus, the trade boards limped along throughout the 1920s under successive Conservative governments. By the 1930s, there were new, albeit largely

---

12 Morris, *Women Workers*, 232.
13 One observer even lists administrative confusion as the major source of dissatisfaction with the whole system of trade boards. Dorothy Sells, *British Wages Boards* (Washington: Brookings Institution, 1939), 263ff.
14 Bayliss, *Wages Councils*, 25.

invisible, movements to expand the system again. Throughout the decade, several trade boards were set up in small industries (such as the "fustian cutting trade," which employed a mere 1,937 workers). Furthermore, some bodies were established under separate pieces of legislation that while not technically trade boards resembled them in all but name. The most important of these enactments was the Road Haulage Act of 1938, which installed a "Central Board" empowered to regulate most aspects of the industry, including wages. Bayliss points out that when the Second World War began in 1939, "1,300,000 workers . . . were covered by Trade Boards, and virtually all of these were in trades for which the boards had been established before 1921. In addition, 200,000 workers in road haulage had a Wages Board."[15]

The policy marginalization of minimum wages paralleled, and was no doubt largely the result of, an important shift within the Labor party. While the party remained steadfastly committed to a "national minimum," it slowly drifted toward public expenditure policies to achieve it. The turning point was the party's 1927 conference. The Independent Labor Party, a strongly left-leaning faction, introduced a living wage resolution at this conclave, but party leaders feared it would cost them at the polls.[16] The compromise was to appoint a committee representing both the party and the Trade Union Congress (TUC) to study the twin ideas of a living wage and child allowances. The committee's 1930 report advocated the latter and ignored the former. Although the manifesto for the 1929 election ritualistically said "workers should have a minimum wage" (without, it should be noted, saying that it should be a "living wage"), the party conference of that same year voted to endorse stand alone family allowances. The public treasury was now to be the mechanism for fighting poverty, and it would remain so for many years. For the 1931 election, the party's manifesto omitted even a mention of a minimum wage; tellingly, it would not reappear until 1987.

At the Fringes, 1940-1979

Two major developments affected the history of the trade boards during the Second World War and in the years afterward. First, industrial relations policy went in an entirely different direction. One aspect of this was the adoption of Keynesian techniques of aggregate demand management for the purpose of maintaining full employment. Another was an abiding concern to protect the right of workers to have an even playing field when it came to

15 Bayliss, *Wages Councils*, 43.
16 Cole, *History of the Labour Party*, 197-202. On the Independent Labor Party, see Robert Dowse, *Left in the Centre: The Independent Labour Party, 1893-1940* (London: Longmans, 1966).

collective bargaining. Second, social welfare policy came to rely entirely on a system of social insurance and public assistance. This shift was driven by the ideas of the new social theorists who believed, as Howard Glennerster has said, that "The main reasons for economic insecurity and poverty had ceased to be low wages and were now unemployment and old age."[17]

When Winston Churchill was made prime minister in 1940, he immediately formed a coalition cabinet. Eager especially to include prominent Labor MPs in important posts, and keenly mindful of the need to maintain industrial harmony, he asked Ernest Bevin to be Minister of Labor. Bevin remained in that post until Labor's election victory of 1945, at which point he moved to the Foreign Office. During the war years, his voice stood above all others when it came to manpower policy.

Bevin was one of those Labor leaders who had come up through the ranks of the trade union movement, and he never forgot that. It is well to recall that trade union leaders of his generation always lived in the shadow of the devastating unemployment and wage reductions of the 1920s and 1930s. While many of them came to embrace Keynesian demand management strategies as a way to maintain high levels of employment, they also sought ways to solidify collective bargaining should those policies fail. In the interwar years, it was not uncommon for one employer to defect from an industry wide collective bargaining system; when it did so, it placed firms wishing to co-operate with the unions in an impossible competitive position. As victory in the war appeared more certain and postwar planning began, Bevin wrote that his central goal was "to safeguard good employers against bad employers who depressed standards of wages and conditions and prevented good employers from progressing in improvements as quickly as they otherwise would because of undercutting."[18] Bevin's mind turned to the trade boards as a way to promote this goal.

He was not unconcerned about the plight of those working for truly low wages in unorganized sectors. Against furious opposition from the industry and many Conservative backbenchers (116 voted against), he secured cabinet backing for and then parliamentary passage of the Catering Wages Bill in 1943, setting up a trade board for what we would today call the entire "hospitality" industry. Since this industry is notoriously plagued by low wages, this was a major accomplishment.

---

17 Howard Glennerster, *British Social Policy since 1945* (Oxford: Blackwell, 1995). 31.
18 Quoted in Peter Weiler, *Ernest Bevin* (Manchester: Manchester University Press, 1993), 137-138.

However, Bevin's most sustained efforts, an echo of the Joint Industrial Council's post-World War I proposals, were devoted to making the Trade Board system a tool to enhance collective bargaining. For this, he drafted and pushed through Parliament what became the Wages Councils Act of 1945. On the surface, part of the act dealt merely with nomenclature, rechristening all the Trade Boards as Wages Councils. But the change of name was significant, for it pointed to the true purposes of the act. Bevin frankly admitted this when he told Parliament that "Many people might ask what is in a name, but as the purpose of the Bill is unfolded it will be seen that the change in the name . . . is a declaration by Parliament that the conception of what was known as sweated industry is past."[19] The most important sections of the new act were the portions dealing with procedures for giving birth to new Wages Councils. Upon the petition of a business or union in any industry, the Minister of Labor could appoint a committee of inquiry to ascertain whether a Wages Council was needed for that industry. The leading criterion for the committee to consider was whether effective collective bargaining had broken down in any part of the industry. Upon receiving the report of the committee, the minister was given authority to create a Wages Council for the industry if he deemed it expedient (whether recommended by the committee or not). The wages it set would then have statutory authority.

Bevin's hope was that the pointed prospect of a wages council being created by himself or a similarly oriented Minister of Labor would be a spur to all businesses to come to the table for serious collective bargaining. As Fred Bayliss has said "This conception of the function of Wages Councils amounted to the use of state power to keep collective bargaining going when economic circumstances tended to destroy it, and was quite different from the simpler, ameliorative purpose of abolishing sweating."[20] The role of the newly dubbed wages councils was therefore transformed, and forgotten entirely in this reshuffle of priorities was any idea of a national minimum wage.

The other critical "non-event" in minimum wage policy of these years was the *Beveridge Report* of 1942.[21] Although this famous report was technically prepared under the auspices of a committee, William Beveridge was the guiding hand throughout. Beveridge was heavily influenced by Seebohm Rowntree's and Charles Booth's attempts to measure poverty and its

---

19 Speaking on the Second Reading Debate, January 16, 1945, quoted in Bayliss, *Wages Councils*, 45.

20 Bayliss, *Wages Councils*, 56.

21 *Social Insurance and Allied Services* (New York: Macmillan, 1942).

causes.[22] Rowntree's path-breaking 1899 inquiry had ascribed much of the poverty he found to the lack of adequate wages. Accordingly, Beveridge had worried a great deal over the problem of low pay, and flirted at least with the idea of a minimum wage.[23] In 1941, however, Rowntree had conducted a series of fresh studies and concluded that very little of the poverty he encountered was attributable to low wages. Of much greater importance, taken together the source of fully five-sixths of total misery, Rowntree argued, were the problems of unemployment, sickness, old age, and the death of a family breadwinner.

Following Rowntree, Beveridge's report listed eight primary causes of poverty: unemployment, disability, loss of livelihood by someone not employed, retirement, marriage needs of women, funeral expenses, childhood, physical disease or incapacity. Society, the report said, needed to create a "national minimum," dredging up the old term of the Webbs. To do so, a massive program of social insurance and public assistance should be created. Given the neglect of low pay, it is perhaps not surprising that no mention whatever was made of a minimum wage.[24]

When published in 1942, a group of Labor MPs forced a vote on accepting the report. Although a combination of Conservative opponents and Labor MPs worried about committing themselves to such broad programs before the war's end defeated the motion, it became widely accepted within the Labor party as a blueprint for postwar social policy. Consequently, when Labor won its landslide victory in 1945, it set about implementing Beveridge's recommendations. When they had finished, therefore, they had erected a welfare state that closely followed what *The Beveridge Report* had proposed.[25] It is interesting to speculate on what would have happened had Beveridge recommended a minimum wage. Given his prestige and the huge Labor majority in the House of Commons, it seems likely it would have been adopted

22 Glennerster, *British Social Policy*, 31-33 discusses Beveridge's faith in Rowntree's studies.

23 The best source of information on Beveridge is Jose Harris, *William Beveridge: A Biography* (Oxford: Oxford University Press, 1977).

24 Beveridge actually mentioned the minimum wage in an obscure memorandum written after publication of the report bearing his name. Addressed to the Advisory Panel on Home Affairs, it provided a laundry list of every conceivable policy to fight poverty, including a "statutory minimum wage." However, the fact that was listed last coupled with the sheer exhaustiveness of the list indicates that it was not a serious proposal. See Harris, *Beveridge*, 431-432.

25 On postwar social policy and the Labor government in general, see Henry Pelling, *The Labour Governments, 1945-51* (New York: St. Martins, 1984); Kenneth Morgan, *Labour in Power, 1945-1951* (Oxford: Clarendon Press, 1984); and Nick Tiratsoo, ed., *The Attlee Years* (London: Pinter, 1991).

alongside the program for social insurance and public assistance. However, that can only remain speculation.

Thus, during the 1950s, it is almost fair to say that Britain had no minimum wage policy. The welfare state was based on other premises and relied on social insurance and public assistance to bring about the "national minimum." At the same time, the trade boards were left in a rather desultory state. Largely stripped of their role to set wages in habitually low-wage sectors, and with the feared postwar slump in employment never materializing, they moved even further to the margins of British politics. Legally, by 1961, they covered about three and one-half million workers, constituting about one half the female work force.[26] Nevertheless, the general full employment and the sustained inflation of the period tended to lift most market wages above the levels set by the extant boards. Catering and retail were partial exceptions, but only partial ones.

The 1960s and 1970s were characterized by only a few minor developments concerning the Wages Councils. The 1968 Royal Commission on Trade Unions and Employers' Associations chastised the councils as impotent when it came to raising low pay and ineffective in encouraging collective bargaining. In 1969, the Wilson Government established a working party to examine the possibility of having a national minimum wage and it published a Green Paper on the subject.[27] However, this effort came to naught, as attention soon became focused on the run up to the 1970 election. The ill-fated Industrial Relations Act of 1971 contained a provision making it simpler to abolish Wages Councils, but it was largely an afterthought. When the Conservative Government came to power in 1979, then, Wages Councils stood nowhere near the center of public policy.

THE ABOLITION OF THE WAGES COUNCILS

Political leaders are often divided into those who have a blueprint in mind upon assuming office and attempt to shape their policy initiatives accordingly and those who face issues and formulate polices on an *ad hoc* basis. Mrs. Thatcher falls decidedly into the former category, even having an *-ism* named after her. There is some dispute, of course, about the exact content of her principles and how devoted she was to some of them. Nevertheless, compared to most politicians, and certainly to most British prime ministers,

---

26 Bayliss, *Wages Councils*, 75.
27 Department of Employment and Productivity, *A National Minimum Wage: Report of an Interdepartmental Working Body.* (London: HMSO, 1969). Green Paper.

she had a core set of beliefs and these guided, if not dictated, her political choices.

Long before she became prime minister, and even before she emerged as a serious contender for the party leadership, she gave a speech that laid bare her thinking, and demonstrated why the Wages Councils would be on the chopping block. She said in 1968 that it was:

> totally unacceptable that government should decide the increases of wages and salaries. Conservatives should arrange to reduce the range of government decision-making and restore individual choice... What we need now is a far greater degree of personal responsibility and decision, far more independence from government, and a comparable reduction in the role of government.[28]

While Mrs. Thatcher and her allies may have been hampered by ambiguity and contradictions as well as disputes among themselves in some areas, on the proper scope of government intervention in the economy they were resolute. Markets were always superior to government in allocating goods and services. Andrew Gamble has said that this belief rested on four propositions: "1) state intervention does not work; 2) all alternatives to markets are deeply flawed; 3) government failure is more prevalent than market failure; 4) anything beyond the minimal state violates individual rights."[29] In principle, the first and third of these are subject to empirical testing, although Thatcherites would probably not accept any contrary findings as valid. In any event, the second and fourth are matters of faith, and therefore unchallengeable. Shirley Letwin has argued that the essence of Thatcherism is a belief that the role of the state is to release the "vigorous virtues" of the people.[30] Ian Gilmour, one of her former cabinet members, stressed the depth of feeling Mrs. Thatcher brought to her task. She "undoubtedly inserted into Conservative policy an ideological, if not religious, fervour and a dogmatic tone that had previously been lacking."[31] And, according to Gilmour, that ideology "largely consisted of nineteenth-century individualism dressed up in twentieth-century clothes."[32]

Thus, despite their marginal position the Wages Councils were a monument, even if only a small and rather rusty one, to state intervention in eco-

---

28 Quoted in Dennis Kavanagh, *Thatcherism and British Politics: The End of Consensus?* (Oxford: Oxford University Press, 1990), 10-11.

29 Andrew Gamble, "Privatization, Thatcherism, and the British State," *Journal of Law and Society* 16 (1989), 5. For further elaboration, see his *The Free Economy and the Strong State: The Politics of Thatcherism* (London: Macmillan, 1989).

30 Shirley Letwin, *The Anatomy of Thatcherism* (New Brunswick, NJ: Transaction, 1993).

31 Ian Gilmour, *Dancing with Dogma: Britain under Thatcherism* (London: Simon and Schuster, 1992), 6.

32 Gilmour, *Dancing with Dogma*, 9.

nomic affairs and therefore vulnerable to attack. In Thatcher's first year in office, Parliament adopted the Wages Council Act of 1979, which "consolidated" a number of councils, but more importantly cut back on the number of inspectors. According to the International Labor Organization, this move meant that the typical establishment would now be visited only every 12 to 14 years.[33] In 1985, the government proposed abolishing the wages councils altogether; however, the House of Commons Employment Committee conducted an independent inquiry, at which considerable opposition surfaced to outright abolition. The government then opted to forego abolition of the councils but still clip their wings dramatically. The Wages Act of 1986 removed those under 21 from coverage, restricted the councils' actions to setting a single minimum wage (which would usually be lower than most of the top-tiers of graded wages, the previous practice), limited accommodations offsets, and eased the procedure whereby individual councils could be terminated. Passing this measure, incidentally, meant that Britain had to renounce adherence to an International Labor Organization convention.[34]

There were still 26 Wages Councils on the books (see Table 3-1), covering in 1990 about 2.5 million workers, mainly in the retail sector. About three-fourths of these employees were women. Antipathy to the wages councils did not end with Mrs. Thatcher's exit from politics in 1990. In 1993, the Major government brought forth the Trade Union and Employment Reform Act, which wound up the remaining Wages Councils.[35] The press release which accompanied the introduction of the act was forthright: "Wages Councils were established in the early 1900s when there were no employment rights, no general health and safety legislation and little social security protection. They have no role to play in the 1990s."[36]

TABLE 3-1 WAGES COUNCILS IN OPERATION IN 1993
Aerated Waters Wages Council
Boot and Shoe Repairing Wages Council
Button Manufacturing Wages Council
Clothing Manufacturing Wages Council

33 International Labor Organization, Labor Administration Branch, *The Role of Consultative and Collaborative Organizations in Selected Areas of Labor Administration, United Kingdom.* (Geneva: ILO, 1994), chap. 3. Report prepared by Robert Husbands.

34 ILO, *Role of Consultative Organizations*, chap. 3.

35 The Agricultural Wages Board, which had been established under a separate statute, was retained in light of opposition to ending it from both employers and employees.

36 Department of Employment, November 5, 1992 press release.

Coffin Furniture and Cerement Making Wages Council
Cotton Waste Reclamation Wages Council
Flax and Hemp Wages Council
Fur Wages Council
General Waste Material Reclamation Wages Council
Hairdressing Undertakings Wages Council
Hat, Cap and Millinery Wages Council
Lace Finishing Wages Council
Laundry Wages Council
Licensed Non-residential Establishments Wages Council
Licensed Residential Establishments and Licensed Restaurant Wages Council
Linen and Cotton Handkerchief and Household Goods and Linen Piece Goods Wages Council
Made-up Textiles Wages Council
Non-food Retail Trade Wages Council
Ostrich and Fancy Feather and Artificial Flower Wages Council
Perambulator and Invalid Carriage Wages Council
Retail Bespoke Tailoring Wages Council
Retail Food and Allied Trades Wages Council
Rope, Twine and Net Wages Council
Sack and Bag Wages Council
Toy Manufacturing Wages Council
Unlicensed Places of Refreshment Wages Council

Passage of this act provides an opportunity to analyze the oft-repeated claim that abolishing minimum wages will lead to more jobs being created. An analysis of the jobs offered at job centers in the sectors covered by the Wages Councils during the nine months following abolition casts considerable doubt on this proposition.[37] True enough, about one third overall and about one half of the jobs on offer in the retail sector paid less than the old minimum wage rates. Part one of the Conservative's goals were clearly accomplished then. However, there was a net loss of about 18,000 jobs in retail and catering. Lower pay and fewer jobs seem to be the result, not the other way around.

REAWAKENING

Much of the credit for the renewed push for a national minimum wage, and indeed for its final passage in 1998, belongs to Rodney Bickerstaffe. Al-

---

37 Low Pay Network, *After the Safety Net* (London: Low Pay Network, 1994).

though certainly not alone in his advocacy for a minimum wage, it was he who provided the major impetus for and much of the energy behind the effort to convince first the unions and then the Labor party that the policy should be adopted. Born into a working class family, he never lost interest in the problems of low pay. In 1981, he became general secretary of the National Union of Public Employees (NUPE), and later the merged union UNISON, and he assiduously used that position as a platform to push for a national minimum wage.

The first problem was that the bulk of the union movement had retained its indifference to or even open hostility toward the idea of a uniform national minimum wage. In 1948, for example, a motion was offered at the annual meeting of the Trades Union Congress (TUC) that "this congress instructs the General Council to urge the government to establish by legislation a statutory minimum wage to guarantee a reasonable standard of subsistence for all adult workers."[38] A spokesman responded that the General Council was strongly opposed to the motion, offering five reasons, summarized by Roger Bowlby:

> 1) It would interfere with the historic functions of trade unions, and amount to asking someone else to do the unions' work; 2) It would do away with the need for unions "to a considerable extent"; 3) The minimum rate so set would in fact oppress the working class, since it would tend in practice to become the maximum; 4) Such a minimum wage would set a dangerous precedent, and might cause the labor movement grave harm if an antilabor government should come to power, which would more than offset any benefits to be derived from a prolabor government; and 5) The adoption of a national minimum wage would shift the scene of negotiations from the shop to Parliament, a bad setting for labor disputes, which might better be fought out on the picket lines.[39]

Following this advice, the motion was overwhelmingly defeated on a voice vote.

In 1953, a new motion was offered to put the TUC on record as favoring a "legalized minimum living wage linked to a revised and accurate retail cost-of-living index."[40] This time it was defeated on a card vote 2,883,000 for and 4,767,000 against.[41] Opponents included some of the largest and strongest unions, especially the Transport and General Workers Union (TGWU) and the Amalgamated Engineering Union (AEU), both of which maintained this position through the years. In 1986, for instance, an official of the TGWU said

---

38 Quoted in Roger Bowlby, "Union Policy toward Minimum Wage Legislation in Postwar Britain," *Industrial and Labor Relations Review* 11(1957), 72.
39 Bowlby, "Union Policy," 72.
40 Quoted in Bowlby, "Union Policy," 74-75.
41 Card votes involved union leaders voting by the numerical strength of their unions.

his organization had a "fear that a statutory minimum could be used to undermine trade union organisation, negotiation, and collective bargaining."[42] As late as 1991, AEU was arguing that "you can't advance free collective bargaining and at the same time advance the National Minimum Wage. The two things must be incompatible."[43]

The early 1980s, though, were witnessing the turning of the tide. Bickerstaffe teamed up with the Low Pay Unit, headed by Chris Pond, an avid proponent of the minimum wage, to create a Low Pay Forum. Meetings with individual union leaders and party elders were steadily used to push the idea of a national minimum wage, while a simultaneous public effort was being made as well. This latter strategy mostly involved offering resolutions at the annual gatherings of the TUC and the Labor party. As another public prong, in 1982, the Low Pay Unit published a tightly argued 63 page tract entitled *The Case for a National Minimum Wage.*[44]

At the Labor party conference of 1982, Bickerstaffe and the NUPE introduced a resolution calling for "a nationally negotiated minimum earnings level, of no less than two-thirds of the average wage in this country, agreed between the Labour government and the TUC, below which no worker should fall," and further "that the commitment to a national minimum wage is placed at the forefront of any socialist alternative economic strategy."[45] In his speech moving the resolution Bickerstaffe was cautious: "We do not ask for a statutory national minimum wage even though I believe in it; all we ask for is a target, two-thirds." Even with the determination of a minimum wage to be fastened firmly to collective bargaining, the motion was voted down.

In 1983, NUPE offered a resolution calling for a statutory minimum wage, set again at two-thirds of median earnings, to the Scottish TUC; however, it too failed. Meanwhile, the national TUC had published a discussion paper on the problem of low pay, and had mentioned a statutory minimum wage. At the 1983 meeting of the TUC, the following resolution passed:

> Congress resolves to continue the discussion among affiliated unions on the introduction of a Statutory National Minimum Wage. To assist the debate the General Council should:
>
> (i) provide a paper summarizing the arguments on both sides put forward by affiliated unions;

---

42 Quoted in George Bain, "The National Minimum Wage: Further Reflections," *Employee Relations,* January 1999, 16.

43 Quoted in Bain, "National Minimum Wage," 16.

44 Chris Pond and Steve Winyard, *The Case for a National Minimum Wage* (London: Low Pay Unit, 1982), Pamphlet No. 23.

45 Labour Party, 1982 Party Conference Program, 192.

(ii) explore further whether a statutory minimum wage would assist to bridge the gap between male and female earnings; the experience of other countries; the relationship with collective bargaining machinery; and the method by which the trade union movement would be involved in negotiation on the level of the minimum wage; and

(iii) prepare detailed targets toward which unions can be encouraged to bargain until legislation exists.

Even though it is riddled with caveats, the resolution seems to be inching toward acceptance of a statutory national minimum wage. The reference to the gap between male and female earnings is especially significant, in that so many of the low paid had always been and remained women.

In 1983 also Bickerstaffe told the Labor party conference that "More and more unions, constituencies, and MPs now hold that a genuine, determined, planned attack on low pay must be underwritten by the will of the entire community in the form of a statutory minimum wage under which no employer shall force and exploit any of our people. And, you know, the two-thirds target is not too much, but what a lift it would be for so many women."[46] The resolution he introduced was bolder and more explicit than the one from the year before, stating that "low pay will only be eliminated by the introduction of a statutory national minimum wage, with a minimum wage target set at not less than two thirds of national average earnings" and that "conference commits the next Labour government to the introduction of such a policy." Many delegates had apparently become convinced, as the resolution carried. However, it did not achieve the two thirds vote needed to make it official party policy. Nevertheless, when the 1983 election manifesto was composed, a whiff of the resolution was on offer. "The next Labour Government," the manifesto pledged, "will launch an offensive against low pay... We will work together with the unions to tackle low pay and extend the concept of fair wages[47] and arbitration ... We will also discuss with the TUC the possibility of introducing a minimum wage." It was an afterthought on the policy wish list, it would only be discussed, and the words "national" and "statutory" were conspicuously absent. Still, Bickerstaffe and the Low Pay Forum had managed a significant step.

Throughout 1984, the Labor party and the TUC were engrossed in licking their wounds from the 1983 election defeat and reeling from Mrs. Thatcher's attacks on the miners' union and Labor-dominated local governments. At the 1985 Labor party conference, though, Bickerstaffe was back, seeking to build on the 1983 resolution. He and the Low Pay Forum had worked tirelessly be-

---

46 Labour Party, 1983 Party Conference Program, 185.
47 "Fair wages" refers to requirements written into government contracts.

fore the conference to lay the ground work. Bickerstaffe's speech was short, only five paragraphs. The first one summed it up adequately:

> It has been a historic, long march to get to today. We have been trying for 20 years to get this Labour Party Conference to pass by a two-thirds majority at least a resolution that commits our party to set up when in power a statutory, national, minimum wage. I shall not be long this morning, because I think that we have got it in the bag. I think that you all know that although we have had trade unionism for these past 150 years, we have never been able to do what we should have done for the low paid of our nation, have we? Of course we have not.[48]

The lengthy resolution made many bows to the large unions, stressing, for example, "that an effective strategy to end poverty must be based on strong trade union organization underpinned by legal rights, and the return of a Labour government, working in partnership with the trade union movement."[49] It also listed a variety of ways to attack poverty, including "a complete review of the social security system to provide a socially just income for all levels of society." Nevertheless, the core of the resolution called for the establishment of a statutory minimum wage.

> Conference calls on the National Executive Committee to consult on proposals for the implementation of a statutory national minimum wage as agreed by Conference in 1983 as part of this programme to fight low pay.

> The minimum wage should take account of the needs of part-time workers by setting a weekly and hourly rate. The Government should ensure that special enforcement machinery be set up, with an adequate number of inspectors, confidential easy access for complaints and stiff penalties for employers who break the law. The minimum wage will not interface with the rights of trade unions to negotiate higher rates of pay.

> Conference further calls on the National Executive Committee to back a public campaign to win support for this programme.

The resolution was approved overwhelmingly. The following year Bickerstaffe moved virtually the identical resolution at the TUC congress, where it also carried by a large majority. However, the TGWU and several other unions remained opposed.

When it came time to draft the 1987 party manifesto, the promise to introduce a minimum wage was straightforward. "We will implement a comprehensive strategy for ending low pay, notably by the introduction of a statutory national minimum wage. This will be of particular benefit to women workers and will help lift families out of poverty."

---

48 Labour Party, 1985 Party Conference Program, 211.
49 Labour Party, 1985 Party Conference Program, 211.

No hedging, no "discussion," no questions about its statutory or national status. Even though Labor lost the election by a significant margin, no one thought the minimum wage proposal was in any way responsible.

When Mrs. Thatcher left office in 1990, Labor's hopes were buoyed. In fact, most opinion polls showed them leading the Conservatives in public favor. In that year the party set up a working group to analyze how best to structure the projected minimum wage. It was clear at this point that minimum wage advocates had reached a critical point in the policy process. Victory was not assured. Labor still had to win an election and the national minimum wage had to avoid the fate of so many policies, being shuffled to the sidelines and dying there a quiet legislative death. However, it was now on the serious agenda.

Both John Smith and Tony Blair, two future party leaders, were on the working group. Smith called Bickerstaffe to a long meeting at the president's lodge at Magalden College, Oxford.[50] The NUPE and the Low Pay Forum had altered slightly the formula they wished to see used. Rather than two thirds of "average" earnings, they were arguing for two-thirds of "median male" earnings. The specifying of "median" for "average" rather than "mean" might actually lower the minimum wage, since in all known income distributions, small numbers of high earners pull up the mean but do not affect the median. However, the use of "male" would raise it considerably, since male earnings outstrip those of females by a substantial margin. Smith told Bickerstaffe that he was strongly in favor of the minimum wage but that he could not carry the two thirds formulation. After several hours of discussion, Smith indicated that one half median male earnings was the best he could do, but that there might be a chance over time to move to two thirds. Smith did agree, though, that overtime should be included in the calculation.

For the 1992 election, Labor included another explicit minimum wage provision in its manifesto.

> Britain's Wages Councils set minimum wages for about 2.5 million people. But there is no minimum wage for all employees. We will end the scandal of poverty pay and bring Britain into line with the rest of Europe by introducing a statutory minimum wage of £3.40 an hour. This is a major but long overdue reform which will benefit around four million low-paid people, 80 per cent of whom are women. We will consult widely to ensure smooth implementation.

The Conservative party, in contrast, touted its "flexible" labor market approach, and firmly repudiated the minimum wage. Their manifesto said:

---

50 Personal interview with Rodney Bickerstaffe, July 30, 2004.

> Over the last 13 years, we have legislated to lift regulatory burdens from
> the shoulders of those who create jobs in Britain. To industry's relief, we
> have shunned the job-destroying European Social Charter. And we reject
> Labour's job-destroying notion of a national minimum wage.

Pollsters were predicting that Labor would win this election; however, for whatever reason, and several have been offered, the Conservatives emerged victorious.[51] Not only would the introduction of the minimum wage now have to wait until after the next election, but, as noted above, the Major government proceeded to kill off the Wages Councils entirely.

The five years following the 1992 election defeat were momentous ones for the Labor party. A cleavage had existed for several years between the traditionalists and the modernizers. The modernizers had a number of targets: symbols, (especially Clause Four of the party constitution, committing the party to "socialism"), internal organization, campaign strategies, and policy commitments. Pointing to polls which showed the electorate thought the party old fashioned, tired, and attached to programs that no longer resonated with the voters, the modernizers intoned that what was needed was a complete overhaul, the building of New Labor. John Smith was selected as leader soon after the 1992 defeat, and while he had sympathies with both camps, he opened the doors for the modernizers. When Smith died suddenly in 1994, Tony Blair won the ensuing leadership contest, and began the overhaul in earnest. In this effort, he relied heavily on his confidante and shadow Chancellor Gordon Brown. By the election of 1997, the transformation to New Labor was complete.

In the area of economic policy, the Labor party had historically been wedded to Keynesian demand management to maintain full employment, progressive taxation, and redistributive expenditures. These were to be buttressed by public ownership of much of the "commanding heights" of the economy and legal protections for trade unions. Blair and his colleagues now jettisoned all of these, stressing markets, no new tax initiatives, restraint in public expenditures, and restrictions on the unions' ability to call strikes. When it came to social policy, Labor's traditional push had been to expand benefit programs. New Labor now spoke of social inclusion and the need for responsibilities to be connected with rights, and the virtue of work. Gordon Brown summed up, for example, much of the new thinking in an interview with the US Public Broadcasting System in 2001.

---

51 See David Sanders, "Why the Conservative Party Won — Again," in Anthony King, ed., *Britain at the Polls, 1992* (Chatham, NJ: Chatham House, 1992), chap. 6.

> We saw in the 1970s and 1980s, when I first became involved in politics, the public reaction to what they saw as an excessive collectivism. In other words, people equated the actions of government with too much taxation, too much bureaucracy, too much collectivism, too much trade union power. They began to believe that government was the source of economic problems or challenges that they faced. It reflected the fact that we had failed to make the distinction between the public interest, which does not require public ownership, and the public ownership that we put forward. Equally, I think in the post-1945 age we were concerned [with establishing] social rights for individuals, and perhaps we distanced them from the responsibilities that people ought to meet when rights are guaranteed. Therefore, in the 1970s and '80s people were reacting against an over-centralization, which was in fact unnecessary, and equally they were reacting against us, probably concentrating too much on rights without responsibilities. In every civilized society that works, rights and responsibilities must go together. If you're getting help to find a job, you've got a duty to look for a job. These are rights that come with responsibilities and not without responsibilities.[52]

The minimum wage meshed neatly into the new policy paradigm. It required no increase in taxation and no public expenditures (aside from some minimal funds for inspectors). It was based on work, and would fit one for social inclusion, both because of the fact that work establishes a strong moral claim to a decent livelihood and because of the virtues imbued by work. At the same time, it could fight poverty and reduce inequality.

Both Gordon Brown and Tony Blair, therefore, heartily endorsed the minimum wage. At the same time, though, both were keen to appear friendly to business interests, and knew that the minimum wage was a potential lightning rod. Maintaining both commitments would require some deft political balancing. Step one in this waltz was to avoid making any firm commitments to a formula regarding the level of the minimum wage. To this end, in 1995, with all the polls showing Labor an almost shoo-in at the next general election, Blair obtained party approval to establish a Low Pay Commission (LPC) to set the wage level when Labor took office. This move provoked rumblings among the unions. UNISON, the public employee union formed in 1993 by the merger of NUPE and several smaller unions, took serious exception to this approach. At their 1996 conference, they reiterated their support for an automatic half male median formula with a goal of two-thirds. Following suit, the TUC endorsed UNISON's position at its 1996 meeting.

The party's manifesto for 1997 mentioned the minimum wage in three places. In the section on labor markets, while praising "a flexible labour market," stress was laid on "flexibility plus," which included "minimum standards of fair treatment, including a national minimum wage." Regard-

---

52 Interview with PBS, July 30, 2001. Transcript available at pbs.org.

ing poverty, the document promised "a comprehensive strategy for ending low pay, notably by the introduction of a statutory national minimum wage." Flying a warning flag to those in UNISON and the TUC who still championed the half male median earnings benchmark, though, an indication itself of how the internal balance of power within the party had shifted away from the unions, the manifesto sounded a note of caution.

> There should be a statutory level beneath which pay should not fall — with the minimum wage decided not on the basis of a rigid formula but according to the economic circumstances of the time and with the advice of an independent low pay commission, whose membership will include representatives of employers, including small business, and employees.

Also, there was a nod to the fact that far more women than men earned low pay, and the potential the minimum wage provided to cut benefits.

> Every modern industrial country has a minimum wage, including the US and Japan. . . Introduced sensibly, the minimum wage will remove the worst excesses of low pay (and be of particular benefit to women), while cutting some of the massive £4 billion benefits bill by which the taxpayer subsidises companies that pay very low wages.

The outcome of the election of 1997 was a foregone conclusion from the beginning, the only question being the size of Labor's majority. Election Day was May 1, and in July a non-statutory Low Pay Commission was created, to which nine people — balanced equally among business, the unions, and academics — were appointed (See Table 3-2). Its charge was to:

- recommend the initial level at which the National Minimum Wage might be introduced;
- make recommendations on lower rates or exemptions for those aged 16-25; and
- consider and report on any matters referred . . . by Ministers.

In accomplishing these tasks, the Commission was "to have regard to the following":

> the wider economic and social implications; the likely effect on the level of employment and inflation; the impact on the competitiveness of business, particularly the small firms sector; and the potential impact on the costs to industry and the Exchequer.[53]

With no mention made whatever of the needs of low-wage workers in the items the LPC was "to have regard to" and the hint that a youth differential was clearly preferred, much of the thrust of the LPC's work was largely set. Given the many contentious issues still remaining, though, and the admittedly complex task of drafting policy details, the commission was

---

53 Low Pay Commission, *First Report*, June 1998, 13-14.

given ten months to complete its work. As is the custom, it began by taking evidence from a wide variety of groups. In addition to those giving formal oral presentations (listed in Table 3-3), 498 other groups and individuals submitted written evidence. Further, the commissioners broke into groups of two or three and paid visits to firms and other installations throughout the country. Naturally, too, they had access to the array of statistical information government departments could provide.

TABLE 3-2. MEMBERS OF THE ORIGINAL LOW PAY COMMISSION	
Name	Occupational Background
George Bain (Chair)	Vice-Chancellor of Queen's University, Former Professor of Industrial Relations
William Brown	Professor of Industrial Relations, Cambridge University
Bill Callaghan	Chief Economist, Trades Union Congress
John Cridland	Director of Human Resources Policy, Confederation of British Industry
Lawrie Dewar	Chief Executive, Scottish Grocers' Federation
Rita Donaghy	Member of UNISON Executive Council Secretary, Students' Union, University of London Institute of Education
Paul Gates	General Secretary, National Union of Knitwear, Footwear and Apparel Trades
David Metcalf	Professor of Industrial Relations, London School of Economics
Stephanie Monk	Director of Human Resources, Granada Group

TABLE 3-3. ORGANIZATIONS PROVIDING FORMAL ORAL EVIDENCE TO THE LOW PAY COMMISSION DURING 1997-1998
Agricultural Wages Board for England and Wales
Amalgamated Engineering and Electrical Union
Belfast Unemployed Resources Centre
Brewers and Licensed Retailers Association
British Apparel and Textile Confederation
British Chambers of Commerce
British Hospitality Association

British Retail Consortium
British Youth Council
Business in Sport and Leisure, Ltd.
Business Services Association
Cleaning and Support Services Association
Commission for Racial equality
Confederation of British Industry
Confederation of British Industry (Northern Ireland)
Convention of Scottish Local Authorities
Equal Opportunities Commission
Federation of Small Businesses (Scotland)
General Assembly Committee on Church and Nation (Church of Scotland)
GMB (General Union)
Hairdressing Employers Association
Independent Care Organisations' Network
Independent Healthcare Association
Joint Care Council
Local Government Association
Local Government Management Board
Low Pay Unit Research Trust
National Advisory Council on Employment of People with Disabilities
National Association of Citizens Advice Bureaux
National Council for One Parent Families
National Council for Voluntary Organisations
National Hairdressers' Federation
National Youth Agency
Northern Ireland Anti-Poverty Network
Northern Ireland Association of Citizens Advice Bureaux
Northern Ireland Committee of the Irish Congress of Trade Unions
Northern Ireland Council for Voluntary Action
Retail Trade Alliance
Scottish Council of Voluntary Organisations
Scottish Trades Union Congress
Trades Union Congress
Transport and General Workers' Union
Unemployment Unit and Youthaid
Union of Shop, Distributive and Allied Workers
UNISON
UNISON (Northern Ireland)

Meanwhile, in November 1997, a bill laying out the framework for the National Minimum Wage was introduced into the House of Commons. A second reading debate was held December 16, at the end of which it passed on a party line vote of 387-145. Margaret Beckett, the President of the Board of Trade and Secretary of State for Trade and Industry was assigned the job of opening the debate. Following Blair's preferences, she took a sober and restrained line. Her arguments were chiefly economic in character, while taking the obligatory pot shots at the previous government.

> The evidence for why we need a national minimum wage is quite clear. Despite the previous Government's assertions, having no floor at all for wages has in itself created considerable problems in the labour market. It has increased costs and pressures on the public purse and it has undermined many efficient and worthwhile companies which are at risk of losing market share as they are undercut by cowboy operators.

> In consequence, we see low standards, not merely becoming the norm, but being reflected in the poor quality, or indeed the lack of any training or of development, in the work force, in levels of productivity that still lag far behind our competitors because improved productivity depends crucially on improved levels of investment, and in consequent reductions in the competitiveness of British industry.[54]

She dredged up Winston Churchill's comments when introducing the Trade Boards Act 1909 concerning how the minimum wage protects the ethical employer. He had said that "where you have what we call sweated trades, . . . the good employer is undercut by the bad, and the bad employer is undercut by the worst."[55] Throughout, she seemed to go out of her way to reassure business interests by noting how many employers were in favor of the bill and stressing that the rate would be set "sensibly" and with "prevailing economic circumstances" the major criterion. "Modern companies," she concluded . . . "depend on stimulating confidence and creativity because those are the principal assets enabling them to compete in the global economy, where a competitive edge is so desperately needed. A policy of a national minimum wage will contribute greatly to such developments."[56]

Some Labor MPs, however, wanted to make the case more in terms of justice. The most forceful of these figures was Ian McCartney, a Minister of State in the Department of Trade and Industry, and himself a former low-paid worker.

> I want to talk about the real-life issues of low pay. Nearly 1 million of our fellow citizens earn less than £2.50 an hour, and 750,000 families

---

54 *Hansard*, House of Commons, December 16, 1997, Col. 163.
55 Quoted in *Hansard*, House of Commons, December 16, 1997, Col. 173.
56 *Hansard*, House of Commons, December 16, 1997, Col. 173.

receive in-work benefits such as family credit. They have a full-time job all week and still cannot afford to live. . .

> Low-paid workers never have a voice; they are powerless and isolated. Throughout this debate, there has not been a clear understanding of what it means to be low paid. . . .

> The low-paid are excluded from the mainstream. They cannot afford school trips for their kids, family outings or days out and sometimes cannot afford a present for their children on their birthday. That is the reality — that is what this is about. This is about feeling valued and having personal dignity when an employer is treating you no better than a dog. We want to introduce respect and fairness.[57]

Conservative opponents concentrated their fire on the old saw of job losses. Shaun Woodward lamented that "The President of the Board of Trade spoke of making work pay, but the danger of the Bill is that it will make the workers pay for it with their jobs."[58] David Prior claimed to be worried about "the thousands of casual and seasonal employees who work in the tourism industry — boys and girls doing holiday jobs, getting training and work experience; women who are topping up their husbands' income; pensioners who are doing extra work to top up their pensions."[59] Some additional charges were also leveled regarding the Government's asking Parliament to debate the bill without a figure for the level of the wage, the supposed lack of small business representation on the LPC, and whether or not regional rates were desirable.

After passage, the bill was assigned to Standing Committee D, at which the Conservatives launched a delaying game by seeking to drag out the proceedings. Over a two week period, only one clause of 53 was completed. In fact, from January 13 to February 17, 1998, the committee met in 19 sessions, including one lasting 26 and a half hours, reportedly an all-time record.[60] In the end, though, Labor leaders had the votes to report the bill out with only a few technical amendments.

Meanwhile, serious fissures were opening both inside the Government and among the measure's supporters outside Parliament. The first row occurred over the Government's own submission to the LPC. The two points of contention reflected the charge to the LPC, what the level of the wage

---

57 *Hansard*, House of Commons, December 16, 1997, Col. 234.

58 *Hansard*, House of Commons, December 16, 1997, Col. 217.

59 *Hansard*, House of Commons, December 16, 1997, Col 221. Labor spokesmen countered that 1)after the abolition of the wages councils, wages and employment had both fallen and 2) evidence from the United States did not back the correlation between minimum wage increases and job losses.

60 Phil Murphy, "Minimum Wage Committee in Marathon Sitting," *The Guardian*, January 28, 1998.

---

should be and whether or not there should be a separate rate for young people (and if so what the cutoff age should be). Beckett and McCartney at the Department of Trade and Industry (DTI) favored higher rates and no separate wage for youths. Gordon Brown and the Treasury, on the other hand, warned against setting the initial rate too high and voiced fears that youth employment could be damaged if they did not have a lower rate. In the end, Brown and his allies carried the day. Although the submission avoided recommending a specific rate it did say that "The higher the level of the minimum wage, the greater the risk of an adverse effect on employment, inflation and the public sector borrowing requirement."[61] The youth differential was more clearly endorsed by way of a statement that rejected a lower wage for trainees but said one for all young people would be a good idea. Ironically, despite her misgivings, it was Margaret Beckett that had to make the official submission through the DTI.

As the LPC continued its work, with regular leaks to the press, union ire was building over both issues. During a Lord's debate in late March, a Government spokesman refused to rule out a youth minimum wage applying to anyone under 26. Moreover, rumors and Treasury briefings were pointing toward an adult rate of around £3.50 per hour. Union leaders had been hoping for a rate of at least £4.00, having already abandoned virtually all hope of achieving the half male median earnings target of £4.61. During the Commons third reading debate — which saw Conservatives again demanding a lengthy debate — several anxious Labor backbenchers took ministers to task over the rate and the exemption.

Although the LPC had to postpone its official report until June, copies were widely leaked. It was clear in late May that it would suggest an adult rate of £3.60 per hour to take effect in April 1999 with a rise to £3.70 slated for 2000. A "Development Rate" of £3.20 (rising to £3.30 in 2000) would apply to all workers 18-20 and for the first six months of employment for everyone over 21. Workers aged 16-17 were to be exempt entirely from the NMW. The Confederation of British Industry pronounced the rate "acceptable."[62] Union reaction ranged from grudging acceptance to outrage. John Monks, the TUC general secretary, said "It is a step in the right direction. It's not as much as we would have wanted — we were pitching for over £4 — but getting a minimum wage properly established in a real step toward eliminating poverty pay is very much our objective." Bickerstaffe was more disturbed. "It

---

61 Quoted in Christine Buckley, "Beckett Warns Against High Minimum Wage," *The Times*, January 31, 1998.

62 This and the following quotes are from a Press Association release of May 28, 1998.

is like 100% marks for the law but rather less than 40% for the level. We are a rich nation and many other countries have got minimum wage levels much higher than this — £3.60 in 1999 is not going to affect employment prospects. We could have expected higher. . . We will continue to campaign. It has taken 100 years to get the law and I hope it is only going to take a matter of months . . . to get a decent minimum wage."

Union disappointment was not at an end. Several senior ministers reportedly believed that even the £3.60 level might be a bit high, and that the youth differential should be extended upwards, even to the 26 point floated earlier (Brown was said to support 24). Several tense meetings were held at Number 10, as rumors swirled in early June that Beckett would either resign or be demoted from the DTI if the LPC's recommendations were not implemented.[63] Then, two more issues emerged: whether or not tips should be included in the calculation of a worker's minimum wage and whether the wage rate should be updated automatically to keep up with inflation.[64] The LPC was set to recommend the former and the Government sent signals that there would be no automatic escalator provision.

At the critical meeting, the prime minister sided with Gordon Brown, a decision that reportedly left Mrs. Beckett "spitting blood."[65] To remain a minister, she had to swallow defeat and tell the House of Commons officially that although the Government accepted the main adult rate, a "transitional" rate of £3.00 (to be uprated to £3.20 in June 2000) rather than £3.20 would apply to young people and that "young" would be defined as 18-21 (contrasted with 18-20 in the LPC report). "We are," she told the House, "at a critical point in the economic cycle. The Government is determined to proceed with all due caution with the introduction of the rate, especially for the crucial group of those aged 18-21."[66] Beckett had managed to wrest a couple of face saving concessions, though. The LPC was to remain in business and the government instructed it to review the position of 21-year-olds in a year. Reportedly, this kept Chairman Bain from resigning in protest.[67]

Many Labor MPs, however, mirrored Lynne Jones (Selly Oak) in feeling "bitterly disappointed" and a large number sat silently while Beckett made

63 Andy McSmith, "Cabinet Split Over Wages," *The Observer*, June 7, 1998.

64 Liam Halligan, "Service Industry Tips Could Count Towards Minimum Wage," *Financial Times*, July 11, 1998; Stephen Castle, "Minimum Wage Rise Rejected," *The Independent*, June 14, 1998.

65 Phillip Webster and Christine Buckley, "Beckett Fury as Brown Triumphs on Teenage Pay," *The Times*, June 18, 1998.

66 *Hansard*, House of Commons, June 18, 1998, Col. 508.

67 Barrie Clement and Colin Brown, "Beckett's Job At Risk in Minimum Wage Row," *The Independent*, June 19, 1998.

her announcement.[68] Bill Morris, general secretary of TGWU, called it "a missed opportunity," "an endorsement of workplace poverty," and a formula "to create second-class citizens at work." John Edmonds of the GMB union called it a "slap in the face," while Nigel de Gruchy of the teachers' union moaned that "The reduced rate for younger workers is probably an own goal." Unfortunately for the Government, UNISON was having its annual conference during this same week. Delegates heard outraged members give inflamed speeches, and there were serious suggestions for calling a protest strike. Hoping to still the waters a bit, the government dispatched McCartney, the unabashed trade unionist and left winger, to the gathering. He told the delegates to stop "whingeing" about the decisions and urged them not to "snatch defeat out of the jaws of victory" by passing hostile resolutions and calling for demonstrations and strikes.[69]

As angry as unionists were, business leaders were obviously pleased. An official of the Institute of Directors told the *Times* "The Government's decision to dilute the Low Pay Commission's proposals for young people are sensible and should lessen the minimum wage obstacle to job creation."[70] Adair Turner, of Merrill Lynch and the CBI, and also soon to become chair of the LPC, also expressed satisfaction, saying the government's policy was a "reasonable and workable way forward" and that anything higher would have been "moving into more dangerous territory."

The Conservative party had not finished its guerrilla war against the bill, however. On July 19, the House of Lords added an amendment to the bill strongly opposed by the Government, endowing ministers with the power to grant far-reaching exemptions to the minimum wage based on geography, firm size, industry, job classification, or age. Although the Lords had already defeated the Blair Government on several matters, this was the first flagship bill to be sabotaged. Angry Labor strategists quickly pointed out that the vote was 161 to 103, but that without the hereditaries it would have passed with an 11 vote margin. An irate Ian McCartney fumed that "The sight of the hereditary peers, the descendants of robber barons and cattle thieves, trying to deny people a national minimum wage is the greatest boost yet to Labour's desire to abolish the heriditaries."[71]

---

68 Phillip Webster and Jill Sherman, "Left Bitterly Disappointed by £3.60 Minimum Wage," *The Times*, June 19, 1998.

69 Webster and Buckley, "Beckett Fury."

70 This quotation and the following one are from Christine Buckley and Alasdair Murray, "Anger at Diluted Minimum Wage," *The Times*, June 19, 1998.

71 Quoted in Press Association release, July 20, 1998.

The Commons quickly reversed the amendment and the Lords backed down on July 28. On July 31 the bill received the Royal Assent.

The rates were scheduled to go into effect April 1, 1999. On that day, Rodney Bickerstaffe and Bharti Patel, who was now head of the Low Pay Unit,[72] stood on the balcony of the Unit's office and released a bundle of balloons into the air.[73] It was a day that been a long time in coming.

---

72 Chris Pond had become the MP for Gravesham.
73 Their photograph is on the cover of the March/April 1999 issue of *The New Review*.

Chapter 4. The National Minimum Wage in Operation

The Policy Making Process

As the National Minimum Wage (NMW) has become bedded in, a more or less regularized policy making process has taken shape. Formally, the process begins in the late summer of each year, when the Government provides the terms of reference for the Low Pay Commission (LPC). From then until early spring, the commission takes evidence and holds a number of meetings. When it completes its work, it forwards any recommendations it has to the Government, which has the option to accept or reject them. Of course, this is only the surface outline, and the actual process of formulating minimum wage policy is both more subtle and more complex.

The LPC was made a permanent statutory body in 2001. Despite this status, though, it can only be called quasi-independent at best, tethered as it is to the Government in so many respects. To begin, the Government has the power of appointment. So far, two considerations have dominated: keeping the Commission balanced and placing people of moderate views on it. Illustrative of the first principle, in June of 2000, when Bill Callaghan, the chief economist of the TUC left to become chair of the Health and Safety Commission, and Lawrie Dewar, the chief executive of the Scottish Grocers Federation, retired, they were replaced by David Coats, the head of the Economic and Social Affairs Department of the TUC, and Ian Hay, the chief executive of the Scottish Association of Master Bakers. Regarding the second, no one who has taken a strong public stance on the NMW, either for or against, has been given a seat. For Labor, moreover, it has also been important to be seen as super sensitive to business interests. When Ian Bain stepped down as chair, for instance, Adair Turner, the vice chair of Merrill Lynch, was selected to replace him. Then when he left the Commission, the chair was assumed by Paul Myners, chairman of Land Securities Group. (Incidentally, the members of the LPC serve without pay.)

Another avenue of Government influence over the LPC is in the setting of the terms of reference. These guides for the LPC control and shape its entire work. The Government can therefore put some matters on the table and send others to the "ignore" bin. The specific terms of reference given the LPC during the various years of its existence are laid out in Table 4-1, and even a superficial reading of them shows how the Government can steer the minimum wage agenda in specific directions. (However, as will be noted below, sometimes the LPC itself will ask to be given certain terms of reference for a subsequent report.)

As the LPC begins its deliberations, various groups make submissions. Many interest groups, of course, take advantage of this opportunity and draft lengthy statements setting out their views. Most of these are quite predictable: the unions, especially those representing low-paid workers, want a higher wage level and expanded coverage while business groups, especially those employing the most low-wage workers, want modest increases at best. Other groups besides unions and businesses are active, though. Charitable and religious groups who work with the poor and organizations engaged in youth work, for example, regularly contribute submissions. However, one of the most important submissions is from the Government itself. While part of this evidence is the usual back-patting (stressing, for example, in its December 2000 evidence how the NMW had closed the gender pay gap by one per cent), it also contains important clues about Government thinking. The LPC cannot afford, consequently, to ignore either the substance or the tone of this evidence.

The LPC then gathers data from the Office of National Statistics (ONS) as well as other sources and deliberates over the elements in its charge. Often, the tentative conclusions are leaked to the press, and stir comment in various quarters. In the end, the commission drafts a detailed report containing their recommendations and transmits it to the Government.

By the terms of the NMW Act, the Government must officially respond to the report. As no Government is a unified entity, though, policy differences and personality clashes over minimum wage policy are inevitable, and the LPC report is often a catalyst for them to erupt. Typically, the report's release is followed by a period of sparring in the cabinet, and the cleavages manifested there frequently spill over to backbench MPs and groups close to the party. In Labor's case, this latter category has meant chiefly the unions, of course. In time, usually a fairly short time, the Government's inner circle determines which of the recommendations to adopt and which to reject. These are announced in a formal statement by the Secretary of State for Trade and Industry. Speeches by him or her and his/her deputies will follow in both houses of Parliament. These are important not only for setting out the actual policies the Government will pursue, but also for their tone. For example, in July of 2000, while explaining the response to the Second Report of the LPC, a Government spokesman told the House of Lords: "The Government's continued awareness of the needs of business has been a key reason why the minimum wage was brought in so smoothly and successfully, and we intend to retain that approach."[1] Only the politically deaf could have missed the message.

Thus, from choosing the members of the LPC and controlling its agenda to making the final decisions on minimum wage policy, the Government is in complete control. Moreover, it is a control that the current Government, at least, has jealously guarded. It has steadfastly refused, for example, to endorse either any tying of the minimum wage to an earnings formula or the development of any mechanism for increasing it automatically (say, with the inflation rate). However, this is not to say that the LPC is without power. It can put the Government in an embarrassing position simply by making recommendations, especially repeated recommendations, it knows that key ministers do not support. For whatever it recommends must elicit a formal response, and a refusal to adopt a recommendation can trigger revolts among other ministers or backbench MPs, as well as make the public face of the Government appear miserly.

POLICY DEVELOPMENT, 1999-2007

Soon after the NMW was launched, the Government handed the LPC a revised set of marching orders for its Second Report. It was to "monitor and evaluate the introduction and impact of the National Minimum Wage" and "to recommend whether 21-year-olds should be covered by the adult rate." (See Table 4-1 for details.)

---

1 *Hansard*, House of Lords, July 14, 2000, Col. 522.

TABLE 4–1 TERMS OF REFERENCE FOR THE LOW PAY COMMISSION
First Report (1998)
Recommend the initial level at which the National Minimum Wage might be introduced.
Make recommendations on lower rates or exemptions for those aged 16-25.
Consider and report on any matters referred to [the commission] by Ministers.
Second Report (2000)
Monitor and evaluate the introduction and impact of the National Minimum Wage.
Recommend whether 21-year-olds should be covered by the adult rate.
Third Report (2001)
Continue to monitor and evaluate the impact of the National Minimum Wage.
[Consider] if there was a case for increasing the main National Minimum Wage rate and the Development Rate and, if so, by how much.
Making any change to the maximum accommodation offset.
Changing the age at which workers become entitled to the adult rate.
Fourth Report (2003)
Continue to monitor and evaluate the impact of the National Minimum Wage.
Review the levels of both the main National Minimum Wage rate and the Development Rate and make recommendations, if appropriate, for change.
2004 Report
(Note: Reports were no longer given numbers.)
Consider whether the October 2004 uprating of the adult and development rates recommended in [the] fourth report remain appropriate in the light of economic circumstances, and if not make any recommendations for change.

Consider the possible advantages and disadvantages of a minimum wage rate for 16- to 17-year-olds.

2005 Report

Continue to monitor and evaluate the impact of the National Minimum Wage.

Review the levels of each of the different minimum wage rates and make recommendations, if appropriate, for change.

Consider whether there was evidence of any significant increase in the number of employers paying 18- to 21-year-old workers lower rates than adults and to advise on the reasons for any such increase. (Note: This issue was added after the LPC had already begun work.)

2006 Report

Consider whether the October 2006 upratings of the adult and development rates recommended in [the] 2005 Report remained appropriate in the light of economic circumstances and the other factors identified as relevant in that report, and if not to make any recommendations for change.

Review the level of the 16- to 17-year-old rate, keeping in mind the position of the youth labour market and the incentives for young people to participate in education and training.

Review the operation of the accommodation offset and, if appropriate, make recommendations for any changes needed to regulations.

Review the treatment of benefits-in-kind, including where those benefits are offered as part of a salary sacrifice arrangement.

2007 Report

Continue to monitor, evaluate and review the National Minimum Wage and its impact, with particular reference to the effect on pay, employment and competitiveness in the low-paying sectors and small firms; the effect on different groups of workers, including different age groups, ethnic minorities, women and people with disabilities; the effect on pay structures; and taking into account the forthcoming changes to the statutory annual leave entitlement.

The LPC began its report by presenting detailed information to demonstrate that, for the most part, all was going smoothly.

> Both employers and workers have adjusted well to the introduction of the minimum wage. Small businesses have been most affected, yet have successfully managed the transition. Each sector has had to adopt its own strategies to cope with the additional pay costs and, for some sectors or types of businesses within them, the adjustment has been considerable. Nevertheless, for the vast majority of employers, the transition has been successful and, consequently, most low-paid workers are receiving their full entitlement.[2]

On the issue of where 21-year-olds should fall, the LPC argued that they should be moved into the adult category and receive "the coverage of the full National Minimum Wage from June 2000."[3] Many ministers, mostly those allied with Gordon Brown, greeted this report by expressing serious reservations about the wisdom of making 21-year-olds eligible for the full adult rate, citing fears of possible youth unemployment.[4] In the end, the skeptics convinced Blair and the cabinet to delay a decision on the issue, while consenting to having the LPC examine the matter further. This move did not please the unions, to put it mildly.

Meanwhile, a more public row was brewing over the projected rise in the basic rate. As noted in the previous chapter, the youth rate was set to move to £3.20 (from £3.00) and the adult rate to £3.70 (from £3.60) in June of 2000. Apparently, though no one was opposed to the increase in the youth (or more accurately, the development)[5] rate, there were misgivings within the Government (again, chiefly among those close to Gordon Brown) about raising the adult rate. Those favoring a more cautious approach wanted to freeze the rate until further economic studies were done concerning the NMW's impact; other ministers, on the other hand, wanted to charge ahead and put the scheduled increase into effect immediately. The former group seemed to be carrying the day in January 2000, and that was promptly leaked to the press. Whirlpools of discontent erupted among Labor activists, as the minimum wage merged with and became a symbol of what many traditionalists in the party were already feeling was a general neglect of "the heartland." In early February, the Minister of Defence resigned and malcontents sent word that they would use the upcoming weekly meeting of the Parliamentary Labor

---

2 LPC, *Second Report*, xii.
3 LPC, *Second Report*, xiv. In addition, a number of technical recommendations were made, all of which were ultimately accepted by the Government.
4 *Times*, January 31, 2000.
5 The development rate applied to 18- to 21-year-olds and new adult hires (although this feature was very seldom used).

Party as a forum to challenge the Government on the minimum wage rise. In mid-February a compromise emerged, with the cabinet agreeing to the 10 pence rise but delaying its effective date until October.

In June, Stephen Byers, the Secretary of State for Trade and Industry, announced that the LPC would be asked to "recommend whether there is a case for increasing the main national minimum wage rate and the development rate, and if so, by how much." To some, this was an attempt to stymie the discontent still lingering over the delayed increase. Then, in October 2000, as the new adult rate was taking effect, the Office of National Statistics (ONS) issued its New Earnings Survey, which painted a rosy picture regarding the impact of the NMW. According to the figures, about 1.5 million people (later lowered to 1.3 million) had benefited from the introduction of the NMW[6], average earnings were up by two per cent (and even more in the most impoverished areas), and the gap between men and women's pay had fallen. This led Byers to crow:

> This shows that the Government's policies to help the low paid, which include the National Minimum Wage and the Working Family Tax Credit, are paying off. For the first time, we have independent, concrete evidence of how the minimum wage is benefiting workers around the UK. The regional breakdown confirms that it is having the biggest impact in those areas most in need and that women in particular have benefited.
>
> All this has been achieved without a negative impact on the economy. Gloom merchants who told us we could not increase the pay of hundreds of thousands of the lowest paid workers without costing jobs and causing inflation have been proven well and truly wrong.[7]

With its membership altered by one third[8] and with new terms of reference, the LPC began work in December 2000 on what may have been its most important report. Aside from some important technical recommendations, this report proposed a major rise in the level of the NMW and, once again, that 21-year-olds be given the adult rate. After citing evidence that there had been no impact on prices or employment (even suggesting at one point that the impact on employment may have been "if anything, mildly positive"[9]), the commissioners recommended a rise in the adult rate to £4.10 in October 2001 and £4.20 in October of 2002. Similarly, they recommended a hike in the development rate to £3.50 in October 2001, to be followed by another 10 pence increase in October 2002.

---

6 This estimate was later revised upward, though, when a different methodology was employed. LPC, *2007 Report*, 27-28.

7 Department of Trade and Industry, press release, October 26, 2000.

8 Margaret Prosser, a TGWU official, had replaced Rita Donaghy of UNISON.

9 LPC, *Third Report*, Vol. II, paragraph 2.16.

The Government accepted the new rates, but demurred again on the status of 21-year-olds. As before, it was mainly Gordon Brown who stood against lowering the age for the adult rate. His rationale, again, was concern over doing anything that might jeopardize employment opportunities for young people. And, as always, it was the subject of intense debate within the Government and among its allies. Presumably, the acceptance of the sharp rise in the adult rate (which was 10.8%) was the compromise necessary for putting to one side the reclassification of 21-year-olds, and was also taken, most analysts believed, at least in part with a view to the upcoming election. Additionally, the Government called for implementing some procedural recommendations from the LPC: that it be made a statutory body (giving it permanent status), that it be empowered to embark on an ambitious research program, and that biennial reviews be undertaken by the LPC that would be published in advance of the budget.

The Fourth Report of the LPC was not due until 2003. More certainties were appearing now, as experience with the NMW grew, certainties reflected in the opening pages of the report.

> In making our new recommendations we have taken into account evidence of the impact of the National Minimum Wage so far, looked at prospects for the economy and considered views of stakeholders. The evidence of the impact shows that the minimum wage has been a success. There have been negligible adverse effects on employment or inflation. . . . [A]s the minimum wage has been in place for almost four years, we can be confident of our assessment. Our aim is to have a minimum wage that helps as many low-paid people as possible without any adverse impact on the economy. We therefore believe there is a strong case for a significant step up in the level over the next few years, contingent on economic circumstances.[10]

Rather boldly, the LPC developed a case 1)that the NMW should be raised at a rate exceeding the growth in average earnings, and 2)that more people should be made eligible for it. For the first, they argued for a hike in the adult rate to £4.50 in October 2003 and £4.85 in October 2004, with corresponding rises in the development rate to £3.80 and £4.10. Increases of this magnitude would make the NMW apply to about 1.7 million workers by October 2004. Regarding the second, once again the LPC recommended that 21-year-olds be given the full adult rate. Reaching further still, they invited the Government to ask them to examine whether or not 16- to 17-year-olds should be given a separate minimum wage.

In March, 2003, the Government accepted the 2003 rates, and also agreed that if economic conditions warranted, the 2004 rates would be implemented as well. The invitation to submit the issue of a 16- to 17-year-old minimum

---

10 LPC, *Fourth Report*, xv.

wage to the LPC was accepted in principle, with a detailed charge slated to be developed later.[11] However, the Government again stood firmly against applying the adult rate to 21-year-olds, repeating the fear "that there would be a real risk of further damaging their employment prospects if they were moved onto the adult rate."[12]

The 2004 LPC report dealt, first, with whether economic conditions warranted keeping the recommended increases on schedule. The commissioners noted the generally optimistic conditions generated by the major economic indicators, and suggested that the new rates be allowed to take effect. However, despite the overall health of the economy and the strong employment picture, the unemployment rate for 18- to 21-year-olds was slightly higher than the overall rate. This led the LPC to conclude that the development rate, therefore, should not rise as fast as the adult rate.

Turning to the adoption of a minimum wage for 16- to 17-year-olds, the LPC heard extensive evidence that very low rates of pay were being offered to these youngsters. For example, a Citizens Advice Bureau in Scotland reported a 17-year-old working 35 hours in a kilt factory who earned £2.30 an hour. Unions presented evidence of a printing company and a car valet firm that paid 16- to 17-year-olds £1.50 per hour, and even worse, a riding school and a decorating firm that paid them only £1.25 an hour. Consequently, the LPC concluded that a minimum wage should be established for these workers, but that the wage level should be set lower than even the development rate. (They suggested £3.00, to be introduced in October 2004). Even more sensitive than in the case of the 18-21 cohort to how this might affect the availability of jobs, the commission took the position that any future increases be considered very carefully, and that the new wage should not be automatically linked to increases in the development rate. The LPC urged, parenthetically, that all 16- to 17-year-olds should be enrolled in education or training, but it acknowledged that only 70% of this cohort are currently full-time students.

In something of an about face, Brown voiced opposition to neither the hefty increases in the regular rates nor the 16- to 17-year-olds' minimum wage. Most believe this was because the economy was booming and there were reported labor shortages in many sectors. There were even leaked reports that he might propose a rate exceeding the LPC sanctioned ones. In

11 Patricia Hewitt said she was personally opposed to this idea, for it might draw students away from school attendance. There is some evidence that high minimum wages for very young people do lead to that result. See Dean Hyslop and Steven Stillman, *Youth Minimum Wage Reform and the Labour Market*, New Zealand Treasury Working Paper, March 2004.

12 Quoted in *Financial Times*, March 20, 2003.

the end, though, the Government accepted both recommendations, to the applause, especially regarding the launching of a 16- to 17-year-old minimum wage, of the unions and most Labor MPs. The general secretary of the TUC declared that "Unions will be delighted that their campaigning has paid off and that young people are to benefit from a minimum wage at last."[13]

In August of 2004, the Government announced the terms of reference for the LPC's 2005 report. These were much more general than before, as reported in Table 4-1[14] When its deliberations were complete, the LPC urged that the adult rate be increased to £5.05 and the development rate to £4.25 in October 2005, and to £5.35 and £4.45 respectively in October 2006, the latter moves being dependent on the continuation of a buoyant economy. The commission also requested that the Government ask them to analyze the operation of the 16- to 17-year-old minimum wage and report in February 2006. Additionally, the LPC repeated its by now almost ritualistic call for 21-year-olds to receive the adult rate. Finally, the commission called for the eventual abolition of the development rate for older workers, pending more study.[15]

On February 25, 2005, the Government disclosed that it would accept the recommendations on new rates and that it would invite further review of the 16-17 minimum wage. However, the Government refused to budge on the status of 21-year-olds, only promising "to look carefully at the issue in the future."[16]

In July 2005, the Government again handed the LPC rather general terms of reference regarding the major issues: the level of the rates (specifically whether the already scheduled October 2006 rates were still justified) and the operation of the 16- to 17-year-old system. The commission concluded in the spring that despite signs of a slowing economy, the increases should nonetheless take effect. It did note that it felt that the period had passed in which increases in the minimum wage should outstrip the growth in average earnings. Concerning the 16-17 minimum wage, the LPC concluded that it was working reasonably well, and that it ought to be increased to £3.30.

There were two other elements of the terms of reference which deserve a brief mention, for they demonstrate how employers, both unscrupulous and scrupulous, can undermine minimum wage policies if great care is not taken in monitoring policy development and implementation. Since its in-

---

13 *The Guardian*, March 11, 2004.
14 Ian Brinkley had also replaced David Coats on the LPC. He too was a TUC official.
15 As they noted, it was hardly ever used anyway.
16 Written Ministerial Statement, Department of Trade and Industry, February 25, 2005.

ception, an "accommodation offset" had been allowed. That is, if an employer furnished housing for employees, such accommodations could count as part of a worker's pay when calculating the minimum wage. It was limited to a certain amount, however (£4.15 per day in 2006), to avoid unfairness. There were recurring complaints, though, that some employers, especially those whose workforces were largely composed of foreign migrant workers, were setting up separate companies to run their accommodation operations. They then charged the employees exorbitant rates, leaving them with little take-home pay. The LPC suggested a major crack down on this practice. More legitimate, but also worrisome to anyone desiring a comprehensive minimum wage, were proposals to allow firms to count certain benefits in kind (here called "salary sacrifice schemes") toward the minimum wage. Examples would be an offer of child care vouchers, say, or the use of a computer. In general, employers favored allowing such plans while unions opposed them. The LPC answered that, while it is true some employees would benefit from such schemes, and some might even prefer them, the benefits would be uneven. Moreover, any such plan would unduly complicate the NMW. Thus, it recommended against allowing any benefit in kind, save the already established accommodation offset. Perhaps giving up, no mention was made this time of paying 21-year-olds the adult rate.

On March 20, 2006, apparently with little intraparty acrimony this time, the Government announced that it was accepting all these recommendations.

The government's June 2006 charge to the LPC opened up some new areas. In addition to the usual requests for monitoring and evaluation, it specifically asked for an examination of the NMW's impact on specific sectors and groups of workers, perhaps most notably on ethnic minorities.

Several economic factors converged to make the LPC rather cautious this time around. First, the overall economy was showing signs of slowing, with growth rates standing at levels somewhat lower than had been anticipated. Perhaps most significantly, the unemployment rate was inching up. In the low-wage sector, there was still job growth, but the rate of growth had declined. Even though the LPC argued that this was caused by an increase in supply factors — more older workers and women entering the labor force and an influx of immigrants since 2004 from the new EU member states — the figures were worrisome. Furthermore, the last two increases had increased the "bite" of the minimum wage, that is, the ratio of the adult NMW rate to the median hourly wage. Because the median wage had grown more slowly than had been predicted, the ratio had risen. In October 2006, it stood at 53% whereas it had been 48% in 1999. Thus, the LPC felt it could not recommend an upgrade that would exceed the revised estimates of median wage growth.

Therefore, they recommended an adult rate of £5.52, a youth rate of £4.60 and a 16-17 rate of £3.40, all to go into effect October 1, 2007. At the same time, they said that given the uncertainty of the economic situation, they would defer any recommendations for October 2008 until later. A good bit of this report was devoted to issues of enforcement.[17] The treatment of migrant workers by employment agencies and "gangmasters" was of especial concern. Furthermore, the fact that there was essentially no penalty for employer violation, he or she merely having to pay the back wages, meant unscrupulous employers had no incentive to comply with the minimum wage. This, the LPC stressed, was not fair to either the employees or law-abiding employers. The LPC welcomed the government's commitment to a 50% increase in funding for enforcement, but noted that it should be used to target certain industries. Finally, once again they forwarded a recommendation that 21-year-olds be paid the adult rate.

On March 21, the government accepted the rates and took the other issues under advisement.

THE NATIONAL MINIMUM WAGE IN OPERATION[18]

The NMW is fairly comprehensive in its coverage, with only small pockets of workers (apprentices, for example) remaining outside its legal reach. Most workers, of course, earn much more than the minimum wage, meaning only a relatively small percentage of the workforce is affected by increases. As each uprating has gone into effect, the ONS has estimated the number of direct beneficiaries. Depending on how steep the rise, the number of these people has varied between one and one and one half million workers. In addition, those workers who are slightly above the new minimum usually also

---

17 The enforcement of the NMW is largely in the hands of Her Majesty's Revenue and Customs (HMRC). David Metcalf has estimated that with the number of inspectors HMRC has, each firm in the country can be expected to be visited once in every 320 years. David Metcalf, *Why Has the British National Minimum Wage Had Little or No Impact on Employment?* London School of Economics Centre for Economic Performance, April 2007, 26. Metcalf points out that what is rather astounding is that there is as much compliance as there is.

18 I am going to use data mostly from the 2005 report. The 2007 report uses some data collected by a slightly different method, making comparisons uneven. The general picture is the same, however.

benefit (the so-called "spillover effect"), as most employers feel they must maintain some measure of differentials in pay.[19]

The numbers affected by the October 2006 increase are not unusual, and can therefore be used to paint a composite picture of the minimum wage work force. As reported in Table 4–2, nearly 1.3 million people, about five percent of all employees, were affected by this increase. If we break them down by gender and whether employed full or part time, we find that the minimum wage workforce is overwhelmingly female and that most work part time. Specifically, over two thirds are women, and, of all minimum wage workers, 60% are part time. The differences between men and women on this score, however, are pronounced. Of women earning the minimum wage, 72% are part-time, while for men the comparable figure is only 36%. Interestingly, the *number* of full time men and women workers is roughly the same (21% of the total minimum wage work force for the former and 19% for the latter).

	Number of Jobs (000s)	Percentage of Jobs
TABLE 4–2 ESTIMATES OF JOBS BENEFITING FROM OCTOBER 2006 NMW RATES		
Adults	1,170	5.1%
Youth (18-21)	110	6.2%
Total	1,280	5.1%

Source: LPC

As Figure 4.1 makes clear, there is also a strong age skew. The 22–24 cohort has more of its members in minimum wage jobs than any other segment of the population, although they are followed closely by other young groupings. Older people also contribute a disproportionate number of workers to the minimum wage pool, undoubtedly the result of many retired people taking part-time jobs. Pronounced trends are also evident if we examine ethnicity and geography. For example, the best estimate available indicates that around 20% of all Pakistani/Bangladeshi workers benefited from the 2004 minimum wage increase, whereas only about nine per cent of whites and blacks did.[20]

---

19 One matter that will come up in the US deserves a note here. Under the NMW, only tips paid by an employer through the regular payroll system can count toward meeting the minimum wage.

20 These numbers must be treated with extreme caution. The other data in this chapter are from the Annual Survey of Hours and Earnings, but these figures are based on the Labor Force Survey (since the ASHE does not collect data on ethnicity). The LFS data are somewhat less reliable for these purposes.

Figure 4.2 contains no surprises, showing the concentrations of low pay exactly where one would expect: in the Northeast, the Midlands, and Yorkshire and Humberside. (Of course, this does not factor in living costs.)

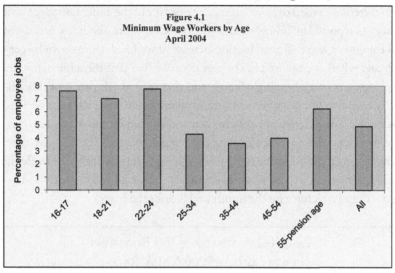

Source: LPC

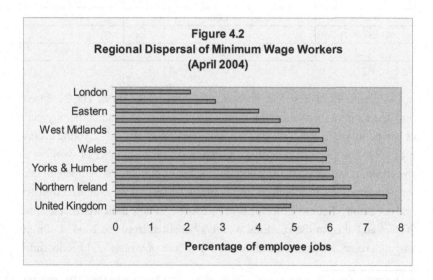

Source: LPC

Minimum wage workers, furthermore, are heavily concentrated in certain economic sectors. As disclosed by Figure 4.3, retail and hospitality, followed by cleaning and social care, are where minimum wage workers are most likely to be found. However, if we look at the percentage of workers in each sector earning the minimum wage, as depicted in Figure 4.4, a rather different picture emerges. Cleaning, hairdressing, and hospitality have the highest proportion of their workforces earning the minimum wage. Given these numbers, it is not surprising that more minimum wage jobs seem to be found in small firms than larger ones. Figure 4.5 presents the best data available, but it is a bit confusing. It provides the percentage of jobs within each size firm that pay the minimum wage (or did so in April 2004). Logically, we would assume that more minimum wage workers as a percentage of the workforce are found in small firms, but that cannot be said from these data, since we do not know how many total workers are employed in various size firms.

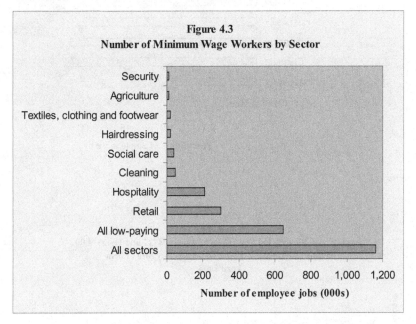

Figure 4.3
Number of Minimum Wage Workers by Sector

Source: LPC

Figure 4.6 turns our attention to the types of households minimum wage workers inhabit. As mentioned in chapter one, the argument is often made that the minimum wage is a clumsy poverty fighting policy in that many who take these jobs are the sons and daughters of middle class, or even affluent, parents just earning a little pocket money. That this assertion is patently false for Britain is clear from the data presented here. Minimum wage workers are heavily concentrated among households at the bottom of the income distribution.[21] The lowest two deciles of working age households with at least one person employed contain over 45% of all minimum wage workers. If you throw in the next lowest decile, you can account for around 60% of all minimum wage workers.

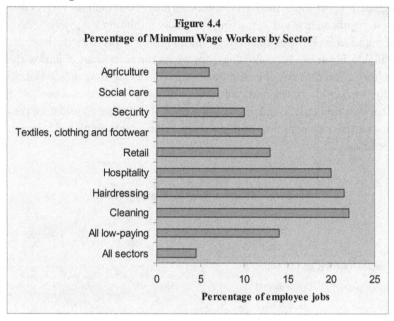

Figure 4.4
Percentage of Minimum Wage Workers by Sector

Source: LPC

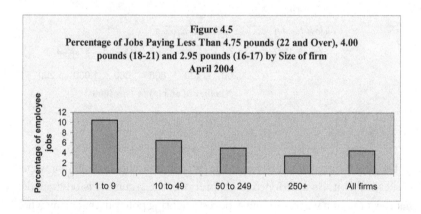

Figure 4.5
Percentage of Jobs Paying Less Than 4.75 pounds (22 and Over), 4.00 pounds (18-21) and 2.95 pounds (16-17) by Size of firm
April 2004

Source:LPC

---

21 A minimum wage household is defined as one that contains at least one minimum wage worker.

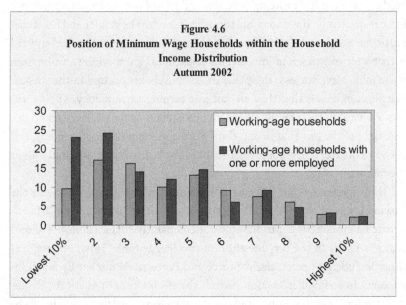

Figure 4.6
Position of Minimum Wage Households within the Household
Income Distribution
Autumn 2002

Source: Bryan and Taylor, *Household Characteristics.*

Further analysis of the research conducted by Mark Bryan and Mark Taylor provides an even more finely grained picture of the demographic breakdown of minimum wage households.[22] Forty percent of such households are
couples with dependent children. Another quarter, 26%, are couples without children. Couples with non-dependent children make up a further 15%.
Only eight percent are lone parents, while seven percent are single without
children. Within the minimum wage household, the minimum wage worker
is not usually the only wage earner, though. Only a little over 20% of such
households have only one person in work. (However, from above, we should
note that 15% of the households are headed by single people.) Over 50%
of minimum wage households have two wage earners, with the remainder
having three or more. Nevertheless, the picture of teenagers earning extra
spending money is wide of the mark. Instead, it is most often the spouse of
the head of household. Considering all minimum wage households, 47% of
minimum wage workers are the spouse of a head of household; however, 33%
are themselves the head of household. If we confine our analysis to couple
households, 57% of minimum wage workers are the spouse of the head of the
household, and 24% are the head of the household. In both types of house-

---

22 Mark Bryan and Mark Taylor, *An Analysis of the Household Characteristics of Minimum Wage
Recipients.* Conducted for the Low Pay Commission, 2004.

holds, "other adults" make up only 17% and 15% of the minimum wage work force respectively. If we combine these figures with the gender and full-time/part-time breakdown offered earlier, the conclusion we are pushed toward is that a lot of women in low-income households are working at minimum wage jobs. Nevertheless, the place these households occupy in the income distribution means that they are not just earning extra money. Their earnings are vital to their family's economic existence. Moreover, we should not lose sight of the fact that in one-third of all minimum wage households, and even in a quarter of the couple households, the head of the household toils at the minimum wage.

How adequate is the National Minimum Wage? Table 4–3 presents the varying levels of the NMW. How, though, should whether or not it is adequate be measured? Let us first look at comparative data. Table 4–4 shows that the UK is in the top one-third of this league table. However, some of those included — particularly Greece and Portugal — are hardly fair comparisons. In an English-speaking match, the UK is closer to Australia, always vaunted for its high minimum wages, than to New Zealand, Canada, or the United States. Compared to the other Western European countries, though, perhaps the most apt comparison, the UK's minimum wage is somewhat, but not dramatically, low.

TABLE 4–3. MINIMUM WAGE RATES, 1999-2006		
Date	Development Rate	Adult Rate
April 1999	£3.00	£3.60
October 2000	3.20	3.70
October 2001	3.50	4.10
October 2002	3.60	4.20
October 2003	3.80	4.50
October 2004	4.10	4.85
October 2005	4.25	5.05
October 2006	4.45	5.35
October 2007	4.60	5.52

Source: LPC

But we might also measure it against a subsistence budget. This is difficult because the cost of living varies so much across the country. However, if we take figures from the Family Budget Unit (FBU), we can at least approximate how well the NMW is doing in helping people climb over the poverty line.[23] The FBU calculates budgets for various regions, but then does an average for the UK; it also tabulates budgets for various sizes and types of households. Let us take the Low Cost but Acceptable budget for a family of four, composed of one adult working full time (38.5 hours) and another working 17 hours, and two children aged ten and four. For 2006, this family would need £359.60 per week if a car, alcohol, and means-tested benefits are included, £329.95 without these three items. At the current minimum wage of £5.35, 55.5 hours of work would produce an income of £296.92. This is 90% of the more modest budget and 83% of the more inclusive figure. Thus, two people working at the minimum wage can get you close but not up to the lowest cost budget.

TABLE 4–4. COMPARATIVE MINIMUM WAGE RATES, 2004 (PURCHASING POWER PARITIES)

Country	Hourly Rate (in £)
Australia	5.37
Belgium	4.92
Canada	3.66
France	5.20
Greece	2.62
Ireland	4.15
Japan	2.71
The Netherlands	5.04
New Zealand	4.01
Portugal	1.99
Spain	2.34
United Kingdom	4.85
United States	3.37

Source: LPC

Equally appropriately, we might examine the level of the NMW against the official poverty line, 60% of median earnings. This hovers around 40-45%, depending on when it is measured (that is, soon after a rise or not). Comparatively, (in mid-2004), Australia's minimum wage was 58.8% of median earnings, while in the US's stood at only 32.2%. The other Western European nations mentioned above were as before, slightly ahead of the UK, France at 56.6%, Belgium 48.5%, and the Netherlands 46.4%.

---

23 Information on how these budgets are constructed can be found on the FBU's website, www.york.ac.uk/res/fbu

THE IMPACT OF THE NATIONAL MINIMUM WAGE

Tracing the impact of any public policy is fraught with analytical difficulties, for in the real world nothing can be held constant. Therefore, segregating the effects of given public policies from the multitude of factors occurring throughout the economy and society cannot be done with precision. Nonetheless, we can offer up some informed conjectures, and make comparisons with informed conjectures offered up under other conditions and in other places. When it comes to the minimum wage, there are three types of analyses that can cast some lights on its effects: examining aggregate economic data; studying specific sectors and even individual firms if possible; and conducting surveys of businesses. Using these sources, we can get at least something of a picture of the NMW's impact on employment, prices, profits, earnings, poverty, and inequality.

Employment Effects

From the opening salvos of the debate over the NMW, its opponents called it a job killer. From the Conservative manifestos to the diatribes of Opposition spokespeople in Parliament, this was a constantly reiterated theme. It is a contention, of course, that is about as shopworn as any assertion in economics.

As discussed in chapter one, the rationale is deceptively simple. The "law" of supply and demand holds that when the price of a product or service increases, less of it will be bought. A minimum wage increases the cost of an hour of labor; therefore, purchasers of the service, employers, will buy less. The experience under the NMW, however, offers absolutely no support for this hypothesis.

Consider the aggregate data first. Figure 4.7 shows the overall unemployment rate since the introduction of the NMW in 1999. It is true that the unemployment rate had been on a downward trend since 1992; however, if the simplistic version of the "minimum wage leads to unemployment" argument were correct, the line would have had to reverse. At an absolute minimum, an objective observer would have to say that, based on this experience, the minimum wage is certainly *compatible* with falling unemployment.

A more sophisticated study was conducted by Mark Stewart.[24] He compared the employment rates for minimum wage workers and a control group further up the income ladder during both the initial implementation of the

---

24 Mark Stewart, "The Employment Effects of the National Minimum Wage," *Economic Journal* 114 (2004), C110–C116.

NMW in 1999 and its first two upratings in 2000 and 2001. He concluded that "No significant adverse effect on employment is found for either the introduction or the upratings for any of the demographic groups considered."[25]

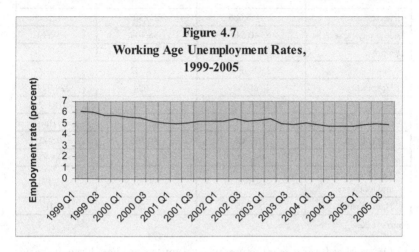

Source: ONS

If we confine our inquiry to the low-paying sectors of the economy, the picture is somewhat more mixed, but on the whole still quite positive. Table 4–5 provides the raw figures. Clearly, the total number of jobs has increased, contrary to predictions of job losses. Some sectors have fared better than others, though. Retail and hospitality have seen strong growth, even though hospitality witnessed a slight reduction in 2004. (This is somewhat deceptive, though, as there was a shift from part-time to full-time jobs in the industry. In 2004, net full-time jobs grew by 48,800 while net part-time jobs shrank by 50,000. Thus, there were more total hours worked.) The big losers, agriculture and textiles, clothing, and footwear, have been in a long-term decline, the former from escalating technology, and the latter from globalization pressures. What is vital to keep in mind is that in the end over 38,000 jobs were *gained* in the low-wage sectors in the fall of 2004 as the minimum wage was rising to new highs. In short, it is simply not true that there is any one-to-one relationship between minimum wage increases and job losses. To stress again, at the least, minimum wage increases are compatible with rising job levels.

---

25 Stewart, "Employment Effects," C116.

TABLE 4–5 JOBS IN LOW-PAYING SECTORS OF THE ECONOMY			
	Total Jobs September 2005	Change in September 2004	Change in March 1999
All sectors	25,948,686	+231,307	+1,742,258
All low-paying sectors	6,740,643	+38,404	+429,610
Of which:			
Retail	2,829,694	+22,552	+305,018
Hospitality	1,781,258	-1,624	+224,024
Social Care	1,076,382	+17,812	+103,252
Cleaning	434,793	+13,426	-19,010
Agriculture	214,008	-10,696	-56,500
Security	161,914	+1,789	+33,840
Textiles, clothing and footwear	130,069	-9,091	-175,436
Hairdressing	112,525	+4,236	+14,419

Source: LPC

On another front, the minimum wage seems to add very little to the aggregate labor factor costs in the British economy. According to the LPC, the 2004 increase only added between 0.06 and 0.07 per cent to the aggregate wage bill employers were forced to pay.[26] Even including the possible impact of differentials, this only rises to a figure between 0.06 and 0.08 per cent. The impact is greater in the low-wage sector, of course, but even there it is fairly low. There, the 2004 uprating, including differentials, only added a little over two per cent to retailer's wage bills and about five per cent to those of the hospitality industry.

There is, admittedly, some evidence that points in the other direction. A study of the home care sector, one of those that most affected by the NMW, was done by Stephen Machin and Joan Wilson.[27] They discovered some job losses which could be reasonably attributed to the 1999 and 2001 increases in the minimum wage, but stated that they were "modest in magnitude and often on the fringes of statistical significance."

Three surveys of firms in the low-paying sectors have been commissioned by the LPC, 2002, 2004, and 2006.[28] All produced similar results, and for brevity's sake, we may concentrate on the one from 2004. The response rate to the survey was 10%, with the respondents heavily skewed toward small

---

26 LPC, *2005 Report*, 43–45.

27 Stephen Machin and Joan Wilson, "Minimum Wages in a Low-Wage Labour Market: Care Homes in the UK," *Economic Journal* 114 (2004), C102-C109.

28 Complete information on the survey is contained in Appendix 3 to the LPC's 2005 report.

firms. This is good in one sense, in that these enterprises employ more minimum wage workers as a percentage of their work forces than larger firms. However, if we utilize the number of firms as the analytical unit for studying the impact this is not the same as the number of workers because, as noted above, we do not know how many people from the total minimum wage work force are employed by small firms. That is, if we get a result that 25%, say, of firms in the survey responded to the minimum wage increase a certain way, that does not mean that that move affected 25% of the minimum wage workers even in that sector. Moreover, there was a tendency for firms affected most to be among the respondents. A random telephone survey of the non-responding firms found that they had been less affected by minimum wage increases than the responding firms. Even with these caveats in mind, though, the data are useful.

The October 2003 uprating led 74% of the reporting firms to face over five percent or higher increases in their total wage bill. A significant amount of this was attributable to the perceived need to maintain differentials, as roughly half the firms reported having to increase pay for people above the new minimum wage rates. Thirty-seven percent of all firms reported decreasing staffing levels (but four percent actually increased them). This reaction varied from 51% of retail firms to only 22% of employers engaged in social care. On the other hand, 10% of security firms reported hiring more people. Nearly a third (31%) of the firms reported decreasing basic hours and 28% cut overtime hours. Thus, at this level, there is some evidence of reduced employment and hours in specific firms. It is interesting, though, how much at variance these results are with the aggregate employment figures in these sectors.

Inflation

A frequently repeated allegation is that a minimum wage will lead to inflation, in that each business will naturally attempt to pass on higher costs to consumers. When these decisions are added together, jolts of inflation are bound to accompany minimum wage increases. The first part of this contention is buttressed by the results of the 2004 LPC survey, as nearly two out of every three firms — 63% — reported marking up prices. However, aggregate inflation has hardly been affected, the overall inflation rate remaining well within the Bank of England's target range of two percent throughout the period of the NMW's operation. Inflation, though, is influenced by so many factors that this is hardly a good measure.

A more rigorous picture is offered by Mirko Draca, Stephen Machin, and John Van Reenen, who, under contract to the LPC, produced two quantitative analyses of price increases in the low-pay sectors following the 2003 NMW uprating.[29] They first analyzed the relationship between the percentage of subminimum wage workers in an industry and producer price increases. If, that is, minimum wage increases lead to price increases, the more affected an industry, the more likely it should be to raise prices. For 240 industrial sectors, they found a 0.034 positive effect; however, this figure was not statistically significant. Second, they examined canteens, restaurants, and takeaways, since these are the firms most labor intensive with low-wage workers. Their conclusion was that there was no indication "that prices in these industries were differentially affected according to their exposure to the minimum wage."[30] However, there are formidable methodological difficulties, acknowledged by Draca and his colleagues, to conducting research of this type. Consequently, the conclusions must be guarded.

Jonathan Wadsworth conducted a further study regarding price fluctuations of goods and services produced by minimum wage workers compared to general price movements. He found that those goods and services did show price increases ranging from 0.5 per cent to two per cent, with an average of 0.8 per cent, above normal after the introduction of the NMW.[31] Minimum wage workers, however, did not consume a complete market basket of these goods; hence the price increases did not affect them across the board. (Even if the price hikes had been absorbed entirely by them, they were still lower than the wage increases they enjoyed from the NMW.)

In sum, while we cannot say that there has been no inflation that is fairly traceable to the minimum wage, we can definitely say that there has been no runaway inflation, even in the sectors most affected by the policy.

Profitability

Once again the respondents to the survey told a depressing story of decreased profits. A full 81% reported a decrease in firm profits. However, other data tend to cast doubt on this. First, the rate of profitability in the economy

---

29 Mirko Draca, Stephen Machin, and John Van Reenen, *The Impact of the National Minimum Wage on Profits and Prices*, Conducted for the Low Pay Commission, February 2005.

30 Draca, *et al.*, *Impact*, 3.

31 Jonathan Wadsworth, *Did the Minimum Wage Change Consumption Patterns?* Research conducted for the Low Pay Commission, February 2007, 54-59.

as a whole has shown little sign of change in any direction. Firm profits as a percentage of GDP have remained virtually stable, as have the gross and net rates of return on capital employed.[32] Draca, Machin, and Van Reenen's study cited above also examined firm profits in the low wage sector. They did find a relationship, although a slight one, between the introduction of the minimum wage and a decrease in profitability. Now, of course, this says nothing about those pre-minimum wage profit levels; they may well have been exorbitant. It is interesting that the study of care homes cited above concluded that there was no evidence of closures. Profits must therefore still be satisfactory.

This finding points to another revealing measure: How many firms are leaving the low-wage sector? If profits are squeezed too much, obviously firms will seek other spheres. Figure 4.8 provides the data for total Value Added Tax Registrations.[33] The LPC perhaps put it best:

> During 2003 there were almost 190,000 registrations, but fewer than 175,000 deregistrations, leading to an increase of 15,500 in the stock of UK businesses. The Figure also shows that the introduction of the minimum wage has had little adverse impact on the number of businesses registered in the low-paying sectors. Indeed, despite the large upratings of the minimum wage in October 2003, the number of businesses in the low-paying sectors increased during 2003.[34]

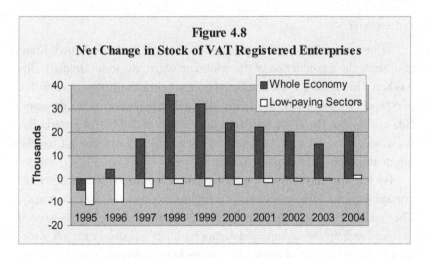

Figure 4.8
Net Change in Stock of VAT Registered Enterprises

Source: Small Business Service

---

32 LPC, *2005 Report*, 42-51.
33 The VAT is a tax collected at each stage of a good's production. Hence, virtually every business is registered.
34 LPC, *2005 Report*, 50-51.

In fact, profitability could well have been positively affected. For example, some firms reported in the survey that they had lower staff turnover (14%) and were able to fill vacancies faster than before (8%). More tellingly, though, 15% informed the survey takers that worker motivation had increased. Perhaps these factors have contributed, in at least a small way, to the overall rise in labor productivity in the UK that has occurred since the introduction of the minimum wage. If so, the NMW is actually helping hold down wage costs per unit of output.

Such an inference is collaborated by an interesting study of employee training.[35] Critics of minimum wage policies often press the charge that employers will cut various benefits, such as training, when they are forced to raise wages. However, data regarding training amassed by Wiji Arulampalam, Alison Booth, and Mark Bryan do not confirm this. "[W]e found no evidence that the minimum wage introduction reduced the training of affected workers and some evidence that it increased it."[36]

It seems safe to conclude, in sum, that the minimum wage has had no measurable negative economic effects. Employment is up, not down; inflation is tamed; and businesses are flourishing, even in the low-wage sector. What about the goals of the policy, though, fighting poverty and softening inequality?

Fighting Poverty

As for the aggregate figures, poverty has indeed fallen in the United Kingdom since the introduction of the minimum wage, albeit not dramatically. As shown in Figure 4.9, the number of people below the official poverty line of 60% of median income has fallen, although it is nowhere near the numbers achieved in the 1970s. Similarly, the number of children in poverty has decreased, as is evident from Figure 4.10. How much, if any, though, has the minimum wage contributed to this trend?

The fact that the minimum wage has been combined with two other important poverty fighting initiatives complicates this question enormously. The first of these programs has been the New Deals. These policies have been designed to help the unemployed obtain both job skills and then job placement. Since being out of work is the single biggest determinant of poverty, these schemes will have helped alleviate poverty if they simply move more

---

35 Wiji Arulampalam, Alison Booth, and Mark Bryan, "Training and the New Minimum Wage," *Economic Journal* 114 (2004), C87–C94.
36 Arulamplalm, Booth, and Bryan, *Training*, C93.

people into work.[37] This effect is compounded if the training the schemes provide produces enhanced job prospects and higher pay. The second initiative is the Working Families Tax Credit, which provides a tax rebate (up to a certain level) for income that is earned. This can obviously generate higher incomes for many people, and move a goodly number above the poverty line.

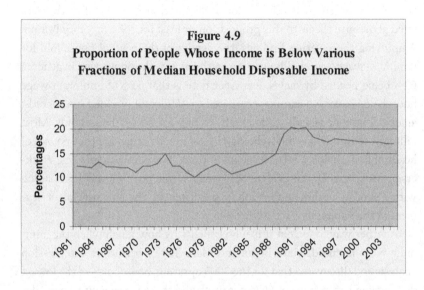

Figure 4.9
Proportion of People Whose Income is Below Various Fractions of Median Household Disposable Income

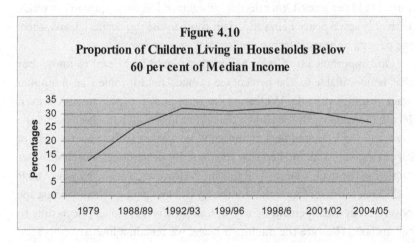

Figure 4.10
Proportion of Children Living in Households Below 60 per cent of Median Income

Source: ONS

---

37 Stephen Nickell, "Poverty and Worklessness in Britain," Presidential Address to the Royal Economic Society, 2004 provides the data.

The first pertinent question regarding the minimum wage's impact on poverty is the type of household in which minimum wage workers reside. As explained before, if it is true, as is often said, that many minimum wage workers are young people merely earning spending money, and, further, that many of them reside in relatively affluent families, then the minimum wage is indeed a largely ineffective if not useless antipoverty tool. But the data cited above give the lie to this proposition, at least for contemporary Britain. Amplifying those earlier findings, the gender of the head of household for minimum wage households almost exactly mirrors the population in general, 63% being headed by males. A further note is that 55% of minimum wage households have two earners, compared to 46% of all working households; among couple households this climbs to 61% for NMW households. Most tellingly, within NMW households 47%, as noted earlier, are the spouses of heads of households. Given the gender breakdown of minimum wage work-ers provided earlier, it is evident that women from poor households residing with a spouse working either full or part time are the most prevalent seg-ment of the minimum wage work force.

Another way to look at it is who benefits by how much when the mini-mum wage is raised. Mark Bryan and Mark Taylor performed a regression analysis and discovered that for the 2003 uprating, households in the lowest decile gained an average of £1.75 per week and those in the next two deciles gained £1.12 per week. Other deciles only gained less than a pound per week, with only seven pence being added for those in the top decile. Clearly, then, the poor gain the most from a minimum wage increase.

One important bit of information that would be helpful to know, but that is unavailable, is the percentage of household income that minimum wage earnings provide. We can make some indirect inferences, however. Jonathan Wadsworth has shown that about 10% of all households with one person in work depend on a minimum wage worker as their main source of earned income, and, further, that in about 5% of working households that worker is the main source of all income.[38] However, a study by Jane Millar and Karen Gardiner found that for the 86% of low paid workers who escape poverty, only eight percent do so through their wages alone.[39] According to the authors, "Despite the minimum wage, we remain a low pay culture in which a large proportion of workers have to get help from other members of

---

38 Wadsworth, *Did the Minimum Wage Change Consumption Patterns?*, ii.
39 Jane Millar and Karen Gardiner, *Low Pay, Household Resources and Poverty.* Joseph Rowntree Foundation, 2004.

their households and from the state to avoid poverty."[40] Nonetheless, given the distribution of benefits spelled out above, the minimum wage is surely helpful to many who try to move above the poverty line.

In sum, poverty has fallen in the UK. Given the sharply differentiated impact of minimum wage increases, the minimum wage must have played some role in this positive development. However, it would take minimum wage increases far above what has been contemplated so far to turn the minimum wage into a living wage and move all who work full time year round out of poverty.

Inequality

Three types of inequality exist in the modern economy: wage inequality, income inequality, and wealth inequality. There is solid evidence that the minimum wage has reduced wage inequality. Richard Dickens and Alan Manning have shown that even in the early years of the NMW there was some melioration of the roaring wage inequality that characterized the 1980s, and that after 2002 the effect was even greater.[41] Their general findings were confirmed in a study of the wage distribution in the nursing home sector.[42] Summing up this and other studies, David Metcalf wrote in 2007 that "This tempering of pay inequality is substantial. Wage inequality rose relentlessly from 1978 to 1996. The diminution of this inequality from 1997 to 2005 caused the 50/10 wage ratio in 2005 to be the same as it was in 1989, reversing around half the growth of the inequality which occurred between 1978 and 1996."[43]

As for income inequality (which counts all income, not only wages), it seems to have subsided somewhat since Labor entered office. The trend of the usual measure, the Gini coefficient, is shown in Figure 4.11. This picture is confirmed by looking at recent gains to income enjoyed by various sections of the population. Figure 4.12 depicts the gains made by various quintiles during the second Blair Government, when the various policies began to have their greatest effect. Clearly the lowest income groups have been enjoying the greatest percentage gains in income (although not anywhere nearly as

---

40 Joseph Rowntree Foundation, Press Release, November 17, 2004.

41 Richard Dickens and Alan Manning, "How the National Minimum Wage Reduced Wage Inequality," *Journal of the Royal Statistical Society*, Series A 167 (2004), 613-626. On the earlier years, see their paper *Has the National Minimum Wage Reduced UK Wage Inequality?* London School of Economics, Centre for Economic Performance, June 2002.

42 Richard Dickens and Alan Manning, "Spikes and Spill-Overs: The Impact of the National Minimum Wage on the Wage Distribution in a Low-Wage Sector," *Economic Journal* 114 (2004), 95-101.

43 Metcalf, *Why Has the British National Minimum Wage Had Little or No Impact on Employment?*, 3.

great a differential as the reverse gains witnessed during the Thatcher years). In an interesting and enlightening exercise, Jonathan Shaw calculated how the Gini would have looked had the 1996-97 policy mix remained in place.[44] It would have simply continued on its pronounced upward trend. In light of this analysis, Labor's policies must be much of the driving force behind the amelioration of income inequality that we have observed since Blair took office.

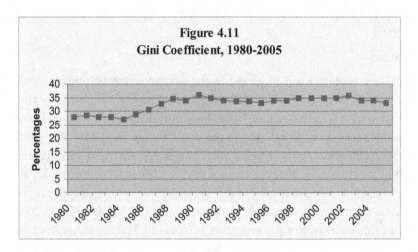

Figure 4.11
Gini Coefficient, 1980-2005

Source: ONS

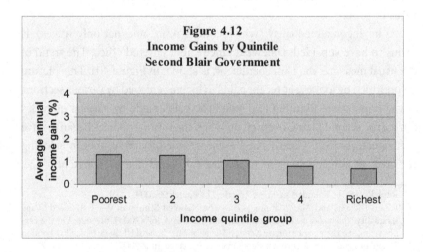

Figure 4.12
Income Gains by Quintile
Second Blair Government

Source: Brewer, Goodman, Shaw, and Sibieta, *Poverty and Inequality*

44 Jonathan Shaw, "Inequality under Labour," *Economic Review* 23 (November 2005).

However, to what degree if any can the minimum wage be handed the credit? As before, this cannot be answered with certainty, but some logical inferences can be made. Since wages are the largest component of incomes for the vast majority of households, any compression at all in wages, as shown by Dickens and Manning has occurred, will reduce income inequality. Additional evidence comes from the differences in gains to women and men's pay attributable to the minimum wage. Clearly, women have enjoyed more wage gains than men in recent years. Overall, women's pay increased 29% between 1997 and 2004, while men's pay only increased 13%. According to the ONS, as noted before, the NMW is at least partly responsible for closing the net gap between men and women's pay. Given the profile of minimum wage workers, this is significant. In sum, more households in the lower parts of the income distribution, that is, are taking home more pay, and this is reflected in the variations in income growth among the various quintiles.

However, neither the minimum wage nor any other government policies have had much effect on wealth inequality. The gaps are simply too large, for one thing. For another, the appreciation in asset values we have witnessed in the last few years disproportionately affects the well-off, since they own most of the assets to begin with. A recent study sponsored by the Joseph Rowntree Foundation found some mixed evidence, but that overall there were no signs that the chasm separating wealth levels in the UK is narrowing.[45]

Conclusion

The policy making process has produced regular increases in the minimum wage, along with a smooth working out of the various technical and administrative issues. This has been accomplished, at least in part, because of the structure of the NMW act. By forcing the matter onto the political agenda, via the work of the LPC, the minimum wage has not become marginalized. Both because it is so controversial and because its beneficiaries are not politically powerful, it is all too easy for a minimum wage to slide to the sidelines of politics, as we will see in the case of the United States. Its opponents, naturally, are quite happy to see this happen; its proponents, meanwhile, may have other fish to fry. The necessity for the LPC to fashion a report, and, even more importantly, the requirement that the Government respond keeps this from happening in Britain.

---

45 Daniel Dorling, *el al.*, *Poverty, Wealth and Place in Britain, 1968 to 200* (Bristol: Policy Press for the Joseph Rowntree Foundation, 2007).

As for the overall impact of the NMW, it is hard not to sound a positive note. It has produced no adverse economic effects that anyone has been able to point to. Employment, inflation, and business health are all on the right side. A case could even be made that not only has the minimum wage produced no ill side-effects, it may have helped create the rosy economic picture. At the same time, both poverty and economic inequality have been mitigated. Whether the minimum wage has had a positive role in these trends cannot be said with certainty. Nevertheless, the circumstantial evidence is that it has surely had some effect.

At the same time, it is important to keep in mind that the minimum wage is more than either just a social policy or part of an economic regulatory regime. It has an enormous psychological dimension. How people feel about their work, about themselves, and about their place in the community are all tied to their level of compensation. Anne Meacock, a barmaid in Swansea, told a reporter for *The Observer* in late 2005, "You can hold your head up high and say that you are earning £5 an hour."[46] In the end, that may be what matters most.

---

46 *The Observer*, November 20, 2005.

CHAPTER 5. THE FEDERAL MINIMUM WAGE

When the Fair Labor Standards Act (FLSA) passed in 1938, it set the minimum wage at 25 cents per hour, but included a provision pushing it up to 40 cents in a series of steps culminating in 1945. Its coverage, though, was far from universal. Only those workers "engaged in commerce or in the production of goods for commerce" that crossed state lines were protected. Further, for the "production of goods" section to apply, the worker had to work in a field "necessary" to such production. Moreover, there were numerous exemptions, the most important of which excluded agriculture and large swaths of the retail industry.

In a series of acts beginning in 1949, Congress steadily raised the level of the wage and extended its coverage. As a result, by the mid-1970s the minimum wage penetrated virtually every corner of the economy. However, though the nominal level of the wage has been raised several times since, its real value peaked in 1968.

Perhaps not coincidentally, it was also during the Johnson administration, when the Great Society programs were being fashioned and implemented, that the minimum wage moved from centerpiece of social reform to the margins. As those who had historically been the stalwarts of minimum wage advocacy turned increasingly to public expenditure programs to attack poverty, the fervor for raising the minimum wage diminished. Since the opponents of the minimum wage lost none of their antipathy to the program, this loss of fervor was all but fatal to keeping the level of the wage in line with increases in inflation, productivity, or other measures of prosperity. To be sure, the battles were still fought, and major victories won, but something was now missing, and that something was how the minimum wage fits into an overall program to alleviate poverty.

POLITICAL DYNAMICS

Historically, when Congress has weighed the minimum wage two issues predominated: what the level of the wage should be and who should be covered. Three subsidiary issues often competed for attention, though: when to implement the scheduled increases (as opponents always tried to delay the effective date of any increase in order to mitigate its effect), how to handle the tip credit, and whether or not there should be any kind of subminimum wage.

Although bills to increase the minimum wage, and until the 1970s to expand its coverage, can be found at every session of Congress, they usually die a quiet death. For a minimum wage measure to move from obscurity onto the active congressional agenda it takes either a Democratic president (although Eisenhower is an exception) or a group of influential Democratic congressional leaders willing to expend precious political capital on its behalf. Until the last two struggles, a typical pattern could be observed. Minimum wage advocates would propose a certain level for the increase and offer up a list of new workers to be covered. Opponents would marshal their forces, concentrated among conservative Republicans and some Democrats (mostly Southerners), to oppose both. A few moderate Republicans would defect, and moderates from both sides would come up with a compromise that reduced the increase, scaled back the increased coverage, tinkered with the effective date, and perhaps addressed the tip credit or some type of subminimum. Some test votes would let everyone know what was possible and what was not. A cobbled together compromise bill would pass both houses with a lopsided majority, and after the usual tidying up through a conference committee be sent to the president. All the while, if a Republican occupied the White House, he would be threatening to veto a bill too distasteful to him, a threat that was occasionally carried out.

This pattern altered in 1996, though. Since coverage was now virtually universal, opponents had fewer bargaining chips. They did bring out the usual small artillery that year, mounting efforts to keep the increase modest, to stall the date the raise would take effect, to emasculate the tip credit, and to create a subminimum wage. However, their new stratagem was to attach totally unrelated items to the bill, in hopes of making the minimum wage advocates either swallow a pill they did not want or run the risk of having to take the blame for not raising the minimum wage. It worked beautifully in 1996, and was broached every time a minimum wage increase was proposed thereafter.

One factor that always plays into minimum wage politics is the measure's immense popularity but low salience. As the polls quoted in the first chapter unmistakably demonstrate, the minimum wage enjoys overwhelming support. However, its support does not run deep within the public. Thus, proponents of the minimum wage can invoke public approval but cannot use it as much of a pressure tool. Lukewarm supporters know full well that they will not pay much of a price for letting the measure fall off the political radar screen, and ardent supporters ordinarily have more pressing items to work on. In consequence, there is always the danger that a minimum wage increase will get pushed to the side. And this has become doubly true as reformers have come to believe that while the minimum wage is a good thing, it is not the mainstay of federal antipoverty policy. Thus, for the increase to win its way onto the statute books, political conditions have to break just right.

EVOLUTION OF THE LAW

Between 1941, when the Fair Labor Standards Act was upheld by the Supreme Court, and 1949, when Congress modified the law for the first time, federal minimum wage policy was characterized by two trends. First, the inflation induced by the war completely obliterated the value of the minimum wage. By 1945, 40 cents was worth very little. Second, the Supreme Court and the lower federal courts decided a number of cases that widened the purview of the law.[1] Populated by New Deal judges, the federal judiciary read the coverage provisions of the statute in a quite expansive way.

President Truman had suggested raising the minimum wage during the 1948 campaign, and reiterated the call during his 1949 State of the Union

---

[1] These cases are discussed in Jerold Waltman, "Supreme Court Activism in Economic Policy in the Waning Days of the New Deal: Interpreting the Fair Labor Standards Act, 1941-1946," *Journal of Supreme Court History* 31 (2006), 58-80.

message.[2] Republicans controlled both houses of Congress, though. Since the early forties, they had been smarting about the courts' reading of the FLSA's coverage provisions, and were in no mood to co-operate with the president. Truman sought a raise to 75 cents, a figure many Republicans were willing to grant if they could cut back on some coverage. Their proposal was to substitute "indispensable" into the definition of "production" in place of "necessary." Truman's floor leaders managed to compromise with "directly essential," but still it was estimated that around a million workers would be removed from the act with that phrase in place. Although Truman was bitter about the new wording, he nonetheless felt he had no choice but to sign the bill. One footnote to this episode was that at this session Republicans proposed indexing the minimum wage to the inflation rate, but Democrats opposed such a step. The reason was that both parties thought a fall in prices was likely in the near future, an event that would have paralleled what happened after World War I. Later, of course, the sides switched.

The Eisenhower years were ones of relative quiet on the minimum wage front. However, Eisenhower's Secretary of Labor urged the president to work for an increase to 90 cents and to bring retail workers inside the act. The president mentioned both proposals in his 1955 State of the Union address, but was only able to get the raise.[3] In the waning days of the Eisenhower administration, when Senator John F. Kennedy was eyeing a presidential run, another battle over the minimum wage erupted. Kennedy proposed covering retail workers in all but the smallest firms and raising the wage to $1.25. (The former was to be accomplished by substituting a sales volume test for the list of specific exemptions in the law at that time.) His opponents countered with an offer to raise the wage to $1.15 and add a sprinkling of new workers through specific enumeration. At several points, he indicated that he was ready to compromise on the wage level, but not on coverage. In the end, the entire bill died, but Kennedy felt he had a winning campaign issue.

When he took office in 1961, Kennedy made increasing and expanding the minimum wage a high priority. His bill would have raised the wage to $1.25 and brought most retail workers under the act's umbrella, by the use of the sales volume test. Though the Senate largely backed his plan, opposition in the House was stiff and vigorous. In the end, the president's allies offered a compromise that adopted the new definition but exempted certain

---

2 The following paragraphs draw on the more complete coverage of the political history of the minimum wage offered in my previous work, *The Politics of the Minimum Wage* (Urbana: University of Illinois Press, 2000), chap. 2.

3 Democrats controlled both houses of Congress.

industries from the sales volume test. A few swing votes were secured by this tactic, and the measure passed. The federal minimum wage was elevated to $1.25 and 3.6 million new workers would now enjoy the act's benefits. Kennedy obviously hoped that this was the first step toward universal coverage and a relatively high wage level, as he announced at the bill's signing, "We can move from this improvement into greater gains."[4]

Almost everyone agrees that Kennedy had been deeply touched by the poverty he had encountered on the campaign trail and that it was a matter which he wished to address. The importance of the minimum wage to his anti-poverty strategy can be seen from three events.[5] First, in addition to the minimum wage bill, his other initial priorities were federal aid to education, hospital insurance for the elderly, housing legislation, and aid to depressed areas. It was, in short, his only income enhancing policy. No mention was made of either public assistance or social insurance programs. Second, while there were some modest changes made in public assistance programs during his years in office, the most important of these were initiated in Congress and support from the White House was lukewarm at best. Third, in early 1963 Kennedy asked Walter Heller to draft some new proposals to address poverty. These new programs were to focus on jobs and human services, not direct cash assistance. Thus, it is safe to say that more jobs at higher wages, buttressed at the bottom by a universal and relatively high minimum wage, was at the core of the Kennedy administration's anti-poverty plans.

The great shift in the place of the minimum wage in the American welfare state came during the Johnson administration.[6] While the muscular Democratic victory of 1964 created a Congress far more than usually hospitable to an increase in the minimum wage, those designing the War on Poverty were clearly looking in other directions. While Johnson's aides were busy fashioning the War on Poverty programs, union leaders began pushing the president to take the lead in raising the minimum wage and expanding its coverage further. Although hesitant, since he was worried about a war-induced inflation, Johnson finally sent Congress a bill in 1966 proposing a raise to $1.60 and vast new coverage. The latter was to be accomplished by low-

---

4 *Congressional Quarterly Almanac, 1961,* 482.

5 See James Giglio, *The Presidency of John F. Kennedy* (Lawrence: University Press of Kansas, 1991), 119-120.

6 Vaughn Bornet, *The Presidency of Lyndon Johnson* (Lawrence: University Press of Kansas, 1983) is a good source on the Johnson administration and the launch of the War on Poverty. Its evolution is masterfully traced in Gareth Davies, *From Opportunity to Entitlement: The Transformation and Decline of Great Society Liberalism* (Lawrence: University Press of Kansas, 1996).

ering the sales volume test, removing some of the industries from the test, and adding certain categories of workers. During the usual wrangling, liberal Democrats managed to add a provision that tipped employees had to be paid at least one-half the minimum wage whatever their level of tips.[7] A coverage regime only slightly scaled back from Johnson's original proposal passed

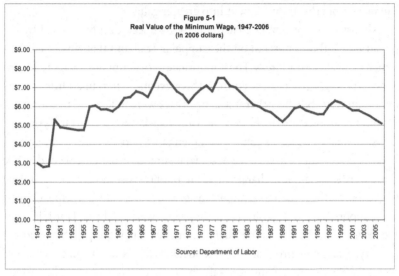

Figure 5-1
Real Value of the Minimum Wage, 1947-2006
(In 2006 dollars)

Source: Department of Labor

both houses, but Republicans did get the raise stretched out over three years. The minimum wage was now close to universal in its application, and with the increase of 1968 was to reach its highest level ever.

In 1971, congressional Democrats began a push to raise the minimum wage to $2.00 and also to include several new categories of workers (for example, domestic household workers, those employed by state and local governments, and some agricultural workers). Opponents, as often in the past, accepted the wage hike, but refused to countenance broadened coverage. Moreover, they countered with a proposal for an 80% youth subminimum wage. Debate dragged on to 1973, when a compromise, including a rather restricted 85% youth subminimum wage, passed both houses of Congress. Citing fears of inflation, Nixon vetoed the measure, and an override fell short. A year later, though, an almost identical measure passed again, and with Nixon's power severely diminished he signed it.

---

7 Up to this point, employers were free to let all an employee's tips count toward the minimum wage. The new provision was especially important, inasmuch as the new coverage rules would bring many more restaurants in particular within the purview of the act.

Jimmy Carter sent a minimum wage bill to Congress in 1977 calling for an immediate increase to $2.65, but more importantly for future increases to be set at half the average manufacturing wage. The administration's index-ing proposal triggered intense debate. In the midst of the bargaining, union leaders pushed for a change in the tip credit to a maximum of $1.00. When the dust had settled, the indexing provision had foundered, a $3.35 minimum wage was to be realized in four steps, and the tip credit was made 40%.[8]

Both Ronald Reagan and George H. W. Bush were natural opponents of the minimum wage, Reagan even once saying that it had "caused more misery and unemployment than anything since the Great Depression."[9] Although they ritually proposed increases in the minimum wage, congressional Demo-crats had too many other fights on their hands during Reagan's presidency to put much energy into the effort. When George Bush assumed office, though, many felt the time was ripe for a try. But Bush wanted a very broad sub-minimum wage, something to which labor was adamantly opposed.[10] Also, the president painted himself into a corner by insisting that the raise be no higher than to $4.25. When Congress sent him a bill with a $4.55 minimum wage, he speedily vetoed it while still aloft aboard Air Force One. In 1989, after further bargaining he got his $4.25 but had to accept only a shadow of his subminimum wage plan.

The events of 1996, in a way, harken back to the Truman years. A Dem-ocratic president faced a Republican Congress, and one filled at that with a number of firebrands who wanted to give the administration no quarter. However, a minimum wage bill passed and became law. The price of the in-crease was high, though.

In the early years of his administration, Bill Clinton elected to fight on other fronts — health care and welfare reform — and ignored those in the White House who were urging him to seek an increase in the minimum wage.[11] He finally made a public request for an increase, but few took it seri-ously, and it went nowhere. What changed the political dynamics was Sena-tor Bob Dole's (then serving as the Senate majority leader) winning of the Republican presidential nomination. To embarrass him, Democratic leaders in the Senate began offering minimum wage amendments to every bill taken

---

8 That is, employers had to pay employees at least 60% of the minimum wage.

9 Quoted in Willis Nordlund, *The Quest for a Living Wage: A History of the Federal Minimum Wage Program* (Westport, CT: Greenwood, 1997), 180.

10 Bush wanted a "training wage" applicable to any new employee. As set out in chapter one, union leaders worried this would lead to employers constantly replacing more experienced workers with new hires in order to cut costs.

11 Waltman, *Politics of the Minimum Wage*, 89-92.

up, a strategy that by all accounts caught Dole off guard. He became mired in political maneuvering, as he had to drag up increasingly arcane rules to keep the issue off the floor, since he knew he would lose a straight up vote. Meanwhile, moderate Republicans in the House, especially those with numerous union members in their constituencies, were quietly seeking ways to get something passed on the minimum wage. In the melee, minimum wage opponents turned the Democrats' strategy around, seeking to attach a totally unrelated provision to any minimum wage bill. Although they considered several possible proposals, what they settled on was a host of business tax breaks.[12] Following a series of intricate maneuvers, congressional majorities belted together a minimum wage increase to $5.15 over two steps with a generous set of tax breaks for business. However, Democratic leaders also had to give in on a Republican demand to keep the base wage for tipped employees at $2.13 (one half the old minimum wage).

THE IMPACT OF THE FEDERAL MINIMUM WAGE

The most comprehensive study of the impact of the federal minimum wage was done after the 1996 and 1997 increases went into effect. Jared Bernstein and John Schmitt conducted a careful analysis of how these increases (from $4.25 to $5.15, in two steps) affected low-income workers and households and whether or not there were any measurable employment effects. They did not, however, examine inflation or business failures.

As for who benefited the most from the minimum wage increase, it is clear that, contrary to what is often asserted, it was the poor. Others gained also, to be sure, but the poor reaped the bulk of the benefits.

> When focusing on the beneficiaries of minimum wage increases, opponents of the policy have suggested that most minimum wage workers are teenagers living in high-income households. Such is not the case. The data presented below contradict this characterization, showing that most workers affected by minimum wage increases are adults, and most reside in lower-income households. At the same time, the results show that the policy is far from perfectly targeted. For example, about one-quarter of the benefits from the increase went to working households in the top 40% of the income scale. Even so, taken as a whole, the results from this section suggest that minimum wage increases are still accomplishing the goal of raising the earnings of low-wage workers in lower-income households.[13]

---

12 The other candidates were repeal of the gasoline tax, a measure allowing employers to grant compensatory time rather than pay for overtime, and a law planting the seed for "company unions."

13 Jared Bernstein and John Schmitt, *Making Work Pay: The Impact of the 1996-97 Minimum Wage Increase* (Washington: Economic Policy Institute, 1998), 5.

Consider the raw numbers.[14] About 8.9% of all American workers were affected, about 10 million employees. Over 7 in 10 (71%) were adults (20 and over) and nearly 6 in 10 (58%) were females. Combining the age and gender variables, 43% of all these workers were adult females and 28% were adult men. Nearly half of all affected workers (46%) work full time.

However, the critical question concerns households. Bernstein and Schmitt focus first on working households headed by someone 25-54. The rationale for selecting this group is that it excludes nonworking households, which by definition cannot gain by the increase and households headed by younger or older people, whose connection to the labor market may not be as strong as prime age adults. Among these households, 35% of the benefits went to the bottom 20% of households, 23% to the next 20%, 15% to the middle 20%, 15% to the next to the highest 20%, and 12% to the top 20%. Thus, 58% of the benefits went directly to the bottom 40% of households. Without question, then, the bulk of the benefits of minimum wage increases flow to those who need them most.

Another pertinent bit of information is that the average minimum wage worker contributes 54% of household income. In fact, even when one-worker households are removed (for whom the percentage is 100, at least for wages), the average minimum wage worker contributes 44% of household income.[15] To put it bluntly, with those percentages there is no way that the earnings minimum wage workers bring home are going for mere extras.

Another interesting matter is whether minimum wage increases can boost the wages of low-wage workers in general. Looking at wages for the workers falling at the 10th percentile in the wage distribution (that is, 90% of wage earners make more, 10% less), Bernstein and Schmitt find a traceable effect. When it is broken down by gender, the effect is quite pronounced for females, but uncertain for males. Given the heavy preponderance of women in the lower reaches of the labor market, though, this is important. Low wage women workers seem to gain markedly when the minimum wage is increased.

Turning to the ever debated question of employment effects, the authors conducted a battery of four tests. The first is a difference-in-differences test, in which a researcher compares employment rates for selected groups of workers before and after a minimum wage increase, with adjustments en-

14 These are the people *directly* affected. That is, no spillover effects were calculated. If, for example, low-wage workers earning up to $6.14 were added in, the percentage of full timers would jump to 63%.

15 These are means. The medians are 41% and 27%. Even if this is a somewhat better measure (debatable here), the general point is still valid.

tered in for extraneous factors such as seasonality and overall growth. The groups chosen by Bernstein and Schmitt are teenagers and adults with less than a high school education, two cohorts that ought to feel unemployment effects first. These groups are then broken down by gender and race/ethnicity. There were some variations in the employment patterns of the different groups; however, they were as likely to be positive as negative. Only two were statistically significant, though, and they were both among the positive outcomes. As Bernstein and Schmitt say, these tests "reveal no significant employment losses from the 1996-97 increase in the minimum wage, either for teenagers or the less-educated adult group. In fact, the only statistically significant results were positive employment effects for Hispanic female teenagers and for less-educated female adults over the full increase."[16]

The differences-in-differences tests have some technical flaws, however. Thus, they turn to three other tests. The first of these is a test developed by economists Donald Deere, Kevin Murphy, and Finis Welch in the mid 1990s, and used to examine the effect of the 1990-91 minimum wage increases.[17] The basic idea is to extend the time horizon in order to control for business cycle effects. The employment rate for adult males was used as a benchmark against which to measure changes in the employment rates of teens and adults who did not complete high school. Using this same benchmark, Bernstein and Schmitt review the employment experiences of these same two groups, but also break them down by gender and look separately at African-Americans. Their conclusions are noteworthy:

> Both minimum wage increases [1996 and 1997] appear to have *raised* less-educated adult male employment (up 2.5% after [the first hike] and then up 2.9% after [the second one]). Employment among less-educated black adults also increased dramatically after the second increase in the minimum wage (up 9.9%). The employment effects of the minimum wage were also, on net, positive for less-educated adult women, female teens, and black teens, though none of these changes was statistically significant. Employment opportunities appeared to decline for male teens, but, again, the change was not statistically significant. Overall these [test] results suggest that the minimum wage increased employment among teens and less-educated adults.[18]

A third test came from the work of David Card.[19] He pointed out that minimum wage increases affect states differently, since some have a greater

16 Bernstein and Schmitt, *Making Work Pay*, 20.

17 Donald Deere, Kevin Murphy, and Finis Welch, "Employment and the 1990-1991 Minimum Wage Hike," *American Economics Association Papers and Proceedings* 85 (1995), 232-237. They found significant disemployment effects.

18 Bernstein and Schmitt, *Making Work Pay*, 21-22. Emphasis in original.

19 David Card, "Using Regional Variation in Wages to Measure the Effects of the Federal Minimum Wage," *Industrial and Labor Relations Review* 46 (1992), 38-54. Card found no effect

concentration of minimum wage workers than others. If there are unemployment effects from minimum wage increases, then they should be more pronounced in states with the highest percentages of minimum wage workers. Consequently, if a comparison were made between the employment rates over time of high and low wage states, we should be able to capture any shrinking employment effects attributable to a minimum wage increase. Running the Card test on the 1996-1997 data produced results similar to those above. Slight differences were recorded in the various groups, but overall wages rose and there were no ill employment effects. "The Card test consistently finds that the 1996 and 1997 minimum wage increases had a strong impact on the wages of teen and less-than-high-school-educated adults. Results from the same test, however, suggest that the minimum wage has no consistent, measurable impact on the employment opportunities of these same two groups."[20]

The final test was the one most commonly utilized in the past, time series analysis. Previous researchers compared the employment rates of teenagers before and after minimum wage increases, while trying to control for other factors that might affect teens' employment patterns. These earlier studies tended to find modest but certain effects, with three economists concluding in 1982 that the best estimate was that a 10% boost in the minimum wage would lower teenage employment by 1% to 3%.[21] However, later analyses tended to cast doubt on this conclusion.[22] Bernstein and Schmitt incorporated some newer methodological features to this approach and reexamined the data beginning in 1954. When the data were subjected to their tests, three conclusions stood out. First, with the improved techniques, the coefficients supposedly measuring the positive correlations dropped markedly, by about half. Second, however measured, the magnitude of the coefficients has diminished over time.[23] Finally, none of the effects cross the significance threshold. "Thus, according to this time-series model, the disemployment effect on teenage workers, while negative, is statistically indistinguishable from zero."[24]

for the 1991-1992 increases.

20 Bernstein and Schmitt, *Making Work Pay*, 30.

21 Charles Brown, Curtis Gilroy, and Andrew Cohen, "The Effect of Minimum Wages on Employment and Unemployment," *Journal of Economic Literature* 20 (1982), 487-528.

22 Allison Wellington, "Effects of the Minimum Wage on the Employment Status of Youths: An Update," *Journal of Human Resources* 26 (1991), 27-46.

23 This could be, of course, because later adjustments in the minimum wage have been more modest than earlier ones. Or, it could be because the nature of the low-wage labor market has changed.

24 Bernstein and Schmitt, *Making Work Pay*, 32.

To sum up, the 1996-97 minimum wage increase went by and large to low-wage earners who reside in low-income households. Given the modest size of the increase, it did not raise these people's total income by a lot, but it undoubtedly helped. Life was a little more comfortable for them than it had been. At the same time, there is no evidence that they faced fewer job prospects than before. If anything, it was the other way around, more jobs — and more jobs at better pay.

Unless there are new or hidden factors at work, the safe bet is that the 2007-2009 increases will produce similar results. But that raise only came after a 10-year drought.

A DECADE OF DETERIORATION — ECONOMIC AND POLITICAL

The decade of 1997-2007 has been a low point in the history of the minimum wage. It was, for starters, the longest period of time ever without any increase whatever. Consequently, low-wage workers watched their living standards erode, in both absolute and relative terms. But, perhaps as importantly, this economic deterioration of the minimum wage was matched by a political deterioration. The precedent of 1996, attaching tax breaks to any suggested minimum wage increase, became a watchword of the Republican-dominated Congress, and the tax proposals grew ever more cynical. There was at least *some* (but really not much) argument in 1996 that the tax breaks were mostly targeted toward small businesses, supposedly the ones who would be paying the increased minimum wage. By 2006, though, that argument had been tossed out entirely, as a minimum wage hike was paired with a reduction in the estate tax.

The freezing of the minimum wage has had predictable economic effects.[25] Even though inflation was relatively modest in these years, the purchasing power of the minimum wage declined precipitously, as shown in Figure 5-1 above. However, it was not only that it declined during these years. It was also that by 2006 the minimum wage was at its lowest level since 1955.

Moreover, the minimum wage shrank when compared to average wages, as shown in Table 5-1. However, we must point out that these data depict "nonsupervisory wages"; they say nothing about average *earnings*.[26] Since overall wages for those without a college degree declined markedly as a per-

---

25 See Jared Bernstein and Isaac Shapiro, *Nine Years of Neglect*, Center on Budget and Policy Priorities and Economic Policy Institute, August 31, 2006.

26 According to Current Population Survey data, about 60% of all workers (part and full time) are paid by the hour.

centage of what college graduates earn, a graph showing the minimum wage and average earnings would be still more disheartening.[27] Furthermore, even this may not present the most accurate picture, for it would say nothing about total income. Specifically, those in the more fortunate brackets derive a significant percentage of their income from dividends, interest, and capital gains, making income figures even more skewed than those for earnings.

TABLE 5-1 MINIMUM WAGE AS A PERCENTAGE OF AVERAGE PRIVATE NONSUPERVISORY WAGE, 1997-2006

Year	Percentage
1997	39%
1998	40%
1999	38%
2000	37%
2001	35%
2002	34%
2003	34%
2004	33%
2005	32%
2006	31%

Source: Economic Policy Institute

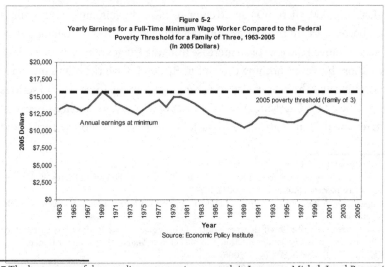

Figure 5-2
Yearly Earnings for a Full-Time Minimum Wage Worker Compared to the Federal
Poverty Threshold for a Family of Three, 1963-2005
(In 2005 Dollars)

Source: Economic Policy Institute

27 The best source of data on disparate earnings growth is Lawrence Mishel, Jared Bernstein, and Sylvia Allegretto, *The State of Working America, 2006-2007* (Ithaca, NY: Cornell University Press, 2007), chap. 3.

Finally, the minimum wage fell further and further short of even the absurdly low federal poverty level, as shown in Figure 5-2.

At the same time, economic inequality continued its sharp rise in the United States. The income Gini coefficient, the most widely used measure of inequality, grew from .42 to .44.[28] Even excluding capital gains (which go disproportionately, of course, to the well-heeled) the top one per cent enjoyed 17.4% of all pretax income in 2005, the highest percentage since 1936.[29] Or, looked at another way, between 1979 and 2004, the bottom 20% gained only 6% in overall after tax income, but the top 20% gained 69%.[30] It is debatable, naturally, and probably unknowable, precisely how much the lagging minimum wage contributed to this dispersion; however, conversely to what happened in Britain when earnings inequality shrank ever so slightly during a period of a rising minimum wage, surely a falling real minimum wage must have played some role.[31]

Even Henry Paulson, George W. Bush's second Secretary of the Treasury voiced concern about the rising tide of inequality in 2006. In his first speech after taking office, he acknowledged that "Amid this country's strong economic expansion, many Americans aren't feeling the benefits."[32] This mirrored an earlier statement by economists at Paulson's old investment firm of Goldman, Sachs that inequality was producing a "drag on consumer sentiment" that was unhealthy for the economy.[33]

Late in 2000, there was an attempt to raise the minimum wage, but it was aborted early in the process. In 2001 and again in 2002, minimum wage advocates moved the idea of an increase from the fringes of politics to serious discussion; however, nothing came of it. By 2004, with the minimum wage languishing and the heat of election year politics in full force, a more serious effort, labeled the Fair Minimum Wage Act of 2004, was launched by several congressional Democrats. Candidate John Kerry picked up the theme and

---

28 The Gini coefficient is regularly calculated by the Census Bureau.

29 Thomas Piketty and Emmanuel Saez, "Income Inequality in the United States, 1913-1998," *Quarterly Journal of Economics* 118 (2003), 1-39.

30 Congressional Budget Office, *Historical Effective Federal Tax Rates: 1979-2004*, December 2006, Table 1C.

31 And, it deserves to be noted that none of the figures given above deal with wealth, which has an even more uneven distribution. See Mishel, *et al., State of Working America*, chap. 5.

32 *Christian Science Monitor*, August 3, 2006.

33 *Christian Science Monitor*, July 17, 2006. However, it deserves to be mentioned that the report seemed to be saying that if nothing is done, there might be demands for even more far-reaching reform.

mentioned it several times on the stump. In the third presidential debate, he all but invoked the question and replied:

> It's a matter of fundamental right that if we raise the minimum wage, 15 million Americans would be positively affected. We'd put money into the hands of people who work hard, who obey the rules, who play for the American dream. If we did that, we'd have more consumption ability in America, which is what we need in order to kick our economy into gear. I will fight tooth and nail to pass the minimum wage.

When it came his turn, George W. Bush said hurriedly that "Mitch McConnell [the Senate Republican whip] had a minimum wage plan that I supported that would have increased the minimum wage." Then, he began talking about education.

It had indeed been rumored that McConnell was going to put forth a minimum wage bill, but no such bill ever materialized. The unique aspect of it, reportedly, was that it would have allowed states to opt out of the increase. This would have in effect terminated the universal minimum wage, undoubtedly the rationale for it in the first place. In any event, despite all the speechmaking, no minimum wage bill of any kind ever got close to passage that year.

By 2006, sentiment was building in many quarters for a minimum wage increase. As we will note in the next chapter, grassroots Democrats were pushing for state referenda, and winning. Analysts from both parties thought this might bring more low-income voters to the polls than normal during off year elections. Senator Charles Schumer of New York, the chair of the Democratic Senatorial Committee, put it straightforwardly, "The average American thinks that the minimum wage ought to be raised, even if they are making more than the minimum wage. Far more importantly from a political viewpoint, it appeals to certain groups of people who don't usually turn out to vote."[34] In June, Senate Democrats garnered 52 votes for an increase to $7.15; however, it needed 60 to break a filibuster. Seeking to keep negative publicity pointed at Republicans, Democrats followed with an effort to block pay increases for Congress until there was an increase in the minimum wage.

If a contest were ever held for the most cynical political move ever, what happened next would have to be in the running. House Republicans paired a minimum wage increase (to $7.25 by 2009) with a further reduction in the already emasculated estate tax, a levy affecting only 3 out of every 1,000 people who die. In 2003, the exemption from the estate tax was $1 million

---

34 Quoted in *New York Times*, July 13, 2006.

($2 million for a couple). Congress had already raised the exemption to $2 million/$ 4 million, and it was set to be pushed up again, to $3.5 million/$7 million by 2009.[35] The 2006 House bill would have increased this to $5 million/$10 million in 2009, and then on top of that added a few additional breaks as well. According to the Center for Budget and Policy Priorities, the beneficiaries of this proposal would be the 8,200 richest Americans; in contrast, about 5.6 million people would have seen higher paychecks from the minimum wage increase.[36]

After the House passed this bill, the minimum wage coalition sought to stop it in the Senate. The estate tax cut was just too bitter a pill to have to swallow to get the increase. Senator Edward Kennedy called the move "contemptible" and "cowardly." Business interests, on the other hand, from the Chamber of Commerce to the National Federation of Independent Businesses stood solidly behind the bill. One business lobbyist was apparently serious when he said that "Every closely held business in America today is either affected by the death tax [opponents' term for the estate tax] or could be affected by it. At the same time, less than 3 percent of the country's workers get paid at the minimum wage." Of course, every business *could* be affected, if, that is, it got big enough.[37] It is rather like saying that everyone *could* be subject to paying the yacht tax.[38] But then he also confessed that "people in the business community understand that it is valuable to Republicans standing for election in November to demonstrate that they have compassion for folks at the lowest end of the economic ladder."[39] At the end of the day, though, the combined bill failed 56-42. Angered, Senate Republican leader Bill Frist said he would not allow separate votes on the two measures, "These issues must be addressed as a package, all or nothing."[40] Republicans, with no apparent embarrassment, even tried to tar Democrats with responsibility for denying minimum wage workers a raise.

---

35 The old rates were set to reappear in 2011, unless the tax cuts were made "permanent." The reason the new rules were set to expire was itself a case study in cynical politics. To contain the size of the tax breaks being enacted, tax cut advocates often set time limits on their proposals. But then, if anyone suggests letting them expire, they can be accused of wanting to "raise taxes" because the rates now in effect will rise.

36 Joel Friedman and Aviva Aron-Dine, *Comparing the House Minimum Wage and Estate Tax Proposals: Who Benefits and By How Much?* (Washington: Center on Budget and Policy Priorities, 2006).

37 In 2006, the Congressional Budget Office showed that if the then prevailing 2006 rates had been in effect in 2000, a grand total of 135 family owned businesses throughout the entire country would have even been subject to the estate tax. Congressional Budget Office, *The Effects of the Federal Estate Tax on Farms and Small Businesses*, 2006.

38 Then, too, more people would be affected by the minimum wage if it were higher.

39 Washington *Post*, August 3, 2006.

40 Kennedy's and Frist's quotes can be found in *USA Today*, August 4, 2006.

The fall elections, though, largely went the Democrats' way, as they took control of both houses of Congress. Although the Iraq War was the major is-sue on voters' minds, the minimum wage was mentioned frequently in Demo-cratic campaigns. When they returned to Washington, the leadership listed the minimum wage as one of their top priorities. President Bush even stated that he might be willing to work with Democrats on this front, *if* he got some more tax cuts. At a news conference after the election, he responded to a question by saying "[An interviewer] asked me about minimum wage. I said there's an area where I believe we can make some — find common ground. And as we do, I'll be, of course, making sure that our small businesses are — there's compensation for the small businesses in the bill"[41] A "clean" bill soon passed the House handily, but stalled in the Senate. The reason was that Re-publicans sought to add tax breaks, as before, and Democratic leaders feared they would be unable to wean away enough moderate Republicans to break a filibuster absent some concessions on taxes. As Jared Bernstein pointed out, very few of these tax modifications had any economic logic to them, and they were poorly targeted in any event.[42] Leading Democrats felt they had no choice, though, and agreed to a bevy of tax cuts being wrapped into the bill. It now passed 94-3, and was endorsed by the president. House Democratic leaders were not prone to accept these measures, however, and negotiations dragged on throughout the spring. There was a real danger that a symbolic gesture made, the bill would be shunted to one side.

While the minimum wage lay becalmed in a conference committee, con-gressional Democrats and the president were struggling over whether Iraq war funding should be tied to a timetable for troop withdrawal. Congress passed and the president promptly vetoed a bill containing such a timetable. As a compromise, Democrats agreed to withdraw the timetable requirement, but then stuck in both the minimum wage increase, burdened this go around by only a handful of tax cuts, and several domestic spending projects as rid-ers. Bush said he would have had liked more tax cuts in recompense for the minimum wage boost, but he quickly signed the bill.

By the new law's terms, the minimum wage goes up in three steps, to $5.85 on July 23, 2007, to $6.55 on July 23, 2008, and to $7.25 on July 23, 2009. According to the Economic Policy Institute, 5.6 million workers (four per cent of the total workforce) earn less than $7.25 per hour, and would therefore directly benefit from the new wage.[43] Another 7.4 million were

---

41 *New York Times*, November 9, 2007.
42 Testimony before Senate Committee on Finance, January 10, 2007.
43 A table is available at the minimum wage section of the organization's website.

expected to receive raises because of the spillover effect. In all, that is 13.0 million workers. Since so many families depend in large part on these earnings, it was an important day for many Americans.

THE STRUCTURE OF THE FEDERAL MINIMUM WAGE

The contemporary federal minimum wage is almost universal in its reach.[44] Technically, the requirement that the worker be engaged in interstate commerce or in the handling or production of goods moving in interstate commerce still stands. However, under modern economic conditions, it is rare for a worker to be completely immunized from interstate commerce. Employees of all schools, state and local government agencies, and institutions engaged in health care are also covered, as are domestic service workers if they earn $1,300 or more per year.

Some employees are specifically exempt. The major categories are executive, administrative, and professional employees, outside sales personnel, and those working for certain seasonal amusement and recreational establishments. In actuality, the overtime provisions of the Fair Labor Standards Act are far more important here than the minimum wage provisions.

Businesses, but not schools or health care organizations (nonprofit and for-profit), are exempt from the act if they have gross sales under $500,000 a year.

Under certain conditions, a firm may employ someone at a subminimum wage. Young people under 20 may be paid less for their first 90 days of employment. Also, if the employer obtains a certificate from the Department of Labor, full-time students and those with physical or mental impairments may be paid less than the minimum wage.

The practicality is, though, that neither the $500,000 exemption nor the allowable subminimums have much effect. Obtaining the certificates takes more time than can usually justify the savings gained by paying reduced wages. But, more generally, the minimum wage tends to set the base in low-wage labor markets, and firms simply comply.

One item that needs to be mentioned is the potential for abuse that exists in the underground economy, especially in sectors utilizing workers who are undocumented. Estimates are that there are approximately 12 million people in the United States illegally, and the bulk of them work in a shadowy world where cash payments are made and few records kept. Naturally, the work-

---

44 Information on the minimum wage's current structure is available at the Department of Labor's website.

ers fear contact with any kind of government official, and are consequently very unlikely to lodge a complaint with the Wage and Hour Division. Undoubtedly, widespread violations of the Fair Labor Standards Act, both its minimum wage and maximum hours provisions (and probably its child labor provisions also), occur daily. To date, however, no one has suggested a convincing strategy to address this problem.

A PROFILE OF THE CONTEMPORARY MINIMUM WAGE WORKFORCE

As the minimum wage shrunk in value throughout the preceding decade, the number of people working at exactly the minimum declined.[45] For instance, between 2002 and 2006, their ranks fell from 2.2 million to 1.7 million. In percentage terms, they made up about 3% of the hourly wage work force in 2002 and about 2.2% in 2006.

The demographic profile, however, is very similar in both years, and therefore we can use the percentages from the 2006 report as a general guide. As the minimum wage increases legislated in 2007 go into effect, more workers will come into this category, and we shall note something about their characteristics momentarily.

One myth we have met before can be dispelled immediately: that most minimum wage workers are teenagers. It is true that 51% are 16 to 24, but only 26% are 16-19. Thus, 74% are 20 and over and 49% are 25 and over. The gender breakdown is overwhelming: 66% are women. Furthermore, this pattern of two women for every man is fairly uniform throughout the age breakdown.

When it comes to race and ethnicity, the numbers are tricky. People can be put into more than one grouping since they self identify. Thus, the numbers do not sum to 100%. The reported identifications are: 85% are white, 13% Hispanic/Latino, 10% African American, and 2% Asian. What is most interesting, however, is an examination of the gender divisions obtaining in the various racial and ethnic groups. Among those categorizing themselves as whites, African Americans, and Asians, the dichotomy is not far off the general numbers, that is, two women for each man. However, among Hispanics/Latinos 43% of minimum wage workers are men.

Another myth also quickly falls, that minimum wage workers are almost all part time. In fact, 39% work full time. But there is an often overlooked phenomenon here when we combine gender with work status. Recall that

45 The standard source of data on minimum wage workers is the Census Bureau's Current Population Survey. Each year they issue a report entitled *Characteristics of Minimum Wage Workers*. It is available on the Bureau's website.

men make up 34% of the total minimum wage work force. They make up, however, a disproportionate share of the full-time workers. Men account for 38% of full time minimum wage workers, but only 31% of part-time employees. In light of the datum on Hispanic/Latino men given above, one possibility is that their overrepresentation here accounts for the disparity.

Regionally, minimum wage workers are more often found in the South than elsewhere. A full 43% reside there, with a further 25% located in the Midwest. Looking at states, one out of every ten minimum wage workers lives in Texas.[46]

The occupational and sector breakdowns produce no surprises. Sixty percent work in "food preparation and serving related occupations," with the next biggest group, 7%, employed in "sales and related occupations." Another 7%, though, are involved in what the Census Bureau labels "production, transportation, and material moving occupations." One cannot help but wonder if this is not the locale for many of the full time Hispanic/Latino male minimum wage workers. When it comes to the economic sectors represented, "leisure and hospitality" claim an expected 63%. "Retail trade" comes in at 8% and "education and health services" adds another 7%. "Local government" and "professional and business services" come in next at 4% and 3% respectively. "Manufacturing" and "state government" are the only other sectors that surpass 1%, with each contributing 2% to the total.

Educational attainments are naturally lower than the population as a whole. Part of this is attributable, of course, to the large number of young people in the minimum wage work force, but that is not the only factor at work. Research studies have found that a lot of people have "minimum wage careers."[47] Over a quarter, 28%, have less than a high school education. College students would fall among the remaining 72% who have earned a high school diploma. However, 32% of all minimum wage workers are high school graduates with no college whatever.

Marital status offers further clues regarding who is really working at the minimum wage. Owing to the age distribution, it is not surprising that 64% have never been married. What is somewhat surprising is that 23% are married with a spouse present, and 20% (of the total) are 25 years and over and married with a spouse present. This composite picture takes on further

---

46 The figures, it should be stressed, relate only to workers paid the federal minimum wage. In states with minimum wages higher than the federal one, there would be very few workers toiling for $5.15. Texas has a state minimum wage, but it is the same as the federal mandate. State minimum wage policies will be discussed in the next chapter.

47 See William Carrington and Bruce Fallick, "Do Some Workers have Minimum Wage Careers?" *Monthly Labor Review*, May 2001, 17-27.

meaning when we break it down by gender. If the two to one ratio regard-ing men and women held, then a little over 7.5% of the minimum wage work force (one third of 23%) should be men with a spouse present and a little over 15% should be women. If fact, though, the percentages are 6% and 17%. Thus, far more women fit into this category than expected, at least from a statistical perspective. Likewise, the 20% of people aged at least 25 with a spouse present should breakdown into 6.7% (again, of the total minimum wage work force) for males and 13.3% for females. However, again, we find women overrepresented here, as the relevant numbers are 5% for men and 15% for women. It would seem that, as we saw in the UK, a goodly number of minimum wage workers, but not as many as there, are married women supplementing their husband's (probably often meager) earnings. This will become clearer when we examine household data.

A more telling portrait can be gathered from examining the people who stand to gain from the 2007 minimum wage increase. This group is composed of both those who currently earn below the target wage of $7.25 and those who will benefit from the spillover effect. The Economic Policy Institute has compiled this information using CPS data.[48] Approximately 12.5 million workers will be affected, 5.3 million directly and 7.2 million indirectly. These people make up almost 10% of the total American work force.

The vast majority of people who will enjoy swelled paychecks are 20 and over. Among all those affected, 79% are 20 and over; among those directly affected, 71% are 20 and over, and a full 85% of the indirect beneficiaries are. Altogether, 59% of those affected are women, but 61% of those directly affected are, pointing to a higher concentration of women at the very low-est reaches of the wage scales. The racial and ethnic breakdown is almost uniform across the categories: 61% of the beneficiaries in both categories are white, 18% Hispanic/Latino, and 2% Asian. A miniscule number of African Americans, 17% versus 16%, are more likely to directly benefit.

These people's work status, occupations, and places of employment provide an interesting profile. Well over half of all those affected, 53%, are full-time workers. But of the indirectly affected more are full-time work-ers, 60% to 43%. This means that there are roughly 6.6 million (12.5 million X 53%) full-time workers earning very low wages. Occupationally, 41% of those directly affected are in service jobs and 21% are in sales. For those in-directly affected, the comparable percentages are 33% and 18% respectively.

48 See the "Minimum Wage Issue Brief" section of the organization's website. The figures are slightly different from those given earlier because two different versions of the CPS were used to make the calculations.

The minimum wage increase, therefore, is going to spill somewhat outside these two areas in the indirectly affected category. The picture is even more dramatic when industrial sectors are brought out. Leisure and hospitality takes in 29% of the directly affected group, and retail trade brings in another 24%. In the indirectly affected category, though, only 18% are in leisure and hospitality and 23% in retail trade. It would seem that a lot of jobs in the retail sector are paying slightly above the minimum wage, a finding that is not surprising.

In sum, 4% of America's workers will receive higher incomes as a direct result of the minimum wage increase that eked by Congress in 2007. On top of that, another 6% will gain by their employers adjusting pay scales in light of the increase. While the raise was long overdue, and very modest by any measure, it will undoubtedly be dearly welcomed.

CONCLUSION

In some ways, the federal minimum wage has been a singularly successful policy. It has periodically raised the incomes of the least well-off and done so without any particular negative side-effects. On the other hand, it is a policy that has fallen short. Its real value has declined precipitously since 1968. Moreover, no mechanism has been established to provide for regular increases, these being subject to the vagaries of congressional politics. These shortcomings are attributable in large measure to the unbending opposition of free market ideologues and their small business allies. However, it is attributable in part also to the fact that those wanting to help the poor came to believe that social welfare expenditure policies, both their social insurance and public assistance variants, held more promise than the minimum wage. The minimum wage became by the early 1970s but a stepchild of the American welfare state.

However, with the end of AFDC in the mid-nineties, an important shift began. Political activists rediscovered the importance of the minimum wage, and, blocked at the federal level, began launching campaigns at the state and local level. Here, they achieved notable successes, and it is to that story that we now turn.

Chapter 6. State and Local Minimum Wage Policies

Between 1997 and 2007, as the Republican-controlled Congress continued to vote down minimum wage increases, political activists were not to be stymied. With increasing frequency, they turned to their state and local governments, and had growing success.

Consequently, in the decade of federal inaction, there was significant movement among state governments. Many raised their own minimum wages to new highs, while others adopted minimum wage laws for the first time. All this rivaled the flurry of action in 1912-1923, as not only were new laws passed, but the issue was kept before the public. By January of 2007, 30 states and the District of Columbia had pushed their own minimum wage levels above what Congress required employers to pay.

At the same time, minimum wage advocates sought and obtained so-called "living wage" ordinances from local governments. These measures usually applied only to firms with government contracts, but the prescribed wage was often considerably above state minimums. Along with the economic gains they brought to low-wage workers, these policies also had an enormous publicizing effect, in part at least because business groups mobilized to oppose them in such stentorian terms.

STATE MINIMUM WAGE LAWS

A summary of these state minimum wage policies is provided in Table 6-1. Three conclusions stand out from an inspection of the table. First, it is not only the usual liberal, or blue, states that have higher minimum wages. Such Republican strongholds as Arkansas, Arizona, North Carolina, and Florida sport minimum wages exceeding the federal level alongside the more expected cases of Massachusetts and California. Second, the vast majority of Americans live in these states. Among the states with substantial populations, only Texas remains outside the fold. Finally, it is almost exclusively only the states of the Deep South that do not have minimum wage statutes at all.

TABLE 6-1 STATES WITH MINIMUM WAGES ABOVE THE FEDERAL LEVEL, APRIL 2007					
State	Minimum Wage	State	Minimum Wage	State	Minimum Wage
Alaska	$7.15	Iowa	$6.20	North Carolina	$6.15
Arizona	$6.75	Maine	$7.00 (10/1/07)	Ohio	$6.85
Arkansas	$6.25	Maryland	$6.15	Oregon	$7.80
California	$7.50	Massachusetts	$7.50	Pennsylvania	$7.15 (7/1/07)
Colorado	$6.85	Michigan	$7.15 (7/1/07)	Rhode Island	$7.40
Connecticut	$7.65	Minnesota	$6.15	Vermont	$7.53
Delaware	$6.65	Missouri	$6.50	Washington	$7.93
District of Columbia	$7.00	Montana	$6.15	West Virginia	$5.85
Florida	$6.67	Nevada	$6.15	Wisconsin	$6.50
Hawaii	$7.25	New Jersey	$7.15		
Illinois	$7.50 (7/1/07)	New York	$7.15		

Source: *U. S. Department of Labor*

The exemplar of a state minimum wage can be found in Washington State. Historically, Washington has usually had the country's highest minimum wage, appropriately enough perhaps since it was the state whose minimum wage law was the first to survive Supreme Court scrutiny.[1] In 1981, while the federal minimum stood at $3.80, Washington's was $4.25, 12% above the federal level. When the 1989 mandated federal increase went into effect, setting the minimum wage at $4.25, the state rate sat still for several years. Then, in 1994, the state rate increased to $4.90, which was eclipsed

---

[1] *West Coast Hotel Company v. Parrish*, 300 US 379 (1938).

by the 1997 federal increase to $5.15. In 1998, however, minimum wage advocates managed to put Proposition 688 on the ballot. It provided that the minimum wage would be raised to $5.70 in 1999, to $6.50 in 2000, and after that indexed to the inflation rate. The measure was hotly debated, and drew a bigger turnout than any other item on the ballot. One estimate concluded that it may have raised turnout four percentage points above normal.[2] It passed by a lopsided 2-1 margin, 1,259,000 to 645,000.

The reach of Washington's minimum wage is correspondingly wide. There is, for example, no tip credit. Furthermore, employers are not allowed to deduct the cost of housing furnished to workers, a provision that most often affects those working in agriculture. According to the Washington Department of Employment Security, jobs paying the minimum wage make up about 2.3% of the state's jobs on a full-time equivalency basis.[3] The absolute number is higher, though, since many minimum wage jobs are part time, varying between 3.5% and 5.0% of the work force, depending on the time of the year (many agricultural jobs in Washington are seasonal) and the time in the cycle of the mandated increases.[4]

Washington's minimum wage workers are only marginally different from those in the country as a whole. According to the Economic Opportunity Institute, 75% are over 20, and less than 30% live with their parents. About 60% are female and about half work full time. They are educationally disadvantaged, as over 65% have 12 years or less of schooling. As for households, the median family income (1998) of households containing a minimum wage worker was $27,203, while 54% of households with a minimum wage worker have incomes under $30,000. Perhaps most startlingly, 39% of minimum wage workers are the only source of income for their households.[5] Now, it is true that minimum wage advocates sometimes massage data like these to paint a more compelling portrait of minimum wage workers than is the case in actuality. In Washington, as elsewhere, there are undeniably some teenagers from relatively affluent families working part time at minimum wage jobs, and they do not really 'need' the money. Nevertheless, the stark fact remains that for many people a minimum wage job is their main job, and their households are heavily dependent on those earnings. No matter how many

---

2 Economic Opportunity Institute, April 2002 release.

3 Scott Bailey, *Nomenclature, Statistics, and the Minimum Wage*, Washington State Department of Employment Security, March 22, 2005.

4 Krista Glen, *Minimum Wage Workers in Washington State*, Washington State Department of Employment Security, May 19, 2003; Seattle *Times*, September 30, 2006.

5 Economic Opportunity Institute, *Washington State's Minimum Wage: The Facts*, February 2003, 1 and *Who Benefits from a Minimum Wage Increase?* An October 1998 release updated on March 23, 2004.

ways you total it up, if you got all the minimum wage workers in Washington in one place at one time, it would be seen that most of them are poor and they do in fact need the money.

As for the industries that employ them, three sectors — accommodation and food services, retail trade, and agriculture — are dominant. Accommodation and food services absorb 29% of all minimum wage workers, while retail trade and agriculture add another 21% and 14% respectively. Looked at another way, minimum wage jobs as a percentage of jobs in that particular sector, 17% of all jobs in both accommodation and food service and retail trade pay the minimum wage, but only six per cent in retail trade do. The size of the firms that employ the most minimum wage workers is more evenly split, about one-third each work in small businesses (0-19 employees), medium-sized firms (20-249 employees) and large (250+ employees), at least calculated on an FTE basis. The heavy use of part-time and seasonal workers by small firms would make the head count different, though.

Turning to the adequacy of the wage, two calculations can be made. First, how does the minimum wage fare in moving or keeping people out of poverty? As far as the federal poverty thresholds are concerned, it fares pretty well. If someone worked 40 hours a week for 52 weeks, in 2006 he or she would have earned $15,870.40 gross. The poverty thresholds for that year were $10,488 for one person under 65, $13,500 for two adults, $13,896 for an adult and one child, and $16,242 for an adult and two children. This means that such a worker would produce an income that is 151%; 118%, 114%, and 98% of the given needed amounts. However, first, the federal poverty levels are ridiculously low.[6] Moreover, living costs in Washington are generally above the national average. Pennsylvania State University's Living Wage Calculator[7] utilizes basic family budgets, and finds Washington's minimum wage more lacking. Their figures show that (on a state-wide average basis) for one adult a Washington minimum wage worker earns only 89% of the amount needed for one adult to live on the most austere of budgets, 62% for two adults, and 47% for one adult and one child (no calculation was made for one adult and two children).

Both these sets of reckonings sidestep an important issue: What is the pertinent family structure and how many people should work? If the model family is two adults both working full time, then the picture changes rather dramatically. If two adults with no children work full time, then at the mini-

---

6 For a discussion, see Constance Citro and Robert Michaels, eds., *Measuring Poverty: A New Approach* (Washington: National Academy Press, 1995). Plus, it is well to keep in mind that the gross figures for minimum wage earnings ignore payroll taxes.

7 This can be found at www.livingwage.geog.psu.edu/

mum wage their earnings are 25% above the budgets used by Penn State's researchers. However, two adults with one child could still produce only 83% of what is needed if both work full time at the minimum wage.

The other way to examine adequacy is to compare the minimum wage to average wages and average earnings. In 2005, median male wages in Washington stood at $18.16 per hour, while median female wages came in at only $13.62.[8] Thus, the $7.35 2005 minimum wage was only 40% of median male wages. If we take overall earnings (counting salaries and wages), the gaps are even wider, of course. In 2004, average male monthly earnings were $4,227; a full time minimum wage worker in 2004 earned $1,241 per month ($7.16 X 40 X 52 ÷ 12), or 29% of male earnings. Compared to total average earnings, the minimum wage still stood at only 36%.

Politically, small skirmishes continue to be fought over the minimum wage. Each legislative session in Olympia sees bills to allow a tip credit or permit farmers to include the value of housing when computing wages. So far, opponents have beaten these efforts back, but they demonstrate that the minimum wage is almost never a settled issue.

The Impact of State Minimum Wages

These state minimum wage increases provide social scientists with an interesting laboratory in which to study the effects of minimum wages. For starters, we have several new instances available to study the before and after effects. But perhaps even more importantly, while this experience does not parallel the experimental method, which involves making comparisons between a "treatment" and "control" group that are matched on all variables save one, the fact that we have a battery of states with higher minimum wages while a number remained at the federal level is about as close to an ideal research site as you are going to have in comparative political economy. What is the evidence regarding the effects of state minimum wages on employment, the numbers of businesses, inflation, and poverty rates?

Employment

Begin with the perpetually most discussed of these, employment. The strongly anti-minimum wage Employment Policies Institute put out a statement in 2003 claiming that "it is perhaps no coincidence that the three states with the highest minimum wages in the nation — Oregon, Washington, and

---

8 Marilyn Watkins, Cara Saunto, and Inga Senftleben, *The State of Working Washington*, Economic Opportunity Institute, October 2006, 33.

Alaska — are among the five states with the highest unemployment rates in the nation."[9] But as Jeff Chapman notes:

> That argument, however, rests on the simplistic observation that some of the states with high minimum wages also have high unemployment rates. Without more examination, this observation is as useful in understanding state job markets as noting that joblessness has been on the rise in New York since the last time the Yankees won the World Series. It might be true, but it doesn't mean one is causing the other.[10]

Two factors have to be analyzed to make any kind of meaningful connection between minimum wages and state unemployment rates. First, you need to look at the national trends in unemployment rates. Assume state A had an unemployment rate of 6% while the national unemployment rate stood at 4% in year 1. State A raises its minimum wage to take effect in year 2, and its unemployment rate falls to 5% while the national rate remains at 4% (and the national minimum wage is unaltered). State A might still have high unemployment compared to the nation as a whole, but it would be absurd to attribute it to the minimum wage increase. Second, you need to examine economic sectors within states that raise their minimum wages (and this is true even if unemployment rates actually go up following a minimum wage hike). Suppose, for example, that high-wage sectors which employ few minimum wage workers lose jobs, but the sectors employing large numbers of minimum wage workers actually gain jobs. If so, one would be hard pressed to find a conceptual rationale for a causal connection between rising minimum wages and higher unemployment. Simply looking at the overall unemployment rates can give, therefore, a highly distorted picture of what is occurring in the real world.

Consider unemployment trends in Oregon, for example, since the national government last raised the minimum wage. Four observations are merited from an examination of Figure 6-1. First, the unemployment rate in Oregon moved above the national rate *before* the state started increasing its minimum wage. Second, after 1997, the trends are closely related. Third, after the 1997 and 1999 increases in the state minimum wage, unemployment actually fell, and in 1999 it fell at a faster pace than the national rate. Fourth, unemployment did go up while the national rate was falling after the 1998 increase, and that certainly warrants further investigation. However, what is manifestly clear is that the fact that Oregon has a higher unemployment rate than

---

9 Quoted in Jeff Chapman, *Employment and the Minimum Wage: Evidence from Recent State Labor Market Trends*, Economic Policies Institute Briefing Paper, May 2004, 2.
10 Chapman, *Employment and the Minimum Wage*, 1.

the nation as a whole says absolutely nothing about the relation between its minimum wage and the comparative number of jobs available.

To add more emphasis to this point, consider a state with an unemployment rate below the national average: Florida. As depicted in Figure 6-2, a slight rise in unemployment did occur soon after the 2006 increase; however, this simply paralleled the national trend. What is most striking is that after the introduction of the 2005 increase, Florida's unemployment rate not only dropped, it dropped even faster than the national rate. Indeed, if one wished to consistently apply the monocausal logic advocated by the Employment Policies Institute, then we could say that the high unemployment rate in the country as a whole compared to Florida must be because the national minimum wage was too low.

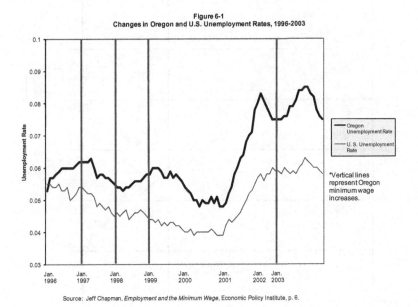

Figure 6-1
Changes in Oregon and U.S. Unemployment Rates, 1996-2003

Source: Jeff Chapman, *Employment and the Minimum Wage*, Economic Policy Institute, p. 6.

Taking apart the components of state unemployment rates sheds further light on the unemployment rate/minimum wage question. Consider, for example, Washington State. Figure 6-3 shows that the number of manufacturing jobs declined sharply as minimum wages went up, but this is a sector in which there are virtually no minimum wage jobs. Compare that to employment levels in the food services and accommodation sectors. As shown in Figure 6-4, the seasonal trend remained remarkably stable, despite regular minimum wage increases. This means that a state could exhibit a rising unemployment rate overall as the minimum wage increases, but there could not possibly be any relationship between the two. Figure 6-4 also strongly supports the proposition that minimum wage increases are perfectly compatible with a stable job picture.

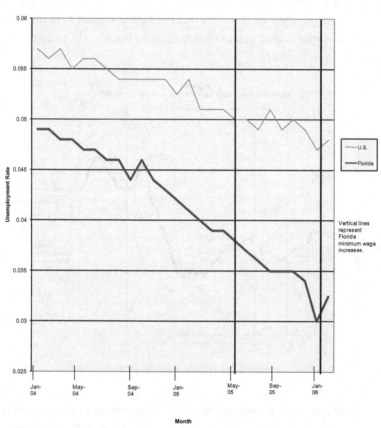

Figure 6-2
Changes in Florida and U.S. Unemployment Rates, 2004-2006

Source: Luke Shaefer and Bruce Nissen, *The Florida Minimum Wage after One Year*, Florida International University, Research Institute on Social and Economic Policy, P.2.

Massachusetts offers further evidence for reading aggregate unemployment figures with great care. Figure 6-5 displays how the employment picture changed in different sectors between 1995 and 2005. There were huge losses in the manufacturing and information sectors, areas where there are few if any minimum wage jobs. In high minimum wage sectors, though, the picture is dramatically different. The retail sector did not lose nearly as many jobs as manufacturing and information services, and the leisure and hospitality industry actually added jobs. This was despite an increase in the state minimum wage in 2000.

Figure 6-3
Employment in Durable Goods Manufacturing in Washington State, 1999-2003

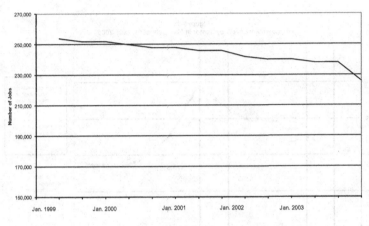

Source: Washington Department of Employment Security/Economic Opportunity Insitute

Figure 6-4
Employment in Eating and Drinking Places in Washington State, 1999-2003

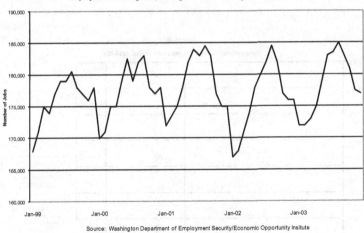

Source: Washington Department of Employment Security/Economic Opportunity Insitute

Or, again, look at Florida, a state where employment has been growing. From Figure 6-6, it is clear that the rate at which jobs were added in the "private services providing" sector, which includes both industries which employ a lot of minimum wage workers and those with few, is almost identical to the overall rate of job creation. In fact, a slight dip in total job creation occurred after the 2005 minimum wage increase, but the "private service providing" sector held its own.

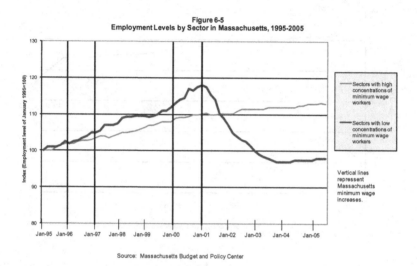

Figure 6-5
Employment Levels by Sector in Massachusetts, 1995-2005

Source: Massachusetts Budget and Policy Center

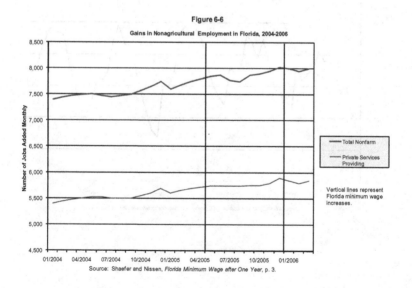

Figure 6-6

Gains in Nonagricultural Employment in Florida, 2004-2006

Source: Shaefer and Nissen, *Florida Minimum Wage after One Year*, p. 3.

To take yet another example, we can examine Oregon. Oregon voters approved a minimum wage of $6.90 (second only to Washington's) in 2002 and indexed it to future cost of living adjustments. Between then and late 2005, Oregon's job growth rate exceeded 41 other states. Furthermore, restaurant jobs grew at a very healthy 7.7% clip and agricultural jobs clocked in at a 6.5% growth rate, numbers which compared to an overall job growth rate of 4.1%.[11]

Turning to the alternative research strategy, at any given moment between 1997 and 2007, there was a set of states with minimum wage levels above $5.15 and a group where merely the federal minimum applied. Two important studies utilized this fact to make a comparison between what was occurring in the two cohorts.

Paul Wolfson compared the 17 states (and the District of Columbia) which had raised their minimum wages between 1997 and 2005.[12] He studied the employment experiences of six groups: teenagers, young adults, adults with less than a high school education, adults with no education beyond high school, African-Americans and young Hispanics. All these groups are usually thought to be especially vulnerable to shifts in low-wage, low-skilled employment. If, as critics claim, they are likely to be laid off because businesses cannot afford to pay them the higher wage, that fact should be reflected in their employment patterns. Further, he analyzed the experience of the eating and drinking establishment sector, the quintessential employer of low-wage workers.

Wolfson utilized data from the Current Population Survey (which are broken down by state) and two techniques known as differences-in-differences and panel regression. Each is designed to answer a different type of question. The first addresses "How different is the dependent variable in these states [the high minimum wage states] from what it would have been if the minimum wage had remained at its 1997 level?"[13] The second approach puts the question "How does the dependent variable respond to the minimum wage?"

Wolfson's analyses reveal the following for the first four of his groups:

> These groups, teenagers and young adults, were chosen because of suspicions that they were unusually vulnerable to adverse effects from the minimum wage. The overall impression from both [analyses] is that em-

---

11 Oregon Center for Public Policy, News Release of December 30, 2005.

12 Paul Wolfson, *State Minimum Wages: A Policy that Works*, Economic Policy Institute Briefing Paper, November 2006.

13 Wolfson, *State Minimum Wages*, 5.

ployment during this period did not suffer from higher minimum wages. If anything, the minimum wage increased employment among teenage boys.

The corresponding elasticity estimates for the two adult groups . . . are slightly larger in absolute magnitude than those for younger workers, but . . . are almost all statistically insignificant. The exceptions are employment and labor supply of men [with a high school education]. As with teenage boys' employment, the minimum wage slightly raises not only employment but also labor supply of these men.

This lack of evidence for a negative employment result is quite striking, especially with respect to teenagers. Both statistical approaches found clear evidence that teenagers' wages were higher as a result of the minimum wage. However, this appears to have had no adverse effect on teenagers' employment. According to the panel analysis, low wages of young adults respond to the minimum wage, yet it is not possible to detect an adverse effect on their employment. Finally, there is no response of labor supply to the minimum wage.[14]

The small sample sizes for African-Americans and Hispanics introduced a number of complications into the data. Furthermore, there is substantial overlap with the categories above. The conclusions, therefore, had to be more guarded. Here, too, though, no evidence exists that employment opportunities shrunk due to higher minimum wages.

As for employment in the restaurant industry, his data show not only that there have been no negative employment effects whatever, but, on the contrary, there may actually be a positive effect: that is, higher wages and more employment.[15] Recall that this is what the Low Pay Commission also found.

Another study was done by the Fiscal Policy Institute in April 2004, then updated in March of 2006.[16] They counted as "high minimum wage states" the 10 states plus the District of Columbia which had minimum wages above the federal level before 2004. This approach provided for a longer time period and a more balanced analysis. On the employment front, they examined both overall employment figures and employment in the retail sector. Their conclusions are unmistakable:

> Over the entire period from January 1998 to January 2006, aggregate employment in the higher minimum wage states (plus DC) increased by 9.7 percent. This is 30 percent higher than the combined job growth of 7.5% for the other 39 states.

---

14 Wolfson, *State Minimum Wages*, 13.

15 Wolfson, *State Minimum Wages*, 16-17.

16 Fiscal Policy Institute, *States with Minimum Wages above the Federal Level have had Faster Small Business and Retail Job Growth*, March 30, 2006, update of April 20, 2004 report.

> Over the entire January 1998 to January 2006 period, retail employment grew by 10.2 percent in the 11 higher minimum wage states (plus DC), nearly triple the 3.7 percent retail job growth in the other 39 states.[17]

A similar study done by the Center for American Progress followed a slightly different methodology, but still reached the same results.[18] They examined small retail businesses (defined as those with fewer than 500 employees) and restaurant employment in states with minimum wages exceeding the federal level compared to the remainder. In addition to compiling the aggregate numbers, they also weighted the results to account for the population disparity between the two sets of states. In the area of small retail business employment, they found 4.8% aggregate growth in employment in the higher minimum wage states compared to only 3.2% in the lower minimum wage states. When the figures were weighted, the comparable figures were 9.2% and 3.0%. Moreover, given that 72% of all retail employment is concentrated in firms with 99 or fewer employees, they examined figures for these establishments separately. Here the unweighted figures came in at 4.5% for the higher cohort and 3.0% for the lower. As for the weighted scores, they were 5.8% and 3.4% respectively. Without question, therefore, employment at small retail businesses was flourishing more healthily in those states with higher minimum wages. When we turn to restaurants, the picture is more mixed, but not decisive either way. Restaurant employment grew 9.0% in the high minimum wage states and 11.2% in the low minimum wage states (unweighted). The comparable weighted figures were 11.0% and 11.4%. Though these figures give the edge to the low minimum wage states, the differences, stated in percentage terms, are much less than for small retail employment overall. That is, the percentage difference in the unweighted retail scores is 50% and in the weighted scores 71% in favor of the higher minimum wage states. For restaurants, the comparable figures are 24% and a mere 4%. In short, in the restaurant area, there is not a lot of difference, especially in the critical weighted scale.

Finally, there was a qualitative comparison done by a reporter for the *New York Times*.[19] He visited business on both sides of the Washington-Idaho (where the federal minimum wage prevailed) line. Washington business owners seemed quite content with the state of affairs, despite their earlier worries. A pizza restaurant owner in Washington admitted he feared the high minimum wage when it went into effect, but said "We're paying the

---

17 Fiscal Policy Institute, *States with Minimum Wages above the Federal Level*, 8 and 9.

18 John Burton and Amy Hanauer, *Good for Business: Small Business Growth and State Minimum Wages* (Cleveland: Policy Matters Ohio, 2006), 12-15.

19 *New York Times*, January 11, 2007.

---

highest wage we've ever had to pay, and our business is still up more than 11 percent over last year." Another said he had considered moving across the river to Idaho, but changed his mind. "To tell you the truth, my business is fantastic. I've never done as much business in my life." Many Idaho workers cross over to work in Washington, forcing Idaho firms to raise their wages to compete. An Idaho restaurateur who had been forced to spike up his wages explained, "At $5.15 an hour, I get zero applicants — or maybe a guy with one leg who wouldn't pass a drug test and wouldn't show up on Saturday night because he wants to get drunk with his buddies." With business up and substantial numbers of workers eager for jobs, there is small wonder that the Association of Washington Business, according to the article, is no longer so hostile to the minimum wage.

Business Growth

The supposed deleterious effect on business profits and business growth posed by the minimum wage can also be studied in the states. If increasing minimum wages reduces profits, then some firms should exit through bankruptcy and others should be deterred from opening.

The results of three major studies, however, refute this gloomy scenario. The first examined business activity in Florida, using the Quarterly Census of Employment and Wages data. This data set, true, only looks at aggregate numbers of business establishments in various categories; thus, it does not capture the number of firms exiting and entering given sectors. However, if the opponents of the minimum wage are correct, the effects should depress the number of businesses generally, and especially those heavily utilizing low-wage labor. The report stated:

> The state minimum wage first took effect during the second quarter of 2005. If critics are correct, then it might be expected that the number of employers would have declined in the following quarter. Instead, the number of private establishments employing workers in Florida grew by over 10,000 in the first full quarter after the state minimum wage took effect. Far from losing businesses, as of the most recent data available, Florida is gaining them at a faster rate than in any quarter since before 2003. Furthermore, during the third quarter of 2005, Florida showed a greater percentage growth in private employing establishments than did the US as a whole.
>
> Looking a bit more closely at sectors and industries that might be expected to take the biggest hit from the state law, growth in employers followed a similar pattern. The number of private service providing establishments grew, and this included growth in retail trade, leisure and hospitality, and food services and drinking establishments. In the same quarter, private accommodations establishments held steady. The number of private

agricultural employers followed a similar pattern to previous years, with a very slight seasonal decline between the second and third quarter.[20]

Another section of the comparative state study conducted by the Fiscal Policy Institute, cited above, looked at business growth in states with minimum wages above the federal level versus those where only the federal minimum obtained. Because there is often more concern about the ability of small businesses to foot the costs of increasing the minimum wage as opposed to larger firms, their study concentrated on small businesses (defined as those with fewer than 50 employees). It looked at the overall rates of growth of small businesses and, critically, small firms in the retail sector. The data base was the Department of Commerce's County Business Patterns reports. Because the Department of Commerce changed its classification system in 1998, the researchers decided to focus on the period between 1998 and 2003 (the latest year for which data were available to them). Throughout this period, 10 states plus the District of Columbia had minimum wages above the federal level. For small business overall, the 11 high minimum wage jurisdictions enjoyed a 5.4% growth in the number of firms compared to an increase of only 4.2% in those states where only the federal minimum wage applied. Interestingly, too, in the former group of states, there was an increase of 6.7% in the number of employees working in small businesses while the other states saw only a 5.3% growth. If we turn to retail small business, the picture is equally dramatic. The high minimum wage states had a growth rate of 0.6% in the number of such establishments, while the lower minimum wage states had to endure a 0.3% *drop* in the number of retail businesses. The number of employees bore a similar pattern. Whereas the higher minimum wage states witnessed a 4.1% gain in the number of small business employees, the lower minimum wage states had to make do with only a 2.6% gain. In other words, for both small business overall and for small firms engaged in retail trade, both the number of businesses and the number of employees working in such firms grew at a much better clip in the states with higher minimum wages.

Confirming these findings, the Center for American Progress study also examined the number of establishments with fewer than 500 employees.[21] The overall growth in total retail establishments was almost identical in the higher and lower minimum wage states, 4.2% in the former and 4.4% in the latter. If weighted scores are calculated, however, the higher minimum wage

20 Luke Shaefer and Bruce Nissen, *The Florida Minimum Wage after One Year* (Miami: Florida International University, Research Institute on Social and Economic Policy, 2006), 5-6.
21Burton and Hanauer, *Good for Business*, 14-15.

states come out ahead at 5.5% to 4.2%. For restaurants, the picture was even clearer. On an unweighted basis, the number of restaurants grew 5.2% in the higher minimum wage states compared to 4.6% in the lower minimum wage states. Calculating the weighted scores led to a 7.0% to 5.7% advantage for the higher minimum wage states.

In short, these data taken as a whole surely demonstrate that minimum wages — at least at the level to which they have been raised to date — are not discouraging people from staying in or going into businesses reliant on low-wage labor. If anything, the opposite is true.

Inflation

One way businesses can respond to the increased costs associated with minimum wage increases is to raise prices. If they do this successfully, that is if they do not meet with consumer resistance, then minimum wage increases contribute to inflation. But, of course, the question is then how much? Recall that the Low Pay Commission found many businesses claiming that they would consider raising prices in response to a minimum wage increase, but that, from the available evidence, overall prices hardly budged.

We have not had as many studies of price increases in the states as policy analysts would like. There are only two, and only one based on past data. The other applied sophisticated models to try to find out what would happen in Arizona should the minimum wage be increased, but it is uncertain how that will play out in the real world.

The data from the past are presented by the Washington state based Economic Opportunity Institute. To quote their findings:

> There is no evidence suggesting Washington's minimum wage has led to significantly higher prices in Washington. Between 1999 and 2002 the rate of growth in general inflation in the Seattle area was identical with other western cities. Between 1999 and 2002, restaurant prices increased in the Seattle area at a slightly higher rate than in other western cities; however, this is not necessarily related to Washington's increasing minimum wage. Labor, after all, typically averages 30 percent of a restaurant's operating costs. To better illustrate the minor difference, a meal that cost $20.00 in Seattle in 1999 increased to $21.88 in 2002 compared to $21.74 in all other western cities, a 14-cent difference.[22]

The other research report was conducted in advance of the 2006 referendum in Arizona.[23] Utilizing a number of sophisticated economic models regarding the ability of businesses to pass on the cost of minimum wage in-

---

22 Economic Opportunity Institute, *Washington State's Minimum Wage: The Facts*, February 2003, 2.
23 Robert Pollin and Jeannette Wicks-Lim, *Economic Analysis of the Arizona Minimum Wage Proposal* (Amherst: University of Massachusetts Political Economy Research Institute, 2006).

creases, the authors concluded that "the average business in Arizona would have to *increase its sales revenue by less than 1/10 of one percent in order to fully cover the additional costs resulting from the minimum wage proposal* (p. 10, emphasis in original). However, that would not be uniform, since businesses are not all affected the same. A retail clothing store would have to raise its prices 0.09% of sales to come out even; in other words, a $20 item would now cost $20.02. Hotels, in contrast, would have to increase prices by 0.8% of sales, making the price of a $100 room $100.80. The restaurant industry, of course, would be the hardest hit, given the high labor intensity and the number of minimum wage workers. Full service restaurants would be faced with a 1.4% increase in sales prices, while limited service restaurants would be forced into a 1.7% increase. This means that a $20 meal at the former would now cost $20.28 and a $5.00 take out at the latter would now cost $5.09. Moreover, these amounts, miniscule as they are, assume no productivity increases related to the minimum wage boost.

In sum, there is not much concrete information about the inflationary effects or lack thereof in states that have raised their minimum wages. However, it seems clear that these states have not experienced any kind of dramatic price increases compared to the nation as whole.

Poverty

It is inordinately difficult to pin down the impact the minimum wage makes on poverty. On the one hand, assigning people to categories of "in" and "out" of poverty is inherently subjective. On the other, the income components of low-income households are diverse. Moreover, the situation is not subject to the kinds of data that can be found in the employment and business fields.

We must immediately dismiss one simplistic approach, correlating state minimum wage levels with poverty rates. Some minimum wage advocates suggest this, and in fact the data show that states with higher minimum wages do tend to have lower poverty rates.[24] However, this is the equivalent of the claim that there is a causal link between high unemployment rates and high minimum wages. It might be true, but much more is needed to say so with any measurable certainty.

The only realistically available way to analyze the effects of the minimum wage on poverty is to examine the profile of people who stand to benefit from a minimum wage increase, both directly and indirectly from the spillover ef-

---

24 Fiscal Policy Project, *An Economic Success Story: Job Growth and Poverty Reduction in States that have Raised the Minimum Wage* (Albuquerque: New Mexico Voices for Children, nd), Table 4.

fect. Much of this type of analysis will necessarily be inferential. Three types of information are pertinent. First, we need to know the pools of workers who receive the raise. If the demographic groups who receive the additional wages match the groups most likely to be in poverty, this is some evidence that the minimum wage is reaching its target. It is not proof, because we don't know what is happening to individuals in the groups; however, it is one useful bit of datum. Second, we need to know the types of households in which beneficiaries of a minimum wage boost reside. The more concentrated they are in the lower quintiles or deciles, the more likely a minimum wage increase is helping them to move out of poverty. Finally, we need to know the percentage of household income minimum wage workers are contributing. It could be that even in relatively low-income households that minimum wage workers do not really contribute that much. If so, then a minimum wage increase will be "wasted." In short, while we cannot be absolutely certain about how the benefits of a minimum wage increase filter out, we can make some knowledgeable estimates.

It is well to recall, at the outset, the studies of Carrington and Fallick and Bouchley, which demonstrated that there are many people who remain in minimum wage jobs for a substantial time.[25] Thus, any increase in the minimum wage will have a decided impact on this cohort of people, most of whom inhabit the bottom reaches of the income distribution.

Reasonably good data are available for six states, and, significantly, the results all point in the same direction. Let us begin with Oregon. A 1999 study of the 1997 and 1998 minimum wage increases found that low-end workers had plainly benefited.[26] Those in the 10th percentile (that is, 90% of workers earned more) enjoyed a 15.5% increase in wages, while those at the 15th percentile saw their wages grow by 9.7%. Of course, it is well to reiterate the caution that this finding says nothing about either who these workers are or the types of households containing them. They could all be affluent teenagers, as far as this data go. Of more relevance, the study also found that "as many as one half" of the state's welfare to work assemblage received a raise when the minimum wage went up.

---

25 William Carrington and Bruce Fallick, "Do Some Workers have Minimum Wage Careers? *Monthly Labor Review* 124 (2001), 17-27. and Heather Boushey, "No Way Out: How Prime-Age Workers get trapped in Minimum Wage Jobs," *WorkingUSA: The Journal of Labor and Society* 8 (2005), 659-670.
26 Jeff Thompson, *Oregon's Increasing Minimum Wage Brings Raises to Former Welfare Recipients and Other Low-Wage Workers Without Job Losses*, Oregon Center for Public Policy, June 1999.

Interestingly, some of the most useful data for Washington comes from a paper designed to attack the state minimum wage.[27] The appendices contain the following information regarding the minimum wage workforce in Washington (some of which was noted above also): 71% are aged 20 or over; 46% work full time; the median family income is $27,203; 54% reside in households with less than $30,000 income; and 39% are the *sole* source of income for the household. The most telling facts among these, perhaps, are the family and household income figures (which it must be stressed say nothing about the size of the household). It is simply not true, at least for Washington, that most minimum wage workers are high school and college students from well-off homes.

New York's profile is even more persuasive.[28] Dividing households up by percentile can be an effective way to look at income shares and who would gain by increases in given income streams. According to the Fiscal Policy Institute, the bottom 40% of New York households receive 15% of the total earnings brought home in the state. An analysis of the proposed 2004 minimum wage hike (to $7.10 per hour) found that 58% of this increase would go to these households. As for the importance of minimum wage workers' wages to family income, in families with children and a minimum wage worker, the worker contributed an average of 55% of total wage earnings. (This is only earnings, it should be noted, not total income.) At the same time, 42% of such families are completely dependent on the minimum wage worker. Additionally, in families with incomes at twice the federal poverty level (not very much income for New York), minimum wage workers bring home an average of 40% of family income.

Michigan data pertaining to its 2006 minimum wage upgrade paint a similar picture.[29] Thirty-eight percent of the state's beneficiaries were full-time workers, a number that made up 7% of the full-time work force. Seventy-five percent were 20 or older, and this was 11% of all workers in this age bracket. Almost a quarter, 23%, are parents. Paralleling New York, among families with both children and a minimum wage worker, 44% are entirely reliant on the earnings of the minimum wage worker.

Texas adds a few more wrinkles and insights, and is particularly important since it contains a larger proportion of minimum wage workers than most states (the third highest, in fact, trailing only New Mexico and Okla-

---

27 David Macpherson, *The Effects of the Proposed 1999-2000 Washington Minimum Wage Increase*, Employment Policies Institute, 1998.
28 Fiscal Policy Institute, *Fiscal Policy Notes*, July 2004.
29 Michigan League for Human Services, *Facts about Michigan's New Minimum Wage*, March 2006.

homa), and because of its size it contributes more than its share to the total national minimum wage work force.[30] Here, 53% of the low-wage work force is Hispanic. Further, more Texans who toil at low wages are older and more work full time than elsewhere, 87.5% being 20 or over and nearly 70% working full time. In addition, nearly 40% are the only source of support for their families. Taken together, these facts indicate that many Texas adults, quite a few of them Hispanic, are working full time at low wages and struggling to support a family. Could it be that this is where many of those adult men working full time we encountered in chapter five are to be found?

The study of Arizona, too, showed a similar breakdown.[31] Among the projected beneficiaries of its new minimum wage, 77% were 20 or older and 42% were Hispanic. Family income averaged $26,323. For all families at less than 150% of the federal poverty level, the minimum wage increase would mean a gain in disposable income (that is, after all taxes, including social security taxes) of 3.5%.

Illinois data resemble that from other states. With a minimum wage increase pending in the legislature, the Center for Urban Economic Development of the University of Illinois at Chicago undertook an analysis of how the law might affect the state's economy.[32] The Center found that two-thirds of those earning between $5.15 and $6.50 (the amount of the suggested increase) were 20 and over and 47% worked full time. Moreover, 30% were married and 32% were the head of a household, while only 25% were students. Any way you put these figures together points to a lot of minimum wage workers helping to support their households, and this is borne out by the analysis of family earnings. The average share of family earnings contributed by an "affected worker" (making between $5.15 and $6.50 per hour) was 48% (the median was 34%). More tellingly, 34% of families received 100% of their earnings from an affected worker.

Finally, perhaps the most direct data comes from a Massachusetts study.[33] The overall profile of Massachusetts' minimum wage earners is not different from that of the other states: 75% aged 20 years and older and about half working full time. What we also have here is some breakdown by income

---

30 Center for Public Policy Priorities, *Getting the Fact Straight: Texas and the Minimum Wage*, February 2005. The Center's study centered on "low-wage" workers, defined as those earning less than $7.50 per hour.

31 Pollin and Wicks-Lim, *Economic Analysis of Arizona Minimum Wage*, 2–3.

32 Ron Baiman, *et al., Raising and Maintaining the Value of the State Minimum Wage: An Economic Impact Study of Illinois* (Chicago: Center for Urban Economic Development, 2003).

33 Massachusetts Budget and Policy Center, *Massachusetts's New Minimum Wage: $8 in 2008*, August 2, 2006.

groups. According to data from the Massachusetts Budget and Policy Center, between 1986 and 1995, while the value of the state minimum wage was shrinking by 13.9%, wages for the lowest 10% of workers declined by 6.1% and for the lowest 20% of workers 4.0%. Then, between 1995 and 2003, as the state minimum wage rose by 31.5%, wages for both these groups of workers rose by 11%.[34] Now this finding, to be sure, does not say anything about the households of these workers. That is, the low wage workers could be mostly from more affluent households. However, given that half work full time and that three-fourths are over 19, this seems highly unlikely. Fortunately, though, we need not speculate. A June 2006 breakdown of the gains that would be made in household incomes by increasing the minimum wage to $8.25 per hour shines a clear spotlight on this question. Of the total change in wages that would result from such a minimum wage hike, 35% would go the lowest quintile and 21% to the next lowest quintile. The top quintile would only realize 11% of the gains, the fourth highest quintile 13%, and the middle quintile 19%. Without question, the minimum wage increase puts most of the money where it is needed most. There are certainly some households in the higher reaches of the income ladder who benefit, most likely by their teens earning a little more. Thus, a state minimum wage does not benefit exclusively those in poverty. However, as with the federal minimum wage and the National Minimum Wage in the United Kingdom, enough of it is targeted at the bottom of the wage distribution to have a measurable impact.

THE POLITICS OF STATE MINIMUM WAGE INCREASES

State minimum wage increases have resulted from two different political processes. In some states, the path has been legislation. In a surprising number of others, though, the increases have come via a referendum. We can learn much about state minimum wage politics by looking, first, at Illinois as an example of a legislature boosting the minimum wage, and then by examining the referenda from 2004 and 2006.

Illinois

Illinois is quintessential Middle America. It contains a large urban area, several mid-size cities, and numerous counties with a heavy agricultural base. It is ethnically diverse, has some strong unions, and possesses a multi-

---

34 Massachusetts Budget and Policy Center, *Facts at a Glance: The Effects of Prior Minimum Wage Increases on Wages, Poverty, and Employment*, November 26, 2004.

faceted economy. Historically, its politics have been mixed, but have leaned slightly conservative most of the time.

Thanks to Luke Shaefer's careful analysis of the steps leading up to the passage of the minimum wage increase in Illinois, we have gained important insight into state minimum wage policy making.[35] As in much legislative policy making, what happened here was hardly "rational" in any sense of the term, and owed much to chance.

Successful Democratic gubernatorial candidate Rod Blagojevich mentioned raising the minimum wage in his 2002 campaign. However, he seems to have regarded it as a low priority item, and did not push it when the legislature convened. The state AFL–CIO decided, though, to make a concerted push for the increase. They were quickly joined by the state chapter of the Association of Community Organizations for Reform Now (ACORN) and the Service Employees International Union (SEIU), two stalwarts in pushing for higher minimum wages. Together, they produced a bill setting the rate at $6.50, omitting a tip credit, and providing for future indexing. The coalition was joined by a familiar array of other reform groups, albeit most with small memberships and resources. Illinois' business lobby, especially the retail section, mobilized to oppose the measure, and enlisted the help of much of the press. According to Shaefer, the ability of the minimum wage advocates to have a research project done by an arm of the University of Illinois at Chicago (the study referenced above) gave them an important supply of ammunition to counter the predictable arguments of the opponents.

Proponents began to lobby members of the state Senate, controlled by Democrats, especially those whose victory margins had been thin. The Senate leadership eventually got a favorable vote on a compromise bill, one removing both the full wage for tipped employees and the COLA. The Speaker of the House, however, now blocked the bill by simply refusing to put it on the calendar. ACORN decided on direct action, and threatened to disrupt a committee hearing. After some disorderly chanting in the committee room, the Speaker announced that he would allow a vote on the bill after all. The bill was stripped down even further during House floor action, directing that the $6.50 wage would take effect in two installments rather than one. It did pass, though, and the governor promptly signed it.

The first lesson to draw from this brief tale is that union support is often critical. Without the unions taking an active part in pushing for the bill, opponents can count on office holders who are only weakly in favor of it

---

35 Luke Shaefer, "State Minimum Wage Laws: Examining the Case of Illinois," *Journal of Poverty* 10 (2006), 67-87.

(which is most of them) to succumb to the temptation of quietly laying it to one side. The second, and closely related, observation is that a campaign promise regarding the minimum wage is not worth much. The issue has too low a salience for most people to make politicians want to put it at the top of their agendas. Finally, minimum wage advocates cannot give up direct protest tactics. They seldom have the political clout to play the inside game alone. As Shaefer says, "after all the compromises were agreed to, it took direct action by organized low-wage workers themselves to move the bill to the front of the agenda."[36]

Referenda

In 2004 and 2006, minimum wage advocates tapped into broad public backing for minimum wage increases and won referenda in several states. In 2004, minimum wage referenda carried the day in Florida and Nevada, despite President Bush winning both states. Then in 2006, wins were scored in Arizona, Colorado, Missouri, Montana, Nevada, and Ohio. (Nevada's measure was a constitutional amendment, which had to be approved at two successive elections.)

TABLE 6-2 STATE REFERENDA IN 2006			
Arizona (Constitutional Amendment)		Montana (Statute)	
Wage rate:	$6.75	Wage rate:	$6.15
Index:	Consumer Price Index	Index:	Consumer Price Index
Tip Credit:	No more than $3.00	Tip Credit:	No tip credit
Vote:	65.4% Yes	Vote:	72.7% Yes
Colorado (Constitutional Amendment)		Nevada (Constitutional Amendment)	
Wage rate:	$6.85	Wage rate:	$6.15
Index:	Consumer Price Index for Colorado	Index:	Consumer Price Index, with 3% maximum
Tip Credit:	No more than $3.02	Tip Credit:	No tip credit
Vote:	53.3% Yes	Vote:	68.7% Yes
Missouri (Statute)		Ohio (Constitutional Amendment)	
Wage rate:	$6.50	Wage rate:	$6.85
Index:	Consumer Price Index for Urban Wage Earners and Clerical Workers	Index:	Consumer Price Index for Urban Wage Earner and Clerical Workers

---

36 Shaefer, "State Minimum Wage Laws," 83.

Tip Credit:	One half of minimum wage	Tip Credit:	One half mini-mum wage
Vote:	76.0% Yes	Vote:	56.2% Yes

Source: *National Conference of State Legislatures and Secretary of State Offices in each state.*

Referenda do not simply appear on the ballot, however. Although state rules vary somewhat, the usual procedure involves, first, drafting a proposal and then securing a certain number of citizen signatures in favor of submitting it to the voters. Of course, once it is on the ballot, the proponents must wage a visible campaign for a yes vote. Sometimes (as when the matter at issue is obscure or technical) this merely means overcoming apathy and ballot fatigue. In cases like the minimum wage, however, where an intense opposition is bound to be launched, proponents must prepare to wage a determined campaign of their own.

Thus, it is necessary for a reasonably well-organized group with at least modest funding to take the lead in, first, drafting the proposal, gathering the required signatures, and filing the necessary documents. Regarding the minimum wage, the normal pattern has been for ACORN to take the lead while simultaneously reaching out to unions and various other reform-oriented groups. Usually, this results in the establishment of an umbrella organization. For example, in Florida, the coalition was called Floridians for All and in Arizona simply the Arizona Minimum Wage Coalition.

Part of the reason ACORN and its allies went the referendum route in so many states was frustration with congressional and state legislative inaction. The Nevada legislature, for instance, rejected a minimum wage increase in 2003 and again in 2005. But another part of the reason was connected to a larger political strategy. The hope was that it would show politicians how popular minimum wage increases, and perhaps by implication other social justice issues, were among the public. At the same time, it was ACORN's belief that allowing people to vote on the minimum wage would increase turnout among the poor and minorities. Conservatives, it was felt, had successfully used this strategy to coax evangelical Christians to the polls by putting anti-gay marriage measures on the ballot in 2004. Both factors, if true, would help more liberal-leaning candidates for Congress and state offices.

How the campaigns began and played out in Florida and Arizona are as typical as any. In Florida, in August of 2004, ACORN build its coalition and sent a staff of forty, sixty canvassers, and over two thousand volunteers out to gather signatures (570,000 were needed and 984,000 were secured).[37] Republicans in the legislature responded by trying to pass a constitutional amendment making it harder to keep the minimum wage increase on the ballot. ACORN managed to check this move by mounting a lobbying campaign of its own among state legislators, including a public rally at the capitol. Once the measure was safely on the ballot, ACORN went to work on a get-out-the-vote campaign and composed several television ads, spending $2 million in the process. Much of this money came from liberal philanthropists, many from out of state. The television spots were needed, they felt, because Florida business interests bought an expensive series of television ads comparing the proposed minimum wage increase to the hurricanes that periodically menace the state. It was, they said repeatedly, a sure destroyer of jobs. The opposition was joined by Governor Jeb Bush and the state Republican Party (whose strength can be measured by the fact that it had control of both houses of the legislature). In the end, though, 72% of Florida's voters opted for the minimum wage hike, and, worthy of note here as elsewhere, it carried in every county.

Arizona, another solidly red state, tells an analogous story.[38] ACORN and its partners began by forming their usual umbrella group, here having the added bonus of persuading a state representative to serve as chair. They drafted the "Raise the Minimum Wage for Working Arizonans Act," which required a constitutional amendment since the state constitution contained a ban on minimum wage legislation. A total of 210,000 signatures were collected, with only 184,000 needed to qualify the measure. Here the unions, especially the SEIU and the United Food and Commercial Workers furnished much of the financial muscle, but they were helped by out-of-state donors as well. The Arizona Restaurant and Hospitality Association, buttressed by contributions from a number of restaurant chains, particularly Outback Steakhouse, spent substantial sums opposing the measure, which they called "cherry pie with dirt filling." An Employment Policies Institute study[39] was produced to claim that job losses would occur, 4,627 in the state as a whole,

---

37 See Peter Dreier, John Atlas, and Kelly Candaele, "Florida Gets it Right: Raising the Minimum Wage," *Commonweal*, June 3, 2005 and John Atlas, "In Red State Florida, Victory for Working People," available at Shelterforce Online, www.nhi.org/online/issues/139.

38 See Becky Pallack, "Prop. 202 would raise Arizona's Minimum Wage to $6.75," *Arizona Daily Star*, October 1, 2006 and Brendan Coyne, "Second Group Looks to Raise Arizona Minimum Wage," *The New Standard*, December 1, 2005.

39 Incidentally, according to the Arizona Secretary of State, the Employment Policies Institute contributed money to the anti-202 campaign.

1,283 in Tucson. As in Florida, though, the measure won overwhelming approval, 65% to 35%, and, as there, carried every county.

The pattern was similar in the other four states: A broad-based coalition led by ACORN and the unions was behind getting the measure on the ballot and then leading the public phase of the struggle; unrelenting opposition by business interests, especially the restaurant industry; substantial to overwhelming public support on election day, varying from 53% approval in Colorado to 76% in Montana. Notably, too, every county in each state voted yes (although it was close in some places, and there was one county in Ohio — Crawford — where the victory was razor thin).

Exit polls were taken in Missouri, Montana, Nevada, and Ohio, providing an interesting glimpse of where support for the measures was strongest. It is vital to recall, though, that even among groups least in favor of higher minimum wages, with only a few exceptions, there is still majority support.

TABLE 6-3 PERCENTAGE VOTING YES IN STATE MINIMUM WAGE REFERENDA 2006				
	Missouri	Montana	Nevada	Ohio
	(State % Yes 76)	(State % Yes 73)	(State % Yes 69)	(State % Yes 56)
Gender				
Male	72	69	63	53
Female	80	79	74	60
Race				
White	73	74	66	52
African-American	95	—	86	82
Latino	—	—	82	—
Age				
18–29	75	77	72	58
30–44	78	71	67	55
45–59	76	75	72	56
60+	75	75	65	58
Income				
Under 15,000	84	86	68	80
30–50,000	77	75	81	60
200,000+	76	—	61	39
Union household				
Yes	84	—	78	63
No	73	—	65	55

Table 6-3 Percentage Voting Yes in State Minimum Wage Referenda 2006				
Education				
No high school	83	81	85	65
H.S. graduate	77	76	77	62
Some college	79	76	68	58
College graduate	69	68	65	50
Post graduate	78	75	65	54
Party identification				
Democrat	93	93	89	76
Republican	58	57	50	33
Independent	79	77	70	60
Religion				
Protestant	73	68	—	60
Catholic	78	79	—	48
Jewish	—	—	—	65
Other	84	82	—	66
None	89	85	—	73
Church atten-dance				
Weekly	71	65	—	51
Occasionally	81	78	—	63
Never	84	82	—	71

Source: *CNN Election Exit Polls. Available at www.cnn.com/ELECTION/2006/pages/results/ballot.measures*

First, gender differences are significant, with women supporting the minimum wage increase more than men in each state.[40] Race is important too, with African-Americans and Latinos far outdistancing whites in their support. Undoubtedly, this is closely tied to the lower incomes experienced by minorities. The age breakdown, on the contrary, is remarkable for its lack of abrupt trends. There was marginally less support among 30- to 44-year-olds in three of the four states, but then in Missouri support topped out among this cohort. In general, though, support was almost uniform across age brackets.

The income pattern is what might be expected, at least in Missouri and Montana. The relatively low support among those in the lowest category in Nevada is rather surprising, although given the size of the state it might be a sampling issue. The most puzzling feature of the income results is the strong opposition evidenced by high income people in Ohio. The vote, of course,

---

40 Comparisons across states would not be valid, since the provisions of the measures varied.

was closer in Ohio, but its high income people were 17 percentage points off the statewide vote, far more than what is found in the other states.

Union households are pronouncedly more in favor of minimum wage increases than their non-union counterparts. However, a clear majority of the latter still support the increases. The educational pattern, since to some degree it so closely parallels income, shows higher support in the lower reaches. It is interesting, though, that in three of the four states, those with postgraduate degrees show higher support than college graduates.

In all three states, the most marked differences are in party identification, Democrats most in favor, independents second, and Republicans last. Only in Ohio, though, did Republican support fall below half, and is also much further from the statewide percentage than in any of the other three states. Their percentage differences (state percentage minus Republican percentage) are 16, 18, and 19, whereas in Ohio it is 23.

In Missouri and Montana, every religious group overwhelmingly marked the "yes" column. Two noteworthy facts stand out, however, about these two states. First, the highest support came from those with no religious affiliation, which was also true for Ohio. This would run counter to those who think religious belief correlates with a greater concern for the poor. Second, support is measurably higher among Catholics in Missouri and Montana than among Protestants. Perhaps this is because the teachings of the Catholic Church emphasize more collective themes than those of Protestantism do. Or, perhaps it is because union membership is higher, at least historically, among Catholics. Then, too, for most of the twentieth century, Catholic income was lower than Protestant income. This meant, in turn, that Democratic sympathies were generally stronger among Catholics than among Protestants. However, Ohio severely complicates the religious puzzle. Why should Catholic support be so low there, falling far behind Protestant levels and eight full percentage points below the state total?

All three states offer a similar (and somewhat disturbing) picture of intensity of religiosity and support for the minimum wage. In every case, the more outwardly devout one is, the less likely he or she is to support minimum wage increases. Part of this picture comes from the fact that the "never" category surely harbors most if not all of the "none" cohort from the religious affiliation question. However, even a comparison between those entering the sanctuaries weekly with the occasional occupants of the pews, presents a cogent contrast. Why, again, this should be so is uncertain, and worthy of a good bit more research.

Indexing

It may well turn out that the hallmark of the 2006 minimum wage referenda will be neither the fact that they passed in relatively conservative states nor the margins by which they secured approval. Instead, it may be the indexing feature. As noted in Table 6-2, in all six, an indexing provision was a central part of the referendum.

Indexing offers four important advantages.[41] First, it is of huge political utility to minimum wage advocates. It means that they do not have to wage episodic battles to have the level of the wage raised, either through legislative action or a referendum. Surely there is a better use of legislative and public time than listening to long-rehearsed arguments. Of course, the fact of indexing does not lead to the legislature and the people losing control of the program, as the law can be altered at any time. But it does shift the burden of having to mount the political initiative to opponents, since the odds in any political struggle always favor the status quo. Perhaps this is an example of "turnabout makes for fair play," in that it is not clear why minimum wage opponents should always enjoy this advantage, as they do now in most places. But there are also good policy reasons for indexing. One, the second advantage, is that it would not compel minimum wage earners to watch their real earnings shrink during the periods between increases. Another is that it would help keep the minimum wage closer to earnings benchmarks, such as the average wage (how close, though, would depend heavily on the index selected). Finally, it would be helpful to many businesses, as they could more readily plan for future costs, thereby creating a more stable business environment.

There are some downsides, the main one being that if the indexing regime is put in place when the wage is at a low level, the move could well harm low-wage workers. It would lock in increases built on a modest base, while simultaneously perhaps making it harder to get the level raised either by legislation or a referendum. Neither politicians nor the public could as easily be persuaded that minimum wage workers were falling behind. The other one is the difficulty of selecting the index. The Consumer Price Index is the most popular choice, and it is probably the most defensible. However,

---

41 For a good discussion of the issues, see Michael Ettlinger, *Securing the Wage Floor*, Economic Policy Institute Briefing Paper, October 2006.

it could lead to minimum wage workers not sharing in productivity gains or losing ground to average incomes.

Nevertheless, these downsides do not outweigh the gains. While on the Supreme Court, Louis Brandeis once wrote "It is one of the happy accidents of the federal system that a single courageous state may, if its citizens choose, serve as a laboratory, and try novel social and economic experiments without risk to the rest of the country."[42] We are now in a period of policy innovation in the states regarding the minimum wage. Indexing is the most important idea currently being incubated there, and, if it proves successful, it may well be that it will emerge as part of the federal program in the future.

Local Minimum Wage Policies

Most of the action at the local level in the last decade and a half has centered on passing so-called "living wage" ordinances, measures which set wages at designated levels for those working for government contractors. These will be taken up in the next chapter. In a few cities, however, activists have managed to secure minimum wages for private sector employees as well.

Technically, Washington, D.C. can be counted as the first city to adopt a general minimum wage. However, the District is usually grouped with the states for minimum wage counting purposes. Excluding the nation's capital, then, as of early 2007 there were three cities with minimum wage policies in place: Santa Fe, New Mexico, San Francisco, California, and Albuquerque, New Mexico.

Ironically, the first two attempts to push mandatory minimum wages into the non-governmentally connected sector failed. This initial push came in Santa Monica, California, when a local coalition calling itself SMART (Santa Monicans Allied for Responsible Tourism), a group with the usual pro-minimum wage profile, worked for three years to get the city council to enact a minimum wage applicable to larger businesses (those grossing over $3 million) in the tourist popular Coastal Zone.[43] Playing on the government benefit theme, their argument was that these firms had profited handsomely from taxpayer funded tourism promotions. In May of 2001, after raising the threshold to $5 million gross, the council passed the measure 5-1. The rejoic-

---

42 *New State Ice Co. v. Liebmann* 285 US 262, 311 (1932). For a critique of this idea, though, see G. Alan Tarr, "Laboratories of Democracy? Brandeis, Federalism, and Scientific Management," *Publius* 31 (2001), 37–46.

43 Copies of newspaper articles relating to the Santa Monica story can be found at the website of the Los Angeles Alliance for a New Economy www.laane.org/pressroom/stories/smart/

ing was short-lived, however, as business interests moved to have the measure put before the voters. After a campaign filled with really questionable tactics — flyers mailed out suggesting prominent Democrats were opposed to the measure who were not in fact opposed and citing unfounded budgetary threats to education and so forth — by opponents (tactics SMART did not take seriously enough until it was too late), the proposal lost 52%-48%. In 2004, the council responded with a more restricted ordinance, applying only to firms with government contracts.

New Orleans' story is somewhat different.[44] Here, after years of work ACORN and other activists managed to put the issue on the ballot in 2002. (The proposal called for the wage to be set at $1.00 above the federal minimum and remain there.) Despite substantial business opposition (and the opposition of ultimately successful mayoral candidate Ray Nagin), the measure passed handily, 63% to 37%. However, opponents turned to the courts, citing a provision of a 1997 Louisiana statute that banned local governments from overturning wage bargains struck in the private sector. The state district court ruled that the city's home rule charter made the state statute void under the state's constitution. The Louisiana Supreme Court, however, overruled the district court and found the city ordinance invalid.

In 2003, a typical umbrella group in Santa Fe, enjoying even stronger than usual backing from the Catholic Church in a city with a substantial Catholic population, convinced the city council by a vote of 7-1 to adopt a general minimum wage law that applies to all firms with 25 or more workers.[45] The level of the wage was initially set at $8.50. Almost immediately, a group calling itself New Mexicans for Free Enterprise filed a suit claiming that only the state could enact minimum wage laws. However, the city won the case.[46]

In San Francisco, ACORN and other groups, but interestingly here with only lukewarm union support (reportedly because they thought the effort futile), collected the needed 26,000 signatures to have a wide-ranging minimum wage, covering all employers in the city, put on the ballot in 2003. A wealthy local businessman, Rob McKay of Taco Bell, provided a significant amount of the funds needed by the coalition, a fortunate turn of events for the activists given the unions' reticence. Although the city's two newspapers

---

44 The best summary of what happened in New Orleans is Oren Levin-Waldman, *The Political Economy of the Living Wage* (Armonk, NY: M.E. Sharpe, 2005), 167-175.

45 See Bobbi Murray, "Minimum Security," *The Nation*, July 12, 2004.

46 *New Mexicans for Free Enterprise v. City of Santa Fe*, No. D-0101-CV-2003-468 (First Judicial District of New Mexico), June 24, 2004.

opposed the measure, the city's business interests did not go all out to defeat it. It won a handy 60% to 40% victory.

Albuquerque adopted its minimum wage, which applies to almost all businesses in the city, by a vote of the city council in 2006.

One complicating factor in analyzing the effects of city minimum wages is political geography. Paul Petersen has argued that a redistributive policy, or in fact any measure perceived as punishing business, will be harder to carry out in a small jurisdiction. Businesses simply have the option of relocating across the line.[47] Thus, in addition to employment, inflation, business bankruptcies, and poverty, some consideration must be given to whether businesses pack up and leave or not.

So far, we have only a handful of studies of city minimum wages. What we do have, though, once again, demonstrates that the gains are significant and that the costs are minimal or non-existent.

San Francisco presents a good research site to analyze a minimum wage's impact, since it is part of a large urban area containing several other municipalities. Thus, a ready comparative control group is at hand. Helpfully, the Institute for Research on Labor and Employment (IRLE) of the University of California conducted such a study of restaurants in the Bay Area.[48]

As for employment, the findings corroborate what we have seen elsewhere. Employment actually grew at a greater clip in San Francisco proper than in the control group. A number of regressions (a procedure which allows researchers to control for various factors such as size of the restaurants and whether or not they are part of a chain) produced the same results: more employment gains in restaurants affected by the minimum wage hike than in the others. While the results were not statistically significant, the fact that they *all* pointed in the same direction is surely indicative. At the very least, it demonstrates, once again, that relatively high minimum wages are compatible with employment growth. Furthermore, these wage gains were accomplished with no cutbacks on critical benefits, such as health insurance.

The data on business closures are equally convincing. Only 3.1% of the restaurant businesses in the affected area (San Francisco) closed, compared to 4.6% throughout other parts of the metropolitan area. In addition, average job tenure and the proportion of full-time workers in restaurants both increased in San Francisco. Having more experienced workers on hand is a

---

47 Paul Petersen, *City Limits* (Chicago: University of Chicago Press, 1981).

48 The full report is Arindrajit Dube, Suresh Naidu, and Michael Reich, *The Economic Impacts of a Citywide Minimum Wage* (Berkeley: University of California, Institute for Research on Labor and Employment, 2006). A more abbreviated form is a January 2006 policy brief from the Institute, *The Economics of Citywide Minimum Wages: The San Francisco Model.*

plus for overall productivity, a fact offering clear benefits to the firm as well as the workers (and the overall economy). Moreover, lower turnover means lower hiring and training costs. There were some price increases, to be sure. Using general industry figures (34% labor cost in a meal and 50% of workers earning the minimum wage), if restaurants passed on 100% of the cost of the 28% minimum wage increase, prices should increase 4.8%. However, overall restaurant prices only increased 2.8%, which was not statistically significant. Limited service restaurants did increase prices 6.2%, which was statistically significant, a fact tied to their heavier use of minimum wage workers. Nonetheless, this is still a net gain for minimum wage workers: a 28% wage hike and a 6.2% price rise in one of the products they might consume.

While the research team did not directly measure the impact on poverty, they did study how pay was affected. They found, first, that the proportion of restaurant workers earning below $8.50 per hour shrunk from 52% to 4%. Further, they found that while average restaurant wages went up 38 cents in the affected area, they rose only 7 cents outside San Francisco. These conclusions, when combined with the shift to full-time work pointed out above, indicate that surely many low-income families gained by the increase.

The only standard economic variable that has been studied in Santa Fe is employment. Two comparisons were made: A before and after comparison for Santa Fe and a matching of particular business sectors with those in Albuquerque (which had not yet passed its minimum wage). The executive summary lays out the findings:

> Overall, employment for businesses in Santa Fe with 25 or more employees was an average of 0.35 employees higher per firm after the living wage than before it. Relative to Albuquerque, these same Santa Fe businesses had an increase of 2.7 employees. The change in specific industries in Santa Fe was not appreciably different from the change in Albuquerque except in the case of construction, for which negative employment changes were consistently found. However, it is difficult to tell whether this loss is due to the living wage ordinance or to falling investment in new buildings. In the accommodation and food services industry, which had the highest portion of its' [sic] workforce earning less than $8.50 before the living wage ordinance (45%), results are actually positive relative to Albuquerque, showing a loss that is an average of 5.5 employees less per firm than in Albuquerque. Overall, this analysis found that the living wage ... had no discernible impact on employment per firm, and that Santa Fe actually did better than Albuquerque in terms of employment changes. [49]

As for the threat of businesses moving away from cities with minimum wages, so far there is no confirmation of that. An IRLE study analyzed re-

---

[49] Nicholas Potter, *Measuring the Employment Impacts of the Living Wage Ordinance in Santa Fe, New Mexico* (Albuquerque: University of New Mexico Bureau of Business and Economic Research, June 30, 2006), 5.

tail establishments in the two cities.[50] For each city, they took the list of the number of stores operated by the country's top 100 retailers before and after the minimum wage went into effect. The results showed gains rather than losses in the number of stores, and while such a finding is merely suggestive rather than conclusive, given the lack of a control group, it is highly suggestive. Large retailers, who have the capacity to relocate, if they so choose, simply do not seem to do so.

CONCLUSION

American federalism presents policy advocates with a number of access points. Foiled at one level, they can turn to another. Even as the Republican majority continued to block minimum wage increases throughout the decade spanning 1997-2007, the hopes for higher minimum wages were not entirely scuttled. State governments proved far more responsive, and minimum wage advocates took full advantage of the opportunity they afforded.

The events surrounding these state policies amplify the political generalizations offered in the first chapter. For it was not low-wage earners themselves who mounted the initiatives on their own behalf. To be sure, ACORN has tried mightily to include low-wage workers in every phase of its operations, and has had a measure of success. Nevertheless, without its relatively well-educated organizers and the contributions from wealthy benefactors, ACORN would be becalmed. As in the Progressive period, getting minimum wage policies on the books depends on the work of middle class activists. And, this demonstrates rather pointedly that political life is not all about pressing one's own self-interest.

From a policy perspective, these state enactments have offered more evidence that minimum wage laws do not have the calamitous effects their opponents have always claimed. On the contrary, they offer reason to think that not only do they help reduce poverty, but that the purely economic effects may be positive as well.

---

50 Arindrajit Dube, *et al., Do Businesses Flee Citywide Minimum Wages: Evidence from San Francisco and Santa Fe*, Policy Brief, September 2006.

Chapter 7. The Living Wage Campaign

The story of contemporary minimum wage policy in Britain and the United States is not complete without an analysis of the living wage campaign.[1] In many ways, it is a part of the push for national minimum wage policies in both countries, as it is decidedly animated by the same general goal, namely the reduction of poverty, and is composed of many of the same organizations that are active in minimum wage politics. However, there are some important differences as well.

First, there is the matter of the specific goal sought, in that a "living wage" is fundamentally different from a "minimum wage." The latter is any legally mandated wage that must be paid by an employer, whereas the former is a wage sufficient to provide a decent living for the affected worker (and perhaps for his or her family, too). Of course, a minimum wage could be set high enough to be a living wage, in which case the two would be synonymous. At the same time, a living wage could be obtained by mechanisms other than legal compulsion, through voluntary action by an employer, for example, or through collective bargaining.

Second, there is the issue of the targets of the campaign. Minimum wage battles have historically been fought at the national level in both countries and at the state level in the United States. Occasionally, as we saw in Santa Fe, San Francisco, and Albuquerque, a local government will enact a general

---

1 On living wage movements in general see Deborah Figart, ed., *Living Wage Movements: Global Perspectives* (London: Routledge, 2004).

minimum wage, but that has been the exception rather than the rule. In contrast, living wage advocates have, so far at least, concentrated their energies more narrowly, focusing on local governments, quasi-governmental entities, and private businesses. In the United States, local governments have been the primary target, with universities receiving some attention.[2] In Britain, more effort has been put into winning wage settlements from private sector firms and the Olympic Delivery Authority, which oversees the financial end of the 2012 Olympics to be held in London. However, a major success was achieved when the Greater London Authority established a Living Wage Unit in 2005.

Third, governmental living wage policies have much more selective coverage than minimum wage laws. They have mostly been restricted to the governmental body itself and to those firms which hold governmental contracts, or in some cases to firms which receive public subsidies, such as incentives provided for economic development.

Finally, the political dynamic is somewhat different on two fronts. First, the smaller scale of local politics and the more restricted scope of activities local governments have on their plates means that if living wage advocates can remain tightly focused and well organized, they have a much better chance of success. Second, living wage advocates have found an especially strong ally in public sector unions. While such unions support national minimum wage policies, they have been an even keener backer of local living wage efforts since the privatization movement has hit public sector unions particularly hard. A living wage policy will help forestall the effects of privatization (in that wages will not be allowed to fall to the "whatever the market will bear" level) when governmental activities are contracted out, and even perhaps allow the unions to recapture some lost ground among already privatized workers.

The living wage campaign has had a string of successes in both countries, but of course it has also suffered some setbacks, and these will be recorded below. However, its most consequential contribution may well have been to keep the plight of those who work at low wages in the public eye. Even when living wage movements fail, the publicity they generate seems to resonate well with the public. Since the modern living wage movement began in the United States, we can consider what has happened there first.

---

2 The State of Maryland was the first to pass a living wage law for an entire state (2007).

THE LIVING WAGE MOVEMENT IN THE UNITED STATES

Although there have been antecedents, the contemporary living wage movement in the United States began in Baltimore in 1994.[3] The incubator of the living wage idea was an organization called Baltimoreans United in Leadership Development (BUILD), a group that traced its lineage to the 1940s and was made up mostly of religious leaders from poor neighborhoods, many of them African-American.[4] Witnessing the continuing deterioration of the local labor market and feeling a sense of unease at city government's revitalization plans for the Inner Harbor area, which they believed would only provide low-wage hotel and restaurant jobs for their constituents, they proposed a "social compact" to guide further development efforts. A part of this master plan would be the requirement that the city and all municipal contractors pay a living wage (then pegged at $7.70). The living wage soon became the main focus of BUILD's campaign, and they joined forces with the American Federation of State, County, and Municipal Employees (AFSCME) to press the issue on the mayor and city council. AFSCME was especially keen to join the campaign in that its members had suffered the brunt of the privatization policies that Baltimore, like many cities, had begun in the 1980s. A living wage ordinance might stymie calls for further privatization as well as allow some of the people working for contractors to recoup a portion of their previous income.

The living wage campaign immediately became entangled in local elections, something to which BUILD was no stranger. Mayor Kurt Schmoke was facing re-election in 1995, and the president of the city council was planning to run also. Schmoke's dilemma was that he had relied heavily on BUILD and its allies in his first campaign and could not alienate them, but also now felt he needed the support of the city's business community. His strategy was to support the social compact and the living wage in principle, but to avoid taking concrete action. Seeking to buy time, he created a commission to study the living wage issue.

---

3 There are several summaries of the American living wage movement. A particularly useful one is Jared Bernstein, "The Living Wage Movement: What Is It, Why Is It, and What's Known About Its Impact?" in Richard Freeman, Joni Hersch, and Lawrence Mishel, eds., *Emerging Labor Market Institutions for the Twenty-First Century* (Chicago: University of Chicago Press, 2005), chap. 3. A more historical view can be found in William Quigley, "Full-Time Workers Should Not be Poor: The Living Wage Movement," *Mississippi Law Journal* 70 (2001), 889-944. On the earlier movements, see Lawrence Glickman, *A Living Wage: American Workers and the Making of a Consumer Society* (Ithaca, NY: Cornell University Press, 1997) and Ellen Matari and Deborah Figart, "Wages and Hours: Historical and Contemporary Linkages," in Figart, ed., *Living Wage Movements*, chap. 3.

4 A summary of the Baltimore campaign can be found in Oren Levin-Waldman, *The Political Economy of the Living Wage: A Study of Four Cities* (Armonk, NY: M.E. Sharpe, 2005), 137-148.

The commission, though, recommended a living wage for city employees and contractors and the city council unanimously endorsed the move (although it only approved a wage of $6.10). Despite making noises about vetoing it, Schmoke ended up signing the measure.

From Baltimore, the living wage movement spread rapidly. As of mid-2007, 140 local governmental entities have adopted living wage ordinances.[5] Although no two living wage campaigns have been identical, there are numerous similarities. One is that ACORN became involved early on. Not only have its local chapters been instrumental in virtually every campaign, but it has also served as an important clearing house for information. It has, for example, published a large manual filled with detailed practical advice on how to organize a campaign, forge alliances, solicit political support, deal with the press, and so on.[6] Second, the campaigns almost always rely most heavily on three constituencies: liberal religious groups and leaders, community organizations, and unions. Each of the three brings something rather different to the campaign: legitimacy, money, affected workers, enthusiasm, political contacts, organizing experience, and so forth. At the same time, each answers to a different call, and there can even be splits within each prong. For example, religious leaders emphasize the moral dimension of economic activity. But they can see this somewhat differently depending on whether they come from traditionally upscale liberal mainline denominations or from churches where the poor occupy the pews. Community organizations usually have several areas of interests other than the living wage, such as housing or health care, and their attention to the cause may waver. Most larger unions have few members who will be affected by the living wage; thus, if their participation is to go beyond a mere formal endorsement, they must have an interest in broader issues of social justice. On the other hand, for unions which see the low paid as potential members, the opportunity afforded to organize will often be paramount. Furthermore, there may well be organizations which will join the living wage coalition chiefly hoping to piggy-back their causes onto it. In short, it can be a powerful but uneasy coalition. Third, normally the campaign will form an umbrella organization, such as Sustainable Milwaukee, the Los Angeles Alliance for a New Economy, or the Western Pennsylvania Living Wage Campaign (Pittsburgh). This can serve several useful purposes, not the least of which is keep-

---

5 ACORN's living wage website provides the latest information.

6 David Reynolds and Jen Kern, *Living Wage Campaigns: An Activist's Guide to Building the Movement for Economic Justice*, Wayne State University Labor Studies Center and ACORN, January 2003.

ing the campaign focused on a single goal. Fourth, it is very often the case that successful living wage coalitions have at least one sympathetic member on the city council. This provides an important conduit to the local political system, and can also serve to keep the idea on the political agenda when it might otherwise fade away. Fifth, winning a living wage campaign is often a slow and arduous business. A year and a half is not uncommon. Thus, the ability to keep the organization together and focused on the eventual outcome is often tested mightily.

The opposition has usually come from the general business community. Sometimes the contractors will be opposed, but in a surprising number of cases they have felt that the ordinances will simply level the playing field. The local Chamber of Commerce, though, will typically sound the alarm of "interfering with the market" and creating an "unfriendly business climate." The most common tactic of the opposition is to mount an advertising and public relations campaign. However, even after a living wage ordinance is adopted, opponents are sometimes not stilled. They can strive to hobble implementation, and have occasionally filed court suits seeking to overturn the measures. These can, at a minimum, delay the ordinance's effective date. A more recent tactic is to have the state legislature, where business interests are normally more powerful, enact a statute prohibiting local living wage ordinances. These have been most successful when it comes to city-wide minimum wage laws, for when local governments act in their contractual capacity they have more flexibility.

Living wage advocates make two central arguments, both of them moral. One is that as the federal minimum wage has shrunk in value, there is a need to tackle wage poverty locally. People who work full time, as William Quigley has put it, simply should not be in poverty.[7] The other is that the public has a right to expect that those who take its money via a contract should not exploit their workers. As Maryland's governor said when signing the state living wage law, "We are going to treat you in a fair and decent way so that you will be able to put food on your family's table for your day of labor on behalf of the people of our state."[8]

Opponents retread some of the same arguments they use against a minimum wage, and then add several others. The retreaded ones are that a living wage will lead to employment losses and firms relocating. Even if these arguments were valid regarding minimum wages, neither of them seems very

---

7 William Quigley, *Ending Poverty as We Know It: Guaranteeing a Right to a Job at a Living Wage* (Philadelphia: Temple University Press, 2003), chap. 1.
8 MSN News report, May 10, 2007.

logical when applied to living wages. When the contract is to perform a specific service, such as cleaning buildings, it is hard to see how much in the way of employment losses would occur.[9] Too, even if a firm moves outside the city, if it is to continue to bid on city contracts, it would still be subject to the living wage proviso. Four arguments with more inherent plausibility do arise, though. One is that it will inevitably lead to higher contract costs, as firms must factor the new wage level into their bids. Thus, the city will be faced with either raising taxes or cutting other services. A related argument is that it will make bidding less competitive, as some firms will elect not to submit bids. This could be because they feel they cannot pay the new wage and make an acceptable profit, or because they fear that workers in the firm doing the same work at other facilities (say private office buildings) will become dissatisfied. A third argument is that it will lead to significant wage redirection. That is, firms will cope by paying their higher-waged personnel less. Thus, there will be gains to low-wage workers at the very bottom of the ladder, but that will be offset by losses to those who are also low-wage but slightly above the prevailing lowest wage. The final argument concerns displacement. If the wage for being a jn

anitor goes up, more qualified people will apply. Employers will naturally prefer the more to the less qualified person, with the end result that those with few skills will suffer job losses. The policy will therefore end up hurting the very people it was designed to help.

As living wage battles have spread across the country, both sides have turned to research and analysis. The pro side can draw on the work not only of ACORN's staff but sympathetic economists and lawyers housed at various institutes. For example, several universities have research arms devoted to labor issues, and some are staffed by experts who favor the living wage. Those at the University of Massachusetts, the University of California at Berkeley, and Florida International University are especially noteworthy in this regard. Further, legal advice can be obtained at the Brennan Center for Justice at New York University Law School. The anti side, always better funded, never lacks for legal talent, since so many lawyers have business connections. But, in addition, the restaurant-funded Employment Policies Institute regularly churns out studies strongly critical of the living wage. Thus,

---

9 It is conceivable that a contractor would force his employees to work harder in the same amount of time and therefore hire fewer workers, but this cannot be pushed very far. If, to take a page from the opponents' book, we assume profit maximization and the entry of new firms into a market when excess profits occur, as the neoclassical model demands, then costs should already be at the lowest possible level. But this is unlikely, which simply illustrates the non-universality of the model.

the battle of ideas regarding the actual effects of living wage laws, something to be discussed below, is not insignificant.

Turning to a few examples, the campaigns in Boston, Los Angeles, and Miami show how diverse the political situation can be. In Boston, ACORN and local unions teamed up with religious leaders to begin their campaign with a small rally on Labor Day 1996.[10] This was to be a prelude to a much larger public rally scheduled for February, at which it was hoped several city council members would endorse the idea. However, the stern opposition of the mayor kept all but one away. Campaigners now began a methodical lobbying effort coupled with an intense public relations drive. Delegations from some combination of ACORN, churches, and unions contacted each council member individually, after careful consideration of what might move him or her, including calling in political chips. Meanwhile, volunteers stood at bus and train stations during rush hour holding signs demanding a living wage. Highly visible rallies were held that attracted important media attention. Petitions were circulated and turned in at city council meetings. When a veto-proof majority of the city council committed themselves, the coalition began bargaining with the mayor. Although he won some minor concessions, he largely capitulated. As a strategic move, the coalition only had the friendly council members introduce the actual ordinance at the last minute.

This last maneuver was calculated to throw the opposition off balance. Although the campaign had lasted over a year, the Chamber of Commerce was slow to take notice, and when it did late in the day it had no specific proposal to attack. However, soon after the measure's passage, business interests launched a vehement counterattack aimed at weakening enforcement. When the dust settled, though, while they had forced living wage advocates to continue the struggle, they had only marginal success.

Los Angeles' living wage movement began in earnest when in 1995 the city publicized plans, largely at the mayor's insistence, to outsource food and other services at the city's airport to non-union contractors.[11] The hotel and restaurant workers union, backed by other local unions, worked to have the city council cancel this move and at the same time pass more union friendly legislation, specifically measures protecting the right to organize. Within

---

10 Boston's case is discussed in Reynolds and Kern, *Living Wage Campaigns*, 12-13.
11 The most thorough coverage of the Los Angeles campaign can be found in Carol Zabin and Isaac Martin, *Living Wage Campaigns in the Economic Policy Arena: Four Case Studies from California*, University of California, Institute of Industrial Relations, 1999. (The other three are San Jose, Oakland, and San Diego.) A briefer version can be found in David Reynolds, "The Living Wage Movement Mushrooms in the United States," in Figart, ed., *Living Wage Movements*, chap. 6.

their proposed package, though, was a living wage ordinance, which they felt would help protect workers even if the non-union policy stood. However, the unions' main interest was organizing.

As the political jockeying began, of critical importance to the Los Angeles campaign was the formation of the umbrella group, Los Angeles Alliance for a New Economy (LAANE). While it contained the usual array of community organizations involved, one of its major backers was Clergy and Laity United for Economic Justice (CLUE). At Christmas over 100 clergy took turns dressing as the ghost of Jacob Marley and went to city hall in chains depicting the mayor's opposition to the living wage ordinance as acting like Scrooge. They went caroling at city restaurants with lyrics written for the living wage campaign. Simultaneously, in a move reminiscent of the Sweated Industries Exhibition in London, community organizations mobilized the low paid to give reporters and public officials tours of their workplaces and to provide stories of injuries that went untreated, crowded housing, and stretched food budgets. In the end, the living wage measure passed handily and the mayor signed it.[12]

Miami's living wage coalition contained very few religious figures, and had to rely almost exclusively on community organizations and unions.[13] Why this was the case is not clear. Nevertheless, the groups involved came together to form the Miami Community Coalition for a Living Wage (CCLW) in 1997. They spent six to nine months gathering information and considering how best to proceed. A few public events followed — a breakfast to announce the launch of the campaign, a couple of meetings, and a rally at the county's headquarters — but all were poorly attended. None of the sponsoring organizations seemed to generate any enthusiasm; in fact, a plan to gather 10,000 signatures of support garnered only 2,000, largely because of the lethargic response of the organizations themselves. However, a few people in the coalition began contacting county commissioners. What they found was surprising. In their initial calculations, CCLW's leaders assumed they would get the support of the four African-American commissioners (of 13), all of whom were Democrats. They had hoped to sway the one Cuban-American Democrat and perhaps the two white Democrats to join them, and then if one of the six Cuban-American Republicans joined in that would be gravy. However, they encountered stiff resistance from two of the African-

---

12 After this victory, the coalition moved to an attempt to secure living wages at local hotels, with some success.

13 Miami's campaign is analyzed in Bruce Nissen, "Living Wage Campaigns from a 'Social Movement' Perspective: The Miami Case," *Labor Studies Journal* 25 (2000), 29-50.

Americans on the commission, a resistance tied to their close alliance with the African-American business community, many of whom were government contractors and feared the ordinance's impact on their enterprises. In contrast, the Cuban-American Republicans were the most receptive to the idea, one even becoming the lead sponsor. Equally puzzling to the living wage coalition, the expected business opposition did not materialize.

In the final month before the ordinance was voted on, the campaign became a bit more high profile, but only marginally so. Living wage T-shirts were ordered by the unions, a few public rallies were held, and phone banks were set up to call supporters. When brought up at a commission meeting, the ordinance passed with little fanfare.

Interestingly, the situation in another Florida setting, Orlando/Orange County, was much more typical.[14] Religious leaders were instrumental in forming the coalition and working in the campaign; business opposition did surface; and a sympathetic candidate for public office won an election and then helped guide the measure's passage.[15]

At a more general level, in 2001 Isaac Martin looked at the cities that had passed living wage ordinances between 1994 and 1999 (22 in all), trying to ascertain what they had in common.[16] His regression analyses pointed to the combined presence of ACORN and high union density. That is, no single factor alone predicted adoption of a living wage ordinance. It was only when strong unions were in place and ACORN was able to till the field that the odds tilted heavily in favor of a living wage. Thus, it is, Martin concluded, a combination of structural features and political acumen and effort that carries the day. However, Margaret Levi, David Olson, and Erich Steinman have cast doubt on this verdict.[17] They point out that the presence of ACORN chapters correlates with city size and that other actors have been important also. Martin's conclusions, in short, may only apply to the early adopters if that, meaning we need several follow-up studies.

---

14 This case is chronicled in Susan Orr, "It's all the Wage: A Qualitative Case Study of the Orange County Living Wage Coalition," Paper presented at the Southern Political Science Association meeting, January 2004.

15 The Orange County Living Wage Coalition had hoped to secure a county-wide living wage; however, it was only able to get an ordinance adopted in the city of Orlando. Orr, "It's all the Wage," 20-21.

16 Isaac Martin, "Dawn of the Living Wage: The Diffusion of a Redistributive Municipal Policy, *Urban Affairs Review* 36 (2001), 470-496.

17 Margaret Levi, David Olson, and Erich Steinman, "Living Wage Campaigns and Laws," *WorkingUSA: The Journal of Labor and Society* 6 (2003), 128-130.

In 2007, Maryland became the first state to enact a statewide living wage law.[18] The measure passed the legislature in 2004 but was vetoed by Republican governor Robert Ehrlich. The movement, led by Progressive Maryland, a typical coalition, did not die, however. Backed by polls showing support running at 67% to 23%, the legislature again passed the bill, this time with the support of new Democratic governor Martin O'Malley. It requires all but the very smallest for-profit contractors to pay wages of $11.30 per hour in the Baltimore-Washington area and $8.50 in other parts of the state. An estimated 50,000 workers stood to be affected by the new law.

Living wage laws and ordinances exhibit a bewildering variety. The level of the wage varies a good bit, and not only in relation to living costs. Plus, there is often a differential if the employer provides certain benefits, most often health insurance. Then, coverage differs on several dimensions. Some ordinances apply only to firms with direct government contracts while others are more expansive, reaching to all firms which receive some kind of subsidy from government. Some ordinances exempt small firms and/or nonprofits. On another front, many have a regular mechanism for updating the wage level, such as indexing it to the CPI, but not all. Finally, the pattern of enforcement, including the penalties for violations, is a patchwork.

In fact, the matter of enforcement has taken on a certain urgency. Stephanie Luce carried on a large-scale research project regarding enforcement, and what she found has to be disturbing both to living wage advocates and those who believe enforcement should follow policy decisions.[19] In many cases, implementation was handed over to an existing agency, one with an already full workload. Then, too, the agency was often one more business than labor oriented (contracting, for example). Luce and her research assistants called each city with a living wage ordinance, and the results are little short of startling.

> Our effort to contact living wage officials in the city of Chicago was typical. We were calling in 2000, two years after Chicago had passed its ordinance. However, the person answering the phone insisted the city had no such ordinance and that we must mean the minimum wage and therefore had to talk to the state Department of Labor.
>
> In most of the calls, the operator transferred us to a department that might possibly know about the ordinance. In a few cases, usually after multiple transfers, we were successful in reaching the responsible department. Sometimes, the multiple transferring was not successful, and we ended up

---

18 See the Washington *Post*, May 9, 2007 and the website of Progressive Maryland.
19 Stephanie Luce, *Fighting for a Living Wage* (Ithaca, NY: Cornell University Press, 2004).

in an infinite loop with no one who could answer basic questions about the living wage.[20]

Even when it was clear which agency was responsible for enforcement, there was seldom one person in charge. With no one directly responsible, and on top of that few or no inspectors, and if there were any they possessed little power, enforcement was anemic at best. This fog of enforcement would be especially daunting to a worker, most likely possessing limited education, who believes he or she was being denied the living wage. In short, living wage advocates' job is not done when the governing authority adopts a living wage, and there are indications they are now taking that seriously.

What of the arguments set out above regarding the actual effects of living wage laws? When they were first being proposed, there were a number of studies projecting what would happen. However interesting, they have now been superseded by studies of what has actually happened. Although there is still much we do not know, some facets of living wage ordinances are becoming clearer.[21]

As for the main objective, reducing poverty, the outcome is a mixed bag. On the one hand, the pay of affected low-wage workers has certainly risen, and the vast majority of those people seem to come from low-income households. Inferences from a Los Angeles study are one source of this conclusion.[22] A survey was done of 320 workers subject to that city's living wage, chosen at random. Among these people, 96% were 20 and over, with 58% 35 and over, 71% had only a high school diploma or less education, and the average worker had been in the work force almost 20 years. Since the survey contained no questions about household income, from this and other demographic data, a panel of researchers examined a set of similar workers drawn from the Current Population Survey. A full 69% of these citizens were living on a budget that did not meet basic needs.[23] The validity of these conclusions is buttressed by a study done in Boston.[24] There, 54% of the affected workers were found to reside in households that did not earn enough to rise to the basic needs level. However, on the other hand, the limited applicability

---

20 Luce, *Fighting for a Living Wage*, 79.

21 The various studies are ably summarized in Jeff Thompson and Jeff Chapman, *The Economic Impact of Local Living Wages*, Economic Policy Institute Briefing Paper, February 2006.

22 David Farris, *et al.*, *The Los Angeles Living Wage Ordinance: Effects on Workers and Employers*, Los Angeles Alliance for a New Economy, 2005.

23 A basic needs budget is somewhat above the poverty level, but still very low. See Farris, *et al.*, *Los Angeles Living Wage Ordinance*.

24 Mark Brenner and Stephanie Luce, *Living Wage Laws in Practice: The Boston, New Haven and Hartford Experiences*, University of Massachusetts Political Economy Research Institute, 2005.

of living wage ordinances severely restricts their impact on overall poverty. A few workers gain, to be sure, but the vast majority of those who are poor remain untouched.

What about depressed employment levels, business relocation, soaring contract costs, less competitive bidding, wage revamping, and displacement? Thompson and Chapman summarize the employment studies as follows:

> In attempting to answer the question of whether or not living wage ordinances have a significant impact on employment, different research-ers have used a variety of approaches, ranging from qualitative interviews with service contractors and affected workers, to detailed before-and-after analysis of impacted firms, to econometric analyses of readily available la-bor market data. Most of the available studies have concluded that there have been either no or only small employment losses as a result of adopting living wages.[25]

For example, Michael Reich and his associates found that despite a 1% decline in overall employment in the San Francisco area and a 9% drop in airport utilization between 1998 and 2001, employment actually rose by 15% at the airport, the focus of the San Francisco living wage ordinance.[26] Several studies by Scott Adams and David Neumark claimed to find pronounced un-employment effects, but the methodology they employed has been subjected to serious question.[27] Moreover, the Adams and Neumark studies are alone in finding any appreciable unemployment effects.

Since living wage policies apply regardless of a firm's headquarters, the relocation argument is hardly applicable. What of contract costs and bid-ding, though?

Even living wage advocates acknowledged that the cost of contracts was likely to rise, but they generally vastly overestimated the expected increases. For example, projections in Berkeley put the increased costs at $479,000, but the actual figure was less than half that. In Los Angeles, the city anticipated $30 to $40 million in increased costs but experienced a boost of only $2.5 million. An Economic Policy Institute study of Baltimore found that contract

25 Thompson and Chapman, *Economic Impact*, 9.

26 Michael Reich, Peter Hall, and Ken Jacobs, "Living Wage Policies at the San Francisco Airport: Impacts on Workers and Businesses," *Industrial Relations* 44 (2005), 106-138.

27 See Scott Adams and David Neumark, *A Decade of Living Wages: What Have We Learned?* Public Policy Institute of California, 2005 for a summary of their work and Mark Brenner, Jeannette Wicks-Lim, and Robert Pollin, *Measuring the Impact of Living Wage Laws: A Critical Appraisal of David Neumark's How Living Wage Laws Affect Low-Wage Workers and Low-Income Families*, University of Massachusetts Political Economy Research Institute, 2002 for a critique of the methods. See also Timothy Bartik, "Thinking about Local Living Wage Requirements," *Urban Affairs Review*, 40 (2005), 269-299.

costs rose just 1.2%, less than the inflation rate.[28] Andrew Elmore conducted a survey of administrators responsible for living wage ordinances and found only modest overall increases (constituting only about 0.1% of city budgets), but of course in those areas of high unit labor costs (cleaners and security guards, for example), the increases were higher.[29] One of the reasons for the lower than expected costs seems to be higher worker morale and decreased employee turnover. A higher wage, so it seems to some economists, induces greater employee effort. This is naturally hard to gauge, but turnover rates are measurable. Since turnover increases costs, when the rate goes down, so do costs. Another reason could be that, pace the Webbs, businesses are simply becoming more efficient.

There is also no evidence for a decline in the number of firms submitting bids. The Baltimore, Los Angeles, and New England studies cited earlier all found the number of bids either remaining steady, or even going up. One manager of a firm bidding for the Baltimore bus contract said "We feel more able to compete against businesses that were drastically reducing wages in order to put in a low bid." In a similar vein, a security firm in Hartford, Connecticut (where the number of bids increased) told researchers that "Most companies with any business sense would concentrate on a higher wage niche, because there is more stability involved, and it gives you better control of the business, and allows you to preserve your reputation."[30]

When it comes to wage redirection and displacement, the evidence again seems to support living wage advocates. Brenner's study of Boston found that the percentage of workers making under $9.75 indeed declined at the affected firms, but that the number earning above $11.75 did not. Similar trends were found by Reich and his colleagues in their analysis of the San Francisco airport. The number of workers making under $10 fell, but the number making over $14 actually went up. The same two studies also found no change in hiring practices after the introduction of the living wages. They did find an increased effort devoted to training, something that has to be good for everyone.

28 Christopher Neidt, *et al., The Effects of the Living Wage in Baltimore*, Economic Policy Institute, 1999.

29 Andrew Elmore, *Living Wage Laws and Communities: Smarter Economic Development, Lower than Expected Costs*, Brennan Center for Justice, 2003.

30 The quotes are from Mark Weisbrot and Michelle Sforza-Roderick, *Baltimore's Living Wage Law: An Analysis of the Fiscal and Economic Costs*, Preamble Center for Public Policy and Brenner and Luce, *Living Wage Laws in Practice*, and are reprinted in Thompson and Chapman, *Economic Impact*, 7.

In addition to the campaigns aimed at local governments, living wage efforts have also sprung up on many college and university campuses across the country, including such high profile institutions as Harvard, George-town, Vanderbilt, Stanford, and the University of Virginia. The main target has been services that colleges and universities often contract out.[31] Almost all of these campaigns, many of which have been successful, have been stu-dent led, and have included hunger strikes and sit-ins.

Without question, the living wage movement in the United States has to be put down as a success. From a local struggle in one city, it has spread nationwide. It has spawned new organizations and given a renewed purpose to others. It has brought together new coalitions and developed a network of activists. And, it has unquestionably raised the wages of many low income workers and their families. But perhaps most importantly it has helped keep the issue of low wages and poverty before the public, and has been more than a little responsible for the hotbed of state action on the minimum wage front in the last few years.

However, the movement faces two serious dilemmas. The first is that no matter how successful local living wage ordinances and university policies are, they affect only a miniscule number of workers. Unless there is a seri-ous horizontal spillover effect to the local labor market, something for which there is no evidence, the wages of most workers will not rise because of living wage ordinances. For this to occur, more general minimum wage laws must win approval. But these measures trigger even more intense opposition than living wage laws, and few living wage movements have the resources to fight such a battle. Furthermore, opposition may sometimes develop among the movement's natural allies, as happened in Chicago. There, a proposed living wage ordinance that would reach big box retailers led several civil rights and other minority community leaders into opposition when Wal-Mart and other chains threatened to open new stores only in the suburbs.[32] From this perspective, state and federal policies are preferable. However, living wage coalitions have difficulty swimming in that arena. The political tools they have to work with are simply less effective there. Success can be achieved, but it is much more problematical.

Second, the living wage has benefited enormously from the way it has framed the issue. Paying people who work hard a fair wage resonates well

31 See Ben Gose, "The Companies that Colleges Keep," *Chronicle of Higher Education*, January 28, 2005.
32 *New York Times*, July 27, 2006. The measure passed the city council 35-14, but Mayor Daley vetoed it. *New York Times*, September 14, 2006.

with American values.[33] Many living wage advocates, however, view the living wage campaign in much broader terms, as the opening salvo in a sweeping campaign to secure economic justice. David Reynolds and Jen Kern, for example, write in ACORN's manual "The actual passage of a living wage law becomes one step in the long-range effort to lay the foundation for a broad social movement around economic democracy" and later that "Historians may very well look back on this up-swell as having laid some of the seeds of the great economic democracy movement of the twenty-first century."[34] However, there is no evidence whatever that the American public would support a march toward the vision of economic democracy. To the extent, then, that the living wage movement seeks to broaden its goals, it risks losing its greatest strength, the overwhelming backing of the public.

THE LIVING WAGE MOVEMENT IN GREAT BRITAIN

The living wage movement in the United Kingdom began in late 2000 when a group of leaders from The East London Communities Organization (TELCO) met to discuss the continuing problems of poverty in East London.[35] They were well aware of the burgeoning living wage campaign in the United States, and finally decided this would be the best place to begin. From that time on, TELCO's signature effort has been its living wage campaign. Its mission statement underlines this commitment:

> Our vision is of a city and country where everyone in work is paid enough to provide adequately for themselves and their family. The Living Wage Campaign aims to make poverty wages history.

Headquartered in a nondescript building in East London, TELCO has a cadre of middle class leaders and organizers; however, it also includes many of the people who live in East London.[36] Much of its success comes from the fact that while it is driven by ideals, it has also been decidedly practical and remarkably patient. Without question, this is a tribute to its dedicated leadership team.

---

33 On the framing of the living wage, see Shehzad Nadeem, "The Living Wage Movement and the Economics of Morality: Frames, Ideology, and the Discursive Field," *Research in Social Movements, Conflicts, and Change* 28 (2008), forthcoming.

34 Reynolds and Kern, *Living Wage Campaigns*, 23 and 91.

35 General information on TELCO and its campaign can be found in Jane Wills, "Organizing the Low Paid: East London's Living Wage Campaign as a Vehicle for Change," in Geraldine Healy, *et al.*, eds., *The Future of Worker Representation* (London; Palgrave, 2004), chap. 13, especially 272-279.

36 TELCO has spun off several other organizations in other parts of London and is affiliated with the Citizens Organizing Foundation. For convenience, I will simply use TELCO to refer to efforts by all these groups.

Two other notes are pertinent. First, since local governments in Britain have not historically had the range of powers possessed by their counterparts in the United States, TELCO began by focusing on the private sector. However, when devolution handed increased power, and a locally elected mayor, to London, they turned their attention to that arena as well. Second, many of the residents of East London are cleaners, and many are recent immigrants to the United Kingdom.[37]

TELCO has employed a wide variety of strategies, and integrated them quite skillfully. First, it has forged important alliances with other bodies. The most significant of these have been with the geography department of Queen Mary's University in London and UNISON. The former has provided important research help, while the latter has provided research, financial help, and organizers. Research, in fact, was the first thrust of the organization, and has remained important. In early 2001 UNISON asked the Family Budget Unit to establish a series of basic family budgets for London. Later in 2001, the study *Mapping Low Pay in East London* was published, demonstrating how inadequate the NMW was for many workers in the city.[38] The report was then used as the centerpiece for a conference held at Queen Mary University. As a result of these efforts, TELCO has always had hard data with which to make its case.

Organizing the low paid has also been a priority. In some cases, this has been done with the goal of helping the workers join unions. However, TELCO has also arranged its own public assemblies and marches at critical points, and has been rather successful in mobilizing the low paid for these events. For example, it organized a "Workers' Mass" at Westminster Cathedral (the Roman Catholic cathedral for London) on May 1, 2006, preceded by a diverse procession of people from around London.

At the same time, it has used some innovative publicity strategies, such as the appearance at the Annual General Meeting (AGM) of HSBC bank discussed below. In both the case of its marches and its publicity "stunts," it has been keenly aware of press coverage, and been able to utilize this to full advantage.

Finally, it has endeavored to work directly with firms. It has frequently sought to meet face-to-face with employers to put the case for increasing

---

37 A good summary of the plight of London's cleaners can be found in the BBC news story by Dominic Casciani, "The Secret Life of the Office Cleaner," September 19, 2005. A more scholarly analysis is contained in Jane Wills, "A Global Workforce in a Global City: The Skills, Experiences and Aspirations of a Group of Contract Cleaners in London, UK," Working Paper No. Three of the ERSC Identities Programme, April 2007.

38 Jane Wills, *Mapping Low Pay in East London*, Queen Mary University, September 2001.

the pay of their cleaners and other low-paid staff. Further, it has recently awarded firms the designation "Living Wage Employer" in an effort to offer them positive publicity.

Canary Wharf in East London was long an area of dilapidated warehouses. In the late 1990s, though, it was "redeveloped" into upscale office complexes for financial services firms. As a result, HSBC bank decided to move its world headquarters there. In early September 2001, TELCO sent a letter to the bank's chair, Sir John Bond, asking to meet with him and requesting that he include a living wage provision in the contracts the bank handed out to firms that cleaned its offices. A rather sharp rebuff was returned, refusing a meeting and saying that it would not "be in order for us to impose a higher minimum wage on our suppliers in East London than is required by statute."[39] In December, TELCO members briefly occupied a branch of the bank in Oxford Street to protest the letter.[40] But the greatest ploy came at the AGM of the bank's shareholders in May 2002. Having purchased a few shares, TELCO showed up at the meeting with the man who cleaned Bond's office and had him request a meeting. The press, having been notified, duly reported the confrontation. Bond later met with a delegation from TELCO, but still rejected their living wage request. Publicity did not stop, though. The singer Billy Bragg held a concert to support the workers, and a TELCO-sponsored demonstration took place outside the 2003 AGM, stressing the fact that the bank had just hired a new director who was to earn £35 million. Both events generated a good bit of favorable media coverage.

Meanwhile, TELCO began meeting with officials from Barclays Bank, another tenant of Canary Wharf. In February 2004, Barclays agreed to require its subcontract cleaning firms to pay £6.00 per hour (and include extra, although still very modest, benefits). Two weeks before their 2004 AGM, HSBC announced a similar package for its cleaners. In a significant development, the Transport and General Workers Union (TGWU) dispatched two organizers to begin work in the Canary Wharf area.

Subsequent developments demonstrate both the fragility of such agreements and the fact that persistence can pay off. Both Barclays and HSBC began to backslide not long after their 2004 announcements. It took strikes by cleaners and negotiations with several other financial firms before the living wage became a more or less permanent part of the Canary Wharf scene

---

39 Letter from Sir John Bond to Father Michael Copps of TELCO, September 26, 2001. (Included in TELCO press pack.)

40 News stories on the events recorded in the next few pages can be found in the quality press the following day. To avoid unnecessary footnotes, unless needed for some specific purpose I will not give the detailed citations.

in 2007. The public shame had largely worked. In the end, Barclays issued a self-congratulatory press release, hailing the policy as one that "ensures that all of our staff in Greater London will earn more than the recommended London Living Wage [only 30p more per hour actually]. Although these employees are not directly employed by Barclays we have a responsibility to ensure that they receive a fair, well-rounded remuneration package, and this deal delivers that."[41] For HSBC's action Sir John Bond received a "Living Wage Employer" designation from TELCO in November 2006. In short, trying for co-operation but keeping the pressure up, and doing so patiently, had paid off.

Another arena in which TELCO took up the cause of cleaners working for subcontractors was East London's hospitals.[42] Pushing privatization in the National Health Service (NHS) was a hallmark of the Thatcher government. While workers employed when the policy went into effect had to be paid at their previous level, new employees were subject to no such stipulation.[43] As a result, in time wages were pressed downward with a vengeance. Morale, and by general agreement efficiency as well, fell. Most workers kept their membership in UNISON, but the union could not do much to affect the bidding and tendering process set up by the Conservative government. In 2001 TELCO began working with the union's local branches. A living wage campaign, with all its attendant publicity, was organized. At one point, a strike was even undertaken at one hospital. By June of 2003 agreements had been reached to put subcontracted staff in several hospitals on a pay and benefits parity with NHS employees, while in others the workers were moved back onto the direct NHS payroll.

A significant milestone for the living wage movement occurred during the 2004 campaign for London's mayorship. Ken Livingstone, the eventual successful candidate, promised to establish a Living Wage Unit within the city's government.[44] Its role would be twofold: 1) to ascertain what a reasonable living wage was for inhabitants of the capital and 2) to implement this wage for all city contractors.[45]

---

41 Barclays Bank, Press Release, June 18, 2007.

42 See Jane Wills, "Subcontracting, Labour, and Trade Union Organization: Lessons from Homerton Hospital and the London Living Wage Campaign," Working Paper No. Two of the ESRC Identities Programme, November 2006 for information on the situation in East London hospitals.

43 This was part of the Transfer of Undertakings Protection of Employment (TUPE) regulations, which were adopted to conform to EU policy.

44 The promise was made at a TELCO-sponsored event.

45 It may be well to recall from chapter 2 that Parliament had passed a Fair Wages Resolution affecting national government contractors while encouraging local governments to follow

Set up immediately after the election, the Unit has issued a report each spring. Its first report, in 2005, was limited to setting a living wage for London and profiling the low-wage work force.[46] The Unit's researchers elaborated two ways to calculate a living wage, what they called the "Basic Living Costs" approach and the "Income Distribution" approach. For the former, they constructed a number of basic budgets for four different family types. Taking into account various state benefits and possible work patterns, and weighting the results by the profile of London's low-wage work force, they came up with a figure of £5.70 per hour. For the latter, the starting point is the median household income calculated in the UK by the Department of Work and Pensions for a couple with no children.[47] An "equivalization" process can then convert this figure into medians appropriate for other family types. Using 60% of the median (the usual measuring rod for poverty in Europe) as the benchmark, and applying the same benefits and weighting formulas as before, the Unit arrived at a figure of £5.90 per hour. Averaging the results of these two exercises provided a poverty threshold wage of £5.80. To convert this to a living wage, though, requires some type of adjustment. The Unit selected a 15% cushion, and raised the wage accordingly to £6.70.

From the Labour Force Survey, they found that 85% of people working full time in London earn above that. Of the remaining 15%, 9% fell below even the poverty threshold. Part-time workers were less fortunate. Around half made more than the living wage; fourteen percent were between the poverty threshold wage and the living wage, though, and a full 35% fell below the poverty wage. Taken together, then, about one in seven employees in London took home less than the poverty wage, and one in five less than the living wage.[48]

Soon after the publication of the 2005 report, the GLA began implementing the living wage in its own procurement activities. In addition to the GLA

---

suit even before it adopted the Trade Boards Act. Mrs. Thatcher's Government had repealed that statute in 1983 (a move which also required renouncing a provision of the International Labor Organization Convention to which Britain had long been a signatory). Further, the Local Government Act 1988 banned local governments from using any "non-commercial considerations" in awarding contracts. Some of the more draconian portions of this act were repealed in 2001. Then, in 2003 Parliament put a new albeit weaker Fair Wages Resolution on the books. See Damian Grimshaw, "Living Wage and Low Pay Campaigns in Britain," in Figart, ed., *Living Wage Movements*, 112-115.

46 These reports are entitled *A Fairer London: The Living Wage in London*, and are available at the Greater London Authority's website.

47 Recall that median income is always lower than mean income because of the presence of a few very high earners. Hence, this figure is already lower than a mathematical "average."

48 This may be slightly misleading in that it does not take account of multiple job holding, but the general picture is clear.

itself, the mayor's writ runs to Transport for London and the London Development Authority, and these entities were also to make sure that their contractors paid living wages. For all GLA units, the living wage requirement was wrapped in a Sustainable Procurement Policy, which contained a number of laudable but vague strictures ("promoting workforce welfare," for example, and "community benefits"). However, it seemed clear that the living wage was the centerpiece of the new procurement policy.

The 2006 report made some minor adjustments in how the calculations were made[49] and updated the figures. The Basic Living Cost wage came in this time at £6.00 per hour and the Income Distribution wage at £6.30, with the difference split as usual at £6.15. The 15% adjustment brought the living wage to £7.05. The new Annual Population Survey was utilized to analyze the prevalence of low pay in London, but the results were broadly similar to those of 2005: 12% of full-time workers made less than the poverty wage while 6% earned something somewhere between the poverty wage and the living wage; 33% of part-time employees made less than the poverty threshold wage with 13% of them receiving a wage between the two levels.

The 2007 report was noteworthy for several reasons, in addition to the annual updating of the wage, now set at £7.20 per hour. First, it reported on the progress of implementing the living wage across the entities tethered to the GLA. Second, it noted that the living wage as set by the Unit was fast becoming a standard used in the London labor market. Employers in a variety of sectors of the economy were starting to use it as the base line for wages (as in the Barclays announcement quoted above). This may well be one of the most important contributions made by the Unit, as it reaches far beyond firms whose main business involves contracting with government. Finally, it mentioned that the Olympic Delivery Authority "has confirmed its support for the London Living Wage for contracts carried out within London's boundaries, that it will encourage its contractors to pay fair wages and that it will monitor implementation" (p. 20). This leads us to the next theater of TELCO's living wage campaign.

When London began preparing to bid for the 2012 Olympics, with much of the venue slated to be in or near East London, TELCO requested and was granted a consultation. Its hope was to have a living wage policy for both the construction and operational phases of the games included. This was granted, and some believe it may well have helped London win the Olympics. In November 2006, though, the Olympic Delivery Authority (ODA), the body

---

49 For example, the methods for computing child care and transport costs were refined.

charged with operating the games, seemed to back off this commitment. (During this period, cost estimates were rising, but it is not clear whether or not this was linked to the dampening of ODA's commitment to the living wage.) In response, TELCO mounted a protest demonstration at a £1,000-a-head event celebrating the games. More meetings followed. On February 15, 2007, the ODA chief executive issued a statement saying:

> We cannot make the London Living Wage a blanket condition. However, for those tenders within London's boundary, we will make it clear that we support the London Living Wage. . . . We now have a mutual understanding with London Citizens [TELCO's parent organization] and will continue to work with them and other key organizations to ensure the Games deliver a lasting economic legacy for east London.[50]

On March 7, 2007, the Procurement Policy was published. The relevant statement read as follows:

> The ODA will make it clear in invitations to tender for ODA contacts that it wants to see contractors adopting the best employment practices including . . . sufficient wage levels. For those tenders within London's boundary, the ODA will make it clear that it fully supports the London Living Wage.

> The ODA is required by Government to demonstrate value for money in all its contracting and has to consider how to achieve its overall objectives on a case by case basis, as it lets each contract. The ODA will ask its contractors if they would be prepared to adopt fair employment measures including the London Living Wage for any work they are doing as part of an ODA contract. These issues will be taken into account when the ODA advertise contracts and considers tenders. They form part of the overall value for money judgment which the ODA must make.[51]

Perhaps the most important part of this passage is the addition of the word "fully" to the earlier statement. Nevertheless, how sternly the ODA will "ask", how much the living wage will be "taken into account" when contracts are awarded and, just as importantly, how much follow-up there will be remains to be seen.

This entire episode demonstrates once again both the power and the limitations of the living wage movement. When narrowly focused, it can win important agreements. Without however a high degree of diligence, there is a perpetual danger that the commitment will slide to the sidelines. Protest demonstrations, and the public sympathy they generate, are the best tool to keep the agreement intact. At the same time, though, it takes diligent attention to detail and an unwavering commitment to follow through.

---

50 ODA Press Release, February 15, 2007.
51 ODA Procurement Policy, Executive Summary, 7.

Two other victories for cleaners involved government itself. The TGWU set about organizing the cleaners in the House of Commons, who were paid less than the London living wage.[52] After two one-day strikes in 2005, the cleaners won the then London living wage of £6.70 per hour (and increased benefits). The other case involved cleaners in London's fire stations, which are governed by the London Fire and Emergency Planning Authority (an entity outside the GLA). A proposal to grant the cleaners the London living wage was put to the Authority's Finance Committee, but it resulted in a tie vote. Accordingly, the entire Authority had to take up the measure. Most Labor leaders, including the Prime Minister, weighed in on the side of the cleaners. Even though a Conservative member of the Authority called paying the London living wage to cleaners "just ridiculous," the vote was 9-8 in favor.

Finally, the living wage movement has spread to campuses in the United Kingdom. Queen Mary University in London became the first living wage campus in the UK in November 2006. The London School of Economics soon followed QMUL's lead, and campaigns sprung up at Oxford and Cambridge, as well as other universities.

In sum, the living wage movement in Britain has been remarkably successful, especially considering the meager base on which it began. It has won significant victories, and continues to spread. Not only are there increased activities on campuses, but TELCO-like organizations are taking root in other cities in the United Kingdom. The annual publication of the GLA's figures is now a major event and elicits widespread public attention. Trade unions have stepped up their efforts, as not only UNISON but also the TGWU and the TUC itself have devoted considerable energy and resources to the campaign.

However, it is important to stress that few if any of the victories would have been possible without broad public support. That support may be passive, but it is real nonetheless. When Sir John Bond's cleaner confronted him at the HSBC's AGM, it was only embarrassing because of the negative publicity it generated for the bank. And that publicity was only negative because the British public by and large cares about the low paid. Likewise, when TELCO demonstrated outside the ODA's gala event, it was only effective because the public was on their side. Without this public support, the living wage movement would simply evaporate.

---

52 Cleaning services for the House of Commons were contracted out, while the House of Lords kept cleaning services in house.

CONCLUSION

The living wage movement is, in sum, a vital component of the contemporary minimum wage narrative. It has not only cultivated a new cadre of activists, brought new coalitions into existence, and kept the issue of low wage poverty before the public. It has also served as a constant reminder that the ultimate goal is to make the minimum wage a living wage.

CHAPTER 8. CONCLUSION

Minimum wage policy seems to be on a more set and stable course in Britain than in the United States. The NMW has to be deemed a success, on both the policy and the political dimensions. It has not only provided real benefits to a significant number of people with few if any negative consequences, but it has also won wide acclaim from the public. Further, even if they are not entirely won over, those who opposed it as though it would be a breach of the barricades have at least become more circumspect. In the United States, the federal minimum wage remains enormously popular, but its politics is as fragmented as ever. Opponents there continue to be as unbending as they were in 1938 and its supporters, not having a coherent vision or rationale for raising it, are always on the verge of stumbling. The almost pathetic deal to attach it to a military spending bill in 2007 is the ultimate example. Nevertheless, the groundswell of support for recent state minimum wage increases and the living wage movement is evidence that the American public sees the issue rather clearly.

Yet, while the efforts of activists, the stances of interest groups, and the actions of political figures are what governs minimum wage policy in the short run, it is the ideas of welfare state theorists that are most important in the long run, for it is their writings that will provide the intellectual frameworks within which future policy is debated. Whether or not they elevate the minimum wage to a central place in their prototypes for the ideal welfare state will determine its future more than any other factor.

CONTEMPORARY MINIMUM WAGE POLICY IN GREAT BRITAIN

By any reasonable evaluative criteria, the NMW has been one of the major successes of British social policy. For starters, it has raised the incomes of the less well off. To be sure, the gains have been modest, but any gain is better than what would surely have occurred in the absence of the minimum wage. In short, more people in Britain have a little more discretionary income than they otherwise would have had. Further, because of the wage compression engendered by the NMW, there has been a slight amelioration of income inequalities. But perhaps most of all it has given many British citizens a renewed sense of dignity. That alone would make the policy worthwhile.

All this has been accomplished, to boot, with no known negative effects, no "tradeoffs" in the language of policy analysis. Repeated studies have failed to turn up any evidence of disemployment effects, the most oft-repeated attack on minimum wages. Employment levels actually rose following the introduction of the minimum wage, and even the recent rise in the level of unemployment is, objective observers point out, attributable to increased supply factors, not the minimum wage. At the most, price increases have been quite modest and easily manageable. Moreover, the health of businesses overall and especially of those firms operating in the low-paid sectors is as robust as ever.

In addition to being a policy success, the minimum wage has been a political success. As Mr. Blair was preparing to leave office, the public was asked "Which three of the following would you judge to have been the greatest successes of Tony Blair's time as prime minister?"[1] Introducing the minimum wage stood way out in front, winning the nod of 54%. Bringing peace to Northern Ireland, at 42%, and providing steady economic growth with low inflation, at 36%, were next, with all other accomplishments scoring only 13% or below. When the final histories of the Blair Government are written, the minimum wage will undoubtedly be given quite a few pages.

Another positive political feature of the NMW is the way its pattern for future policy development is structured. By creating the Low Pay Commission and arranging its operation the way it did, the Blair Government avoided having the minimum wage become captive to the parliamentary timetable. Had they simply put the NMW on the books and left future increases up to parliamentary legislation, they would have created the very situation that exists in the United States. When the party friendly to the minimum wage is in power there is the danger that other pressing matters will allow it to be

---

1 YouGov Poll, May 2, 2007. Nine items were listed.

pushed to the periphery; when the party hostile to the minimum wage is in power, they can ignore it entirely. In contrast, having the Low Pay Commission's schedule demand a charge from the Government and then requiring that the Government respond publicly insures that the minimum wage cannot be put out of mind. There is no guarantee that the recommendations of the Low Pay Commission will be adopted, as the recurring story of the status of 21-year-olds shows; however, the design does at least place the minimum wage perpetually on the agenda.

Moreover, bringing the deliberations regarding minimum wage increases inside government has largely defanged business opposition. To some degree, this has to flow from the mountain of high quality studies commissioned by the Low Pay Commission and the results of its own inquiries. It is simply harder to mount any kind of convincing case that the minimum wage is causing harm to the economy. Thus, business submissions to the LPC concentrate on the scale of the increase, not whether there should be one. The CBI, for example, has endorsed the indexing of future minimum wage increases to the inflation rate, rather than take a chance on their being pushed up faster than the rise in median wages. This is a far cry from British business's position as the NMW was under consideration, and from the approach taken by their American counterparts.

Given the high public approval enjoyed by the NMW and its acceptance by the business community, the Conservative party has also shifted its stance. In February of 2000, then Shadow Chancellor Michael Portillo announced that the party was officially ending its opposition to the minimum wage, although it remained "concerned at the costs for business."[2] In February of 2005, the party announced that if it won that spring's election, it would implement the LPC's recommended increase. Then in December 2005, David Cameron, the party's new leader, said "I think the minimum wage was been a success, yes. It turned out much better than many people expected." This is hardly a ringing endorsement, but it does signal that an outright repeal is very unlikely.[3]

---

2 This and the following quotations are from articles in the quality press or websites.

3 It may be that Labor will, for a while at least, gleefully point out earlier Conservative statements. In 2001, for example, during Prime Minister's Question Time, a Labor M.P. asked "[D]oes [the P.M.] remember receiving a piece of advice in March 1998 from a very influential source, saying that the minimum wage is the height of irresponsibility? In light of that advice, will he please help my memory by informing us who that might have been?" Blair replied, "It was plainly not that influential a source of advice, since we proceeded with the minimum wage. It is worth pointing out what those in the Conservative party said. The shadow Chancellor said 'I think the Minimum Wage is an immoral policy.' The Leader of the Opposition said that the minimum wage is the height of irresponsibility. . . . We are

However, despite significant public backing, which if American experience is any guide, may be wide but not deep, and moderated opposition, the favorable political atmosphere that now envelopes the minimum wage could dissipate. It is uncertain at the moment how the Brown Government will deal with the matter, for example. Brown, recall, was always cautious about the minimum wage, both when it came to setting the rates and expanding the reach of the adult rate. Furthermore, he has appointed a businessman to his Cabinet who had earlier unburdened himself of the view that the NMW should be frozen. Of course, it could be that Brown will see the minimum wage as a way to mollify if not win the support of some of his more left-leaning Labor doubters. It is well also to remember that it supports his bed-rock approach to welfare policy, making work pay. That fact, coupled with the now all but overwhelming evidence that it has had no adverse economic effects, might well lead him to view it rather favorably.

More worrisome for the future of the NMW is how a future Conservative Government might handle it. Although the statements quoted above indicate a lessening of overt hostility to the idea, there are other ways to subvert a policy. The control over appointments to the LPC, the power to craft the charge, and, finally, the ability to adopt, modify, or reject the LPC's recommendations give a governing party ample levers to shape minimum wage policy. In short, a Conservative administration could simply allow the NMW to wither by ignoring it. For minimum wage workers, the immediate effect would then be largely the same as repeal. At least, though, unlike the Wages Councils, it would still be on the books when the political wheel turned again.

A weathervane for Conservative thinking is the two reports from the party's Social Justice Policy Group issued in 2006 and 2007, *Breakdown Britain* and *Breakthrough Britain: Ending the Costs of Social Breakdown.*[4] These documents reflect what appears to be a genuine concern with poverty, and lack any touch of the harshness of the Thatcher years. In the second, we find 190 policy recommendations. Many focus on encouraging stable families and attacking various maladies of the educational and substance abuse systems, areas sorely needing attention. However, when it comes to the incomes of the poor, the focus is solely on two fronts: manipulating the tax and benefit system and securing jobs and training for those currently dependent on ben-

---

delighted that those sinners have come to repentance now." *Hansard*, House of Commons, March 7, 2001, Col. 292-293.

4 The Social Justice Policy Group was chaired by former party leader Iain Duncan Smith. The reports are available on the party's website.

efits. "Our aim must be that every working-age household capable of earning a decent living must be able and obliged to do so. Government policy must, therefore, focus on getting those who are unemployed and long-term economically inactive people, into employment."[5] The second sentence is the key; apparently once people are employed the government's responsibility ends. In short, the phrase "capable of earning a decent living" carries no flip-side when it comes to government policy. That is, using the minimum wage to secure "a decent living" for the employed poor appears nowhere. This lends credence to the conclusion that while the Conservative party may have made its peace with the minimum wage in principle, it has no plans to make it part of its policy regime when it returns to power.

Two aspects of the NMW will also pose challenges for the LPC and any Government. One is the problem of enforcement. As the level of the NMW has gone up, the temptation to evade it has risen. This is worrisome for both the government and law-abiding business firms. It is significant in this regard that the Federation of Small Business is eager for the government to step up its enforcement efforts, since they feel that honest and legitimate companies are suffering. Achieving a greater degree of compliance, though, will mean more inspectors and increased penalties, neither of which is always popular. However, if the policy is to retain the backing of business, and indeed of the public, fair and effective enforcement is absolutely necessary.

The second issue involves the changing nature of the low-wage work force. With the accession of new members to the EU, Britain has had a wave of new immigrants, many of whom have eagerly taken low-wage jobs. Not only does this complicate the law's enforcement, since many of these people are unfamiliar with UK employment law, speak little English, and are not members of unions (to say nothing of those in the country illegally), it could also change the politics of the minimum wage. Will the public still support the minimum wage as strongly if minimum wage workers are increasingly seen as members of ethnic minorities hailing from Eastern Europe? Could an eruption of anti-immigrant feeling sweep away support for the minimum wage?

CONTEMPORARY MINIMUM WAGE POLICY IN THE UNITED STATES

The federal minimum wage remains an enormously popular policy. In fact, it may be the most popular policy ever enacted by the federal government. Nevertheless, Democrats show little or no inclination to give it a prominent

---

5 *Breakthrough Britain*, Section on Economic Dependency and Worklessness, 20.

place in their policy playbook. They ritualistically support it, certainly, but this is done by most with little real enthusiasm. This is shown most clearly by the near fiasco of the 2007 congressional session. After saying repeatedly that raising the minimum wage would be a central part of their first 100 days in office, they indeed brought it up early on and guided it past the House. But then they willingly let it slide to the margins in the Senate, where it languished almost unnoticed. It was only when Democratic leaders had a military spending bill they knew the president would not veto that they attached it as a rider, and then almost in silence. Democrats, it seems, needed something to attach to the measure so that they would not appear to be giving in completely to the president, and the minimum wage increase was as good a candidate as any. Even then, they stretched the increase over three years and did not recalibrate the tip credit. But that is not the only instance. During Bill Clinton's administration, Secretary of Labor Robert Reich had to press the president to support any kind of minimum wage increase, even after welfare reform was on the statute books. Finally, Clinton agreed to ask Congress for a modest increase, but in his public statement he showed little passion for it, speaking, according to Reich, "the same way he'd make the case for extending patents on hybrid corn."[6]

Congressional Democrats' lukewarm endorsement of the minimum wage is mirrored by their progressive supporters among the political elite. To take but one example, the Center for American Progress, a self-described progressive think tank, published a 267 page book in 2005 entitled *Progressive Priorities: An Action Agenda for America*.[7] Its stated goal is to be the blueprint for a latter day New Deal. A wide variety of topics — from health care, taxes, the racial divide, energy, and a wide array of national security issues — are given sustained attention, and there are many laudable ideas in the report. However, there is no mention of the minimum wage. In April of 2007, before Congress passed the minimum wage boost, the Center issued a report dealing solely with poverty.[8] After reciting the usual grim figures, it lays out 12 recommendations. To be sure, raising the minimum wage (then at $5.15) is listed first, and they propose setting it at half the average wage (making the minimum wage $8.40) and indexing it for the future. Of the remaining 11 proposals, nine of them call for increased governmental expenditures.[9] In a

---

6 Robert Reich, *Locked in the Cabinet* (New York: Knopf, 1997), 237.

7 (Washington: Center for American Progress, 2005).

8 Center for American Progress, *From Poverty to Prosperity: A National Strategy to Cut Poverty in Half*, April 25, 2007.

9 The two that do not are making it easier for employees to form unions and helping former prisoners find productive employment and reintegrate into the community. Of course, the

sense, it could be said that the minimum wage *is* given pride of place since it is listed first (although this is not stated); however, its importance is clearly diminished by putting it in such a laundry list. One cannot help but wonder if it would have been listed first had the report come after the most recent increase in the minimum wage passed rather than before.

To put the contemporary American scene in perspective, though, we have to look beyond Washington, to the states and to localities. Movements to increase state minimum wages, and equally important, to index them, is where the future is being formed. Activists are honing their arguments and their strategies, and experience is accumulating to show that minimum wages pay off on several fronts. If they keep the momentum going, and politicians learn the political benefits to be gained from supporting higher minimum wages, the opposition may find itself in further retreat. Then, there is the living wage movement, the real breeding ground for citizen politics and for the public education effort needed to put and keep the issue of low wages in the public eye. The only danger here is that the living wage movement will yield to those who want to use it as a vehicle to promote other causes. Though many of these may indeed be worthy, to broaden the agenda is to risk losing the public support that is the essential bedrock of the movement itself.

Perhaps it will be the move to index state minimum wages that will prove most important in the long run. The greatest defect in the federal minimum wage is the lack of a mechanism to upgrade it regularly. It would certainly be possible constitutionally to establish an independent regulatory commission with the power, under congressionally imposed guidelines, to adjust the minimum wage from time to time (say annually). This may be too ambitious, however. Nevertheless, some Low Pay Commission-type body would be enormously helpful. The haphazard way increases are now handled would give way to at least a somewhat more rational system. Should a Democratic Congress and Democratic president assume power, this would be an excellent item for discussion.

WELFARE STATE THEORY

A fitting place to conclude is a brief survey of three of the most prominent contemporary theorists of the welfare state, Joel Handler, Lawrence Mead, and Stuart White, and note how their ideas relate to the minimum wage.[10]

latter initiative could well entail expenditures also.

10 Because my focus has been on Britain and the United States, I am omitting the French theorist Pierre Rosanvallon. See his important book *The New Social Question: Rethinking the Welfare State* (Princeton, NJ: Princeton University Press, 2000). Translated by Barbara Harshaw.

Handler is perhaps the best known of contemporary apologists for the Marshall three-tiered citizenship approach.[11] He believes that Americans continue to mentally separate the deserving and undeserving poor. From this position, it is easy for them to develop hostile attitudes toward the undeserving, and even banish them to some state of semi-citizenship. The corrective to this is to adopt the idea of universal citizenship, which would erase the difference between the two groups of the poor. Even though this is a hard sell, it is the best, indeed the likely only, way to build a foundation for a humane and justifiable welfare state, according to Handler.

The granting of universal citizenship will carry with it certain rights and entitlements, one of which will be a claim on a reasonable share of the economic product the society produces. In an ideal world, this would include a basic income grant along the lines advocated by Philippe van Parijs.[12] In this program each citizen would receive a periodic grant from the public treasury, with no conditions attached.

In the more immediate practical world, Handler discusses the impact of welfare reform in the United States. After reviewing the studies that show incontestably that while the welfare rolls have indeed shrunk, the income of former welfare recipients is still woefully inadequate. He then offers his reform plan to address this inadequacy. His first proposal indeed involves the minimum wage.

> Since the great majority of welfare recipients are presently working, have recently worked, are trying to work, and will eventually leave welfare via work, the most obvious reforms involve improving the low-wage labor market so that more jobs are available, and earnings and benefits are increased and there is less need for welfare. In other words, make present jobs better. Nationally, this means job creation where unemployment is still high or even when unemployment begins to rise and jobs become less available, continuing to support the EITC, modest raises in the minimum wage, providing health and child care benefits, and reforming unemployment insurance and disability.[13]

In the ensuing pages, he discusses the importance of job creation, expanding the EITC, changing unemployment insurance (to allow for "family responsibilities, child care, and transportation needs" to count as involuntary unemployment), making Food Stamps more accessible, and new programs for child care, child support, health care, and transportation. However, not another word is said about the minimum wage. Moreover, there is surely

---

11 A good summary of his ideas can be found in *Social Citizenship and Workfare in the United States and Western Europe: The Paradox of Inclusion* (Cambridge: Cambridge University Press, 2004).

12 See Philippe van Parijs, *Arguing for Basic Income: Ethical Foundations for a Radical Reform* (London: Verso, 1992).

13 Handler, *Social Citizenship*, 62.

irony in the call for only "modest" increases in the minimum wage. There is certainly no suggestion to make the minimum wage a living wage. In sum, in this view of the welfare state, there is certainly a place for the minimum wage, but it is at the periphery.

Lawrence Mead's ideas address the minimum wage only indirectly.[14] Mead is most famous for his contention that it is perfectly defensible for society to make demands of welfare recipients, in particular that they engage in paid work. There are two bases for this approach. One is contractual: Society is justified in saying that if you take this money we may demand this of you. The second is communitarian. Work is not only good for the individual; it is part of the definition of citizenship. With work, you become a full member of the body politic. In company with civic republicans, Mead believes that work entitles even the poor to look other citizens in the eye. By moving former welfare recipients into paid work, welfare reform has not impoverished people but rather given them status. With full citizenship the poor may now press legitimate demands on the state. Mead explains further:

> When adult citizens enter the workforce, they not only obtain higher incomes; more important, they gain the trust and respect of fellow citizens. From this higher rewards will follow, from both the public and the private sectors. Create citizens first and a solution to poverty will follow. That is the implication of welfare reform to date. Politics, not economics, is the master science.[15]

Now, suppose the poor all go to work and avoid being on public assistance. But they discover that the "market" has channeled them into dead end jobs at low wages. (Mead ignores this possibility, implying that work itself will raise one's income.) By Mead's lights, they may now press a legitimate demand that the state underwrite their pay levels by enacting a minimum wage. Of course, they may be told this is not economically wise, but Mead has already asserted the primacy of politics over economics.

Moreover, two other factors enter. Civic republicanism has long held that both poverty and perverse levels of inequality are incompatible with sustainable citizenship.[16] Therefore, using high minimum wages as a tool to attack poverty and abate economic inequality is a perfectly logical outgrowth of the civic republican position itself. Then, return to the contractual. If society has

---

14 Mead's ideas can be found in *Beyond Entitlement: The Social Obligations of Citizenship* (New York: Free Press, 1986) and "Welfare Reform and Citizenship" in Lawrence Mead and Christopher Beem, eds., *Welfare Reform and Political Theory* (New York: Russell Sage Foundation, 2005), chap. 8.

15 Mead, "Welfare Reform and Citizenship," 194.

16 See Phillip Petit, *Republicanism: A Theory of Freedom and Government* (Oxford: Oxford University Press, 1997) and Richard Dagger, *Civic Virtues: Rights, Citizenship and Republican Liberalism* (Oxford: Oxford University Press, 1997).

the right to say that if we provide you with X, you must do Y, then surely it works the other way around as well. If a citizen provides a full, honest contribution to the production of the society's stock of material goods, then he or she ought to be able to stake a claim to a minimum share.

Stuart Whites' theories are the most pertinent, for they are built around the construction of a "civic minimum."[17] White begins by arguing for what he calls "democratic mutual regard." Citizens, in the shortest of shorthands, must respect each other, and society's institutions must be built to maintain that respect. From there we get to the idea of justice as "fair reciprocity." Part of this concept involves making a contribution to economic production. This, it is perfectly valid for society to demand that everyone who is able make an actual contribution through work, a "fair dues" obligation.[18] It follows that everyone will then become an economic citizen.

The commitment citizens have to each other obligates society to take certain concrete steps to ensure a system of "fair reciprocity." In the economic sphere, one is the eradication of discrimination. A second is that it must "prevent, correct, or appropriately compensate for significant forms of brute luck disadvantage."[19] Three of the main forms of brute luck disadvantage are the uneven distribution of initial wealth (choosing your parents badly, in essence), the discrepancies in marketable talent, and the existence of handicaps. A third obligation is to protect citizens from the consequences of the dependency and exploitation that can accompany market vulnerability. To accomplish all this, we need to construct a "civic minimum" applicable to all citizens. By offering up their contribution, citizens have earned a right to a certain basic level of material well-being.

White then offers up an ideal and a non-ideal way to do this, of which the latter is more important.[20] His reform program has five components.[21] For our purposes, the first, "making work pay," is the most important:

> All those who are expected to satisfy a minimum work expectation must receive a decent minimum income in return for doing so. This includes not only a level of post-tax earnings sufficient to cover a standard set of basic needs, but also a decent minimum of health care and disability coverage. . . . The model of a minimum wage combined with in-work

---

17 Stuart White, *The Civic Minimum* (Oxford: Oxford University Press, 2002).

18 Two notes: 1) White includes in this requirement those wealthy enough to avoid paid employment; 2) He includes care giving as an acceptable contribution.

19 White, *Civic Minimum*, 48.

20 The former is basically a form of taxation and redistribution. See White, *Civic Minimum*, 78–85.

21 He is assuming that the state provides a universal, high-quality educational system.

benefits for the low-paid, including child-care subsidies for low earners, is certainly one credible approach to this task.[22]

The others are making "participation" (mostly through care-giving) equivalent to paid work; setting up a two-tiered public assistance program, with one similar to Mead's conditional welfare payments and another given with no work expectation, but one that could not continue indefinitely; a "capital grant" scheme whereby everyone had some type of endowment available to draw on; and heavy taxation of inherited wealth (used most likely to finance the capital grant scheme). All five, however, are separable from each other.

White would probably accept that some of these ideas might prove impracticable or have unforeseen negative consequences. Or, that there might be better ways to achieve his goals. But those are arguments over means, not ends. The important point for welfare state theory is obtaining wide acceptance of the "civic minimum." Were that to be done, it is hard to believe that the minimum wage, indeed a living wage, would not be among the central components of the welfare state policy mix.

With Mead and White, then, welfare state theory is inching back toward its New Liberal and Progressive parentage (something White approvingly discusses directly). As it does so, the minimum wage should recover its central role in the effort to alleviate poverty and to temper inequality.

---

22 White, *Civic Minimum*, 202.

BIBLIOGRAPHY

Adams, Scott and David Neumark. *A Decade of Living Wages: What Have We Learned?* San Francisco: Public Policy Institute of California, 2005.

Arulampalam, Wiji, Alison Booth, and Mark Bryan. "Training and the New Minimum Wage." *Economic Journal.* 114 (2004): C87-C94.

Bain, George. "The National Minimum Wage: Further Reflections." *Employee Relations,* January 1999, 15-28.

Bartik, Timothy. "Thinking about Local Living Wage Requirements." *Urban Affairs Review.* 40 (2005): 269-299.

Bayliss, Fred. *British Wages Councils.* Oxford: Basil Blackwell, 1962.

Bernstein, Jared. "The Living Wage Movement: What Is It, Why Is It, and What's Known About Its Impact?" In *Emerging Labor Market Institutions for the Twenty-First Century.* Edited by Richard Freeman, Joni Hirsch, and Lawrence Mishel. Chicago: University of Chicago Press, 2005.

_____ and John Schmitt. *Making Work Pay: The Impact of the 1996-97 Minimum Wage Increase.* Washington: Economic Policy Institute, 1998.

_____ and Isaac Shapiro. *Nine Years of Neglect.* Washington: Center on Budget and Policy Priorities and Economic Policy Institute, 2006.

Bernstein, Michael. *A Perilous Progress: Economists and Public Purpose in Twentieth Century America.* Princeton, NJ: Princeton University Press, 2001.

Blackburn, Sheila. "Ideology and Social Policy: The Origins of the Trade Boards Act." *The Historical Journal.* 34 (1991): 43-64.

Bowlby, Roger. "Union Policy toward Minimum Wage Legislation in Postwar Britain." *Industrial and Labor Relations Review.* 11 (1957): 72-84.

Brenner Mark and Stephanie Luce. *Local Living Wage Laws in Practice: The Boston, New Haven and Hartford Experiences.* Amherst: University of Massachusetts Political Economy Research Institute, 2005

Brown, Charles, Curtis Gilroy, and Andrew Cohen. "The Effect of Minimum Wages on Employment and Unemployment." *Journal of Economic Literature.* 20 (1982): 487-528.

Bryan, Mark and Mark Taylor. *An Analysis of the Household Characteristics of Minimum Wage Recipients.* Research conducted for the Low Pay Commission, 2004.

Bulkley, Mildred Emily. *The Establishment of Minimum Rates in the Boxmaking Industry under the Trade Boards Act of 1909.* London: Bell, 1915.

Bythell, Duncan. *The Sweated Trades: Outwork in Nineteenth Century Britain.* London: Batsford Academic, 1978.

Card, David. "Using Regional Variation in Wages to Measure the Effects of the Federal Minimum Wage." *Industrial and Labor Relations Review.* 46 (1992): 38-54.

_____ and Alan Krueger. *Myth and Measurement: The New Economics of the Minimum Wage.* Princeton, NJ: Princeton University Press, 1995.

_____. "Minimum Wages and Employment: A Case Study of the Fast-Food Industry in New Jersey and Pennsylvania: Reply." *American Economic Review.* 90 (2000): 1397-1420.

Carrington, William and Bruce Fallick. "Do Some Workers have Minimum Wage Careers? *Monthly Labor Review,* May 2001, 17-27.

Chapman, Jeff. *Employment and the Minimum Wage: Evidence from Recent State Labor Market Trends.* Washington: Economic Policy Institute, 2004.

Citro, Constance and Robert Michaels, Editors. *Measuring Poverty: A New Approach* Washington: National Academy Press, 1995.

Cole, G.D.H. *A History of the Labour Party from 1914.* London: Routledge and Kegan Paul, 1948.

Committee on Social Insurance and Allied Services. *Report.* London: HMSO, 1942. (*Beveridge Report*)

Croucher, Richard and Geoff White. "Enforcing a National Minimum Wage: The British Case." *Policy Studies.* 28 (2007): 145-162.

Deere, Donald, Kevin Murphy, and Finis Welch. "Employment and the 1990-1991 Minimum Wage Hike." *American Economics Association Papers and Proceedings.* 85 (1995): 232-237.

Department of Employment and Productivity. *A National Minimum Wage: Report of an Interdepartmental Working Body.* London: HMSO, 1969.

Dickens, Richard and Alan Manning. *Has the National Minimum Wage Reduced UK Wage Inequality?* London School of Economics Centre for Economic Performance, 2002.

_____. "How the National Minimum Wage Reduced Wage Inequality." *Journal of the Royal Statistical Society,* Series A. 167 (2004): 613-626.

_____. "Spikes and Spill-Overs: The Impact of the National Minimum Wage on the Wage Distribution in a Low-Wage Sector." *Economic Journal*. 114 (2004): 95-101.

Douglas, Paul and Joseph Hackman. "The Fair Labor Standards Act of 1938, I and II." *Political Science Quarterly*. 53: 1938, 491-515; 54: 1939, 29-55.

Draca, Mirko, Stephen Machin, and John Van Reenen, *The Impact of the National Minimum Wage on Profits and Prices*. Research conducted for the Low Pay Commission, 2005.

Drier, Peter, John Atlas, and Kelly Candaele. "Florida Gets it Right: Raising the Minimum Wage." *Commonweal*, June 3, 2005.

Dube, Arindrajit, Suresh Naidu, and Michael Reich. *The Economic Impacts of a Citywide Minimum Wage*. Berkeley: University of California Institute for Research on Labor and Employment, 2006.

Eisenach, Eldon. *The Lost Promise of Progressivism*. Lawrence: University Press of Kansas, 1994.

Elmore, Andrew. *Living Wage Laws and Communities: Smarter Economic Development, Lower that Expected Costs*. New York: Brennan Center for Justice, 2003.

Ettlinger, Michael. *Securing the Wage Floor*. Washington: Economic Policy Institute, 2006.

Eyraud, Francois and Catherine Saget. *The Fundamentals of Minimum Wage Fixing*. Geneva: International Labour Office, 2005.

Freeden, Michael. *The New Liberalism*. Oxford: Oxford University Press, 1978.

Freeman, Richard. "Fighting for Other Folks' Wages: The Logic and Illogic of Living Wage Campaigns." *Industrial Relations*. 44 (2005): 14-31.

Friedman, Joel and Aviva Aron-Dine. *Comparing the House Minimum Wage and Estate Tax Proposals: Who Benefits and By How Much?* Washington: Center on Budget and Policy Priorities, 2006.

Friedman, Milton and Rose. *Free to Choose: A Personal Statement*. New York: Harcourt Brace Jovanovich, 1980.

Glennerster, Howard. *British Social Policy since 1945*. Oxford: Blackwell, 1995.

Glickman, Lawrence. *A Living Wage: American Workers and the Making of a Consumer Society*. Ithaca, NY: Cornell University Press, 1997.

Greater London Authority. *A Fairer London*. (Annually)

Grimshaw, Damian. "Living Wage and Low Pay Campaigns in Britain." In *Living Wage Movements: Global Perspectives*. Edited by Deborah Figart. London: Routledge, 2004.

Grossman, Jonathan. "Fair Labor Standards Act of 1938: Maximum Struggle for a Minimum Wage." *Monthly Labor Review*, November 1978), 22-30.

Handler, Joel. *Social Citizenship and Workfare in the United States and Western Europe: The Paradox of Inclusion*. Cambridge: Cambridge University Press, 2004.

Harris, Jose. *William Beveridge: A Biography*. Oxford: Oxford University Press, 1977.

_____. "Political Thought and the Welfare State, 1870-1940: An Intellectual Framework for British Social Policy." *Past and Present*. 135 (1992): 116-141.

Hart, Valerie. *Bound by Our Constitution: Women, Workers, and the Minimum Wage*. Princeton, NJ: Princeton University Press, 1994.

Higgins, H.B. *A New Province for Law and Order*. London: Constable and Co., 1922.

Hobson, J.A. "The Living Wage." *Commonwealth*. 1 (1896): 128-129; 165-167.

_____. *The Social Problem*. London: Nisbet and Co., 1902.

Hohman, Helen. *The Development of Social Insurance and Minimum Wage Legislation in Great Britain*. Boston: Houghton Mifflin, 1933.

Holcombe, Arthur. "The Legal Minimum Wage in the United States." *American Economic Review*. 2 (1912): 21-37.

Hyslop, Dean and Steven Stillman. *Youth Minimum Wage Reform and the Labour Market in New Zealand*. New Zealand Department of the Treasury, 2004.

Kloppenberg, James. *Uncertain Victory: Social Democracy and Progressivism in European and American Thought, 1870-1920*. New York: Oxford University Press, 1986.

Leuchtenberg, William E. *Franklin D. Roosevelt and the New Deal, 1932-1940*. New York: Harper and Row, 1963.

Levi, Margaret, David Olson, and Erich Steinman. "Living Wage Campaigns and Laws." *WorkingUSA: The Journal of Labor and Society*. 6 (2003): 111-132.

Levin-Waldman, Oren. *The Case of the Minimum Wage: Competing Policy Models*. Albany: State University of New York Press, 2001.

_____. *The Political Economy of the Living Wage: A Study of Four Cities*. Armonk, NY: M.E. Sharpe, 2005.

Low Pay Commission. *Annual Report*. (Various titles)

Low Pay Network. *After the Safety Net*. 1994.

Lowe, Rodney. "The Erosion of State Intervention in Britain, 1917-24." *Economic History Review*. 31 (1978): 270-286.

Luce, Stephanie. *Fighting for a Living Wage*. Ithaca, NY: Cornell University Press, 2004.

Machin, Stephen and Joan Wilson. "Minimum Wages in a Low-Wage Labour Market: Care Homes in the UK." *Economic Journal*. 114 (2004): C102-C109.

Macpherson, David. *The Effects of the Proposed 1999-2000 Washington Minimum Wage Increase*. Washington: Employment Policies Institute, 1998.

Marshall, T.H. *Citizenship and Social Class*. Cambridge: Cambridge University Press, 1950.

Martin, Isaac. "Dawn of the Living Wage: The Diffusion of a Redistributive Municipal Policy." *Urban Affairs Review*. 36 (2001): 470-496.

Matari, Ellen and Deborah Figart. "Wages and Hours: Historical and Contemporary Linkages." In *Living Wage Movements: Global Perspectives.* Edited by Deborah Figart. London: Routledge, 2004.

Mead, Lawrence. *Beyond Entitlement: The Social Obligations of Citizenship.* New York: Free Press, 1986.

_____. "Welfare Reform and Citizenship." In *Welfare Reform and Political Theory.* Edited by Lawrence Mead and Christopher Beem. New York: Russell Sage Foundation, 2005.

Metcalf, David. *Why Has the British National Minimum Wage Had Little or No Impact on Employment?* London School of Economics Centre for Economic Performance, April 2007.

Millar, Jane and Karen Gardiner. *Low Pay, Household Resources and Poverty.* London: Joseph Rowntree Foundation, 2004.

Mishel, Lawrence, Jared Bernstein, and Sylvia Allegretto. *The State of Working America, 2006-2007.* Ithaca, NY: Cornell University Press, 2007.

Morris, Jenny. *Women Workers and the Sweated Trades: The Origins of Minimum Wage Legislation.* Aldershot: Gower, 1986.

Nadeem, Shehzad. "The Living Wage Movement and the Economics of Morality: Frames, Ideology, and the Discursive Field." *Research in Social Movements, Conflicts, and Change.* 28 (2008): forthcoming.

National Anti-Sweating League. *Report of a Conference on a Minimum Wage held at the Guildhall, London, October 24, 25, and 26, 1906.* (Pamphlet)

Neidt, Christopher, et al. *The Effects of the Living Wage in Baltimore.* Washington: Economic Policy Institute, 1999.

Nissen, Bruce. "Living Wage Campaigns from a 'Social Movement' Perspective: The Miami Case." *Labor Studies Journal.* 25 (2000): 29-50.

Nordlund, Willis. *The Quest for a Living Wage: A History of the Federal Minimum Wage Program.* Westport, CT: Greenwood, 1997.

Orr, Susan. "It's All the Wage: A Qualitative Study of the Orange County, Florida Living Wage Campaign." Paper presented at the 2004 meeting of the Southern Political Science Association, New Orleans, LA.

Paulsen, George. *A Living Wage for the Forgotten Man.* Selingsgrove, PA: Susquehanna University Press, 1996.

Pew Research Center. *Maximum Support for Raising the Minimum Wage.* April 19, 2006.

Pollin, Robert and Jeannette Wicks-Lin. *Economic Analysis of the Arizona Minimum Wage Proposal.* Amherst: University of Massachusetts Political Economy Research Institute, 2006.

Pond, Chris and Steve Winyard. *The Case for a National Minimum Wage.* London: Low Pay Unit, 1982. Pamphlet No. 23.

Potter, Nicholas. *Measuring the Employment Impacts of the Living Wage Ordinance in Santa Fe, New Mexico.* Albuquerque: University of New Mexico Bureau of Business and Economic Research, 2006.

Powell, David. "The New Liberals and the Rise of Labour, 1886-1906." *The Historical Journal.* 29 (1986): 369-393.

Powell, Thomas Reed. "The Constitutional Issues in Minimum Wage Legislation." *Minnesota Law Review.* 2 (1917): 1-21.

Prasch, Robert. "American Economists in the Progressive Era on the Minimum Wage." *Journal of Economic Perspectives.* 13 (1999): 221-230.

Quigley, William. *Ending Poverty as We Know It: Guaranteeing a Right to a Job at a Living Wage.* Philadelphia: Temple University Press, 2003.

Reich, Michael, Peter Hall, and Ken Jacobs. "Living Wage Policies at the San Francisco Airport. *Industrial Relations.* 44 (2005): 106-138.

Reynolds, David. "The Living Wage Movement Mushrooms in the United States." In *Living Wage Movements: Global Perspectives.* Edited by Deborah Figart. London: Routledge, 2004.

_____ and Jen Kern. *Living Wage Campaigns: An Activist's Guide to Building the Movement for Economic Justice.* Detroit: Wayne State University Labor Studies Center, 2003.

Rodgers, Daniel. *Atlantic Crossings: Social Politics in a Progressive Age.* Cambridge, MA: Harvard University Press, 1998.

Rowland, Peter. *The Last Liberal Government.* Volume I: *The Promised Land, 1905- 1910.* New York: Macmillan, 1969.

Seager, Henry. *Social Insurance: A Program for Social Reform.* New York: Macmillan, 1910.

_____. "The Minimum Wage as Part of a Program for Social Reform." *Annals of the American Academy of Political and Social Science.* 38 (1913): 3-12.

Sells, Dorothy. *British Wages Boards.* Washington: Brookings Institution, 1939.

Shaefer, Luke. "State Minimum Wage Laws: Examining the Case of Illinois." *Journal of Poverty.* 10 (2006): 67-87.

_____ and Bruce Nissen. *The Florida Minimum Wage after One Year.* Miami: Florida International University Research Institute on Social and Economic Policy, 2006.

Sheldrake, John. "The Sweated Industries Campaign." *Socialist History.* 3 (1993): 37-54.

Smith, Constance. "The Working of the Trade Boards Act in Great Britain and Ireland." *Journal of Political Economy.* 22 (1914): 605-629.

Stewart, Mark. "The Employment Effects of the National Minimum Wage." *Economic Journal.* 114 (2004): C110-C116.

Storrs, Landon. *Civilizing Capitalism: The National Consumers' League, Women's Activism, and Labor Standards in the New Deal Era.* Chapel Hill: University of North Carolina Press, 2000.

Stromquist, Shelton. *Reinventing "The People": The Progressive Movement, the Class Problem, and the Origins of Modern Liberalism.* Urbana: University of Illinois Press, 2006.

Sykes, Alan. *The Rise and Fall of British Liberalism.* New York: Longman, 1997.

Tawney, R.H. *The Establishment of Minimum Rates in the Chain-Making Industry under the Trade Boards Act of 1909.* London: Bell, 1914.

_____. *The Establishment of Minimum Rates in the Tailoring Industry under the Trade Boards Act of 1909.* London: Bell, 1915.

Thies, Clifford. "The First Minimum Wage Laws." *Cato Journal.* 10 (1991): 715-746.

Thompson, Jeff and Jeff Chapman. *The Economic Impact of Local Living Wages.* Washington: Economic Policy Institute, 2006.

Toynbee, Polly. *Hard Work: Life in Low Pay Britain.* London: Bloomsbury, 2003.

Vinson, Adrian. "The Edwardians and Poverty: Towards a Minimum Wage?" In *Edwardian England.* Edited by Donald Read. New Brunswick, NJ: Rutgers University Press, 1982.

Wadsworth, Jonathan. *Did the Minimum Wage Change Consumption Patterns?* Research conducted for the Low Pay Commission, 2007.

Waltman, Jerold. *The Politics of the Minimum Wage.* Urbana: University of Illinois Press, 2000.

_____. *The Case for the Living Wage.* New York: Algora, 2004.

_____. "Supreme Court Activism in Economic Policy in the Waning Days of the New Deal: Interpreting the Fair Labor Standards Act, 1941-1946." *Journal of Supreme Court History.* 31 (2006): 58-80.

Webb, Sidney and Beatrice. *Industrial Democracy.* London: Longmans, 1897.

Weiler, Peter. *Ernest Bevin.* Manchester: Manchester University Press, 1993.

Wellington, Allison. "Effects of the Minimum Wage on the Employment Status of Youths: An Update." *Journal of Human Resources.* 26 (1991): 27-46.

White, Stuart. *The Civic Minimum.* Oxford: Oxford University Press, 2003.

Wills, Jane. *Mapping Low Pay in East London.* London: Queen Mary University, 2001.

_____. "Organizing the Low Paid: East London's Living Wage Campaign as a Vehicle for Change." In *The Future of Worker Representation.* Edited by Geraldine Healy, et al. London: Palgrave, 2004.

Wolfson, Paul. *State Minimum Wages: A Policy that Works.* Washington: Economic Policy Institute, 2006.

Wooden, Mark. "Minimum Wage Setting and the Australian Fair Pay Commission." *Journal of Australian Political Economy.* 56 (2005): 81-91.

Zabin, Carol and Isaac Martin. *Living Wage Campaigns in the Economic Policy Arena: Four Case Studies from California.* Berkeley: University of California Institute of Industrial Relations, 1999.

In addition to the research reports cited above, a variety of material relevant to minimum wage issues is published by the following institutes and think tanks:

Brennan Center for Justice

Center on Budget and Policy Priorities

Center for Public Policy Priorities (TX)

Center for Urban Economic Development (Illinois)

Economic Opportunity Institute (Washington State)

Economic Policy Institute

Employment Policies Institute

Family Budget Unit (UK)

Fiscal Policy Institute (US)

Florida International University Research Institute on Social and Economic Policy
    Institute for Fiscal Studies (UK)

International Labour Office

Joseph Rowntree Foundation

London School of Economics Centre for Economic Performance

Massachusetts Budget and Policy Center

Michigan League for Human Services

Oregon Center for Public Policy

University of California Institute for Research on Labor and Employment (formerly
    Institute of Industrial Relations)

University of Massachusetts Political Economy Research Institute

INDEX